PORTRAIT OF AVON

Portrait of
AVON

JOHN HADDON

ILLUSTRATED AND WITH MAP

ROBERT HALE · LONDON

ISBN 0 7091 8361 5

Robert Hale Limited
Clerkenwell House
Clerkenwell Green
London EC1R 0HT

Photoset by
Kelly Typesetting Limited
Bradford–on–Avon, Wiltshire
and printed in Great Britain by
Lowe & Brydone Ltd.,
Thetford, Norfolk
Bound by Weatherby Woolnough Ltd.,
Wellingborough, Northants

CONTENTS

MAPS AND MAP REFERENCES

The geology of the area is covered by the 1 inch Bristol District Geology sheet, obtainable from the Ordnance Survey.

The topographical Ordnance Survey map which covers most of the area is the 1:50,000 Sheet No. 172 (Bristol and Bath), but for the extreme south see Sheet No. 182 (Weston-super-Mare and Bridgwater), and for the south-east Sheet No. 173.

For most of the villages map references are given in the text. These relate to the grid lines on the O.S. maps and their use is explained in the margin of the map sheet.

ILLUSTRATIONS

PICTURE CREDITS

Pictures supplied by: Bath City Planning and Architects
Department: 16, 17, 18; West Air Photography: 1, 2, 3, 5,
6, 19, 22, 23, 24, 28, 29, 33, 34; West Country Tourist
Board: 10, 15, 20, 21, 25, 26, 27; Geoffrey N. Wright: 4,
7, 8, 9, 11, 12, 13, 14, 30, 31, 32.

MAPS ETC.

INTRODUCTION

In 1972 the British Government, imbued it would seem with the spirit of Dr Frankenstein, began an operation in which large chunks were severed from the living bodies of Gloucestershire and Somerset and stitched on to an unwilling City and County of Bristol to create a new political creature, the County of Avon. This came creakingly into life on All Fools' Day 1974, and opinion is divided as to whether it is a child of promise or a freak.

Physically it is attractive and full of a pleasant variety which is given some cohesiveness by the focus of the lower Avon valley and the bounding limits of the Cotswolds, Mendips and Severn Sea, and as an economic unit it has a functional structure already recognized in the 1967 Report of the South West Regional Economic Council, which defined a Bristol-Severnside Area identical except for small extensions north and south-west to the new county. It is not, of course, a law of nature that Economic Councils are always right, and there are grounds for arguing that the county should have taken in part of west Wiltshire, as was originally proposed by the Royal Commission, but there is little doubt that Avon has a pros-perous, balanced, attractive and reasonably integrated economic base with a good potential for future development.

What is questionable, however, is whether it was necessary to create a new local government area at all and whether, once formed, it was given the most effective administrative struc-ture. These are issues which have been clouded by attendant circumstances which render difficult any clear-cut assess-ment of the situation. There has been, for example, an in-built resentment from the previous administrations, particularly in Bristol, which deplored its loss of autonomy and was in any case politically at odds with the rest of the county to which it contributes more than half the rateable value. Many new 'Avonians' discovered in themselves previously unsuspected

9

and unvoiced regional loyalties to the old counties, and there was a sense of disorientation when carefully nurtured relationships with old County Halls and District Councils were suddenly severed at a time when the delicate web of relationships, often informal and unspecified, was still in process of formation within the new administration. It is hardly surprising that the machinery creaked, and in any case it is difficult to escape the conclusion that it was a mistake to set up a new system when the country was struggling to maintain its economic life and when central government was cutting its financial support to local administration. After all, if you take a new-born baby, put it in a straitjacket and cut down its air-supply, you should not be surprised if it does not seem particularly vigorous.

The theme of this book, however, is topography not politics, a stock-taking of the landscapes of Avon and a consideration of the forces which have shaped them through time, and it is hoped that some service has been done by gathering together within a single regional framework information which was previously scattered through numbers of record offices, libraries, local studies and books about the old counties, linked with personal observation of all parts of the new county. It is an attempt to see the county as a regional entity and a contribution to the process of re-orientation required in 'thinking Avon'.

It cannot be a static picture, for a basic feature of all landscapes is that they are undergoing a process of change. There are rhythms, daily and seasonal, whether they be the growth of plants or the movement of traffic, the shifting of sunlight from dawn to dusk or the switching on and off of lamps; there are constant variations in movement as the wind ripples the grass, the sea breaks against the shore, or birds erupt from woods, children from schools, workers out of factories. Change may be slow, as in the crumbling of rocks, or rapid, even violent, as in the action of fire or flood or the activities of construction companies. Everywhere there are forces at work, acting, counteracting, interacting—human and physical. Nothing is permanent, nothing stable.

The major agent in this process is Man himself, for the landscape is an artificial creation whether it be urban or rural, and whenever Man has been the cause of drastic change, his actions have aroused controversy. Today, because of the enormous acceleration in human powers of interference and the consequent weakening of natural restraints, the rate of change and the range of options have become so large that concern has become acute, but the present situation is part of a process which has extended throughout history, a process to which landscape itself bears testimony, carrying within itself relicts of the past. It is with the historical development of Man/Land relationships that this book is partly concerned.

The human motives for the manipulations which produce a particular landscape are various, complex and not always clearly understood. In many cases they are economic and designed to increase the wealth of a particular person or class of society, but this is not the only motive, and land-use can be affected, for instance, by aesthetics, as in the landscaped parklands of the eighteenth century, or by strategy, as in the sealing-off of land under RAF runways, or by politics, as in the direction of industry to areas populated by underprivileged voters. Then there are actions which arise from pride, from guilt, from pity or from fear. And in every case there are limitations imposed by incomplete information and human fallibility.

Actions are affected by personal opinion, contemporary fashion in thought, and the power-structure within society. The rapidly rising contemporary concern for environmental quality has, for example, given power to the conservationist lobby and produced a considerable increase in relevant legislation, particularly since the Civic Amenities Act of 1967 introduced the designation of Conservation Areas. It is a concern very different from the 'Behold we make all things new' optimistic utopianism of planning in the 1950s, and it has resulted from a complex variety of interacting causes. There is a reaction against reconstruction and a lack of confidence in forecasts, promises, expert opinions and the ability of politicians and administrators to make satisfactory decisions. There is a frightening feeling of rootlessness, of being cut off from the support of the past. There is anger at the loss of the familiar surroundings of childhood. There is fear that we are wasting assets and damaging natural gifts at such a rate that our grandchildren will face deprivation and disaster.

Rural Avon is a green land of hedged or walled fields,

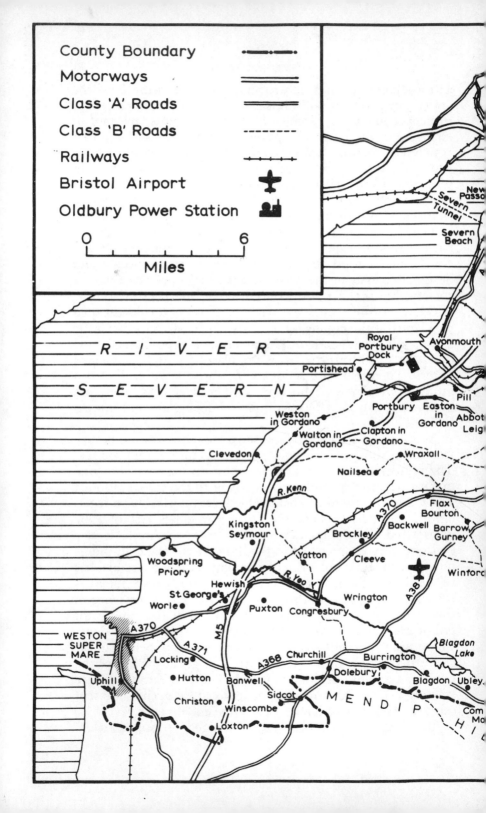

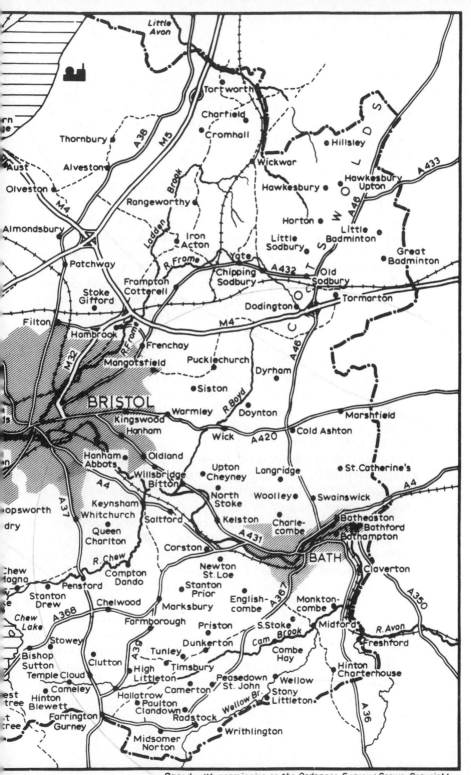

Based with permission on the Ordnance Survey : Crown Copyright

comfortable rather than spectacular, wearing a settled and a peaceful air. Yet change is active as the motorways slash through the pattern of the rural fabric, as Bristol spreads a skirt of buildings southward to Dundry Hill, as the commuters take over the villages and developers suburbanize the old stone settlements with acres of red brick, while the boaters and sailors and fishermen and riders and walkers struggle for supremacy along the banks of the Avon, and the big new metal barns of the farmers and the big new warehouses of the distributors go up in a landscape where elms die in the hedgerows, replaced rarely and with reluctance, where sprays and machines subdue the variety of the roadside verges, and where foxes forsake the countryside for suburbia.

Townscape has suffered much more evident interference, from the laying waste of acres of minor Georgian building in Bath to the ring-roads, office blocks and housing towers of Bristol, and it is in the cities that the critics of change have been most active. That is something we shall look at in more detail in the section on Bath and will give some thought to in relation to Bristol and Weston-super-Mare. Unfortunately problems of landscape management are never easy and are particularly difficult in towns, so it is not surprising that simplistic or single-minded proposals for a solution often make matters worse instead of better.

For one thing, the death of flowers, the infestation of the soil with chemicals, the sealing of agricultural land by acres of housing, the pollution of air, water and land by industry, the loss of visual identity brought by new housing estates, the disruption of urban communities by motorways, are all products of that irrepressible urge of mankind to have more material comfort for less work, an urge which has created, destroyed and re-created patterns of town and country since the first fields were cultivated. It is no mean achievement that a factory worker living in a council house has a standard of living and an expectancy of life-span far above that of a medieval prince. For better or for worse, we have eaten of the fruit of the Tree of Knowledge, and if now we want a Garden of Eden, we have to create it for ourselves by harnessing our ever-increasing scientific knowledge and technical ability to a satisfactory system of values.

But what values? It is clear from the beginning, when

mankind made not only tools but also ornaments, built both houses and temples, not only buried the dead but left them with implements for use or as a sign of after-life, and throughout history where people have sacrificed personal gain to further an abstract principle, that human values are not solely material. Because of this, landscape should not be evaluated purely in economic terms. One of the non-material factors is symbolism: the Old Court House at Keynsham was useless, dangerous and not attractive, yet it meant something to somebody, for when it was about to be demolished there appeared on it the bold letters "SAVE ME". Pedestrians dislike Bristol's Inner Ring Road not only because it is noisy and smelly and makes them walk a long way and climb onto spidery bridges before they can cross it but also because it makes them feel that human beings have been subordinated to motorcars. Much of the distaste expressed about the new cathedral in Clifton arises from the feeling that it does not 'look like a church'. To some the atomic power-station at Oldbury-on-Severn is a sign of hope, to others a symbol of menace.

This symbolism is one reason why many of us are attracted by elements in the landscape which are witnesses to the past, for they act as powerful symbols of continuity, helping us to feel that we belong to an unbroken stream of life, that we are not just initiators but also inheritors, that we have roots. There is a particular pleasure in identifying within the landscape some work of men long dead—an Iron Age hill-fort, perhaps, or a Norman church, a great bridge or an abandoned canal or the pattern of field enclosures—not only because it increases our knowledge but because it also stirs our imagination and gives us a feeling of kinship with the past. At a time when so much is disappearing so fast, there would seem to be some virtue in taking stock of what still remains.

Although the emphasis in this book is on Man and his works, the study would be incomplete, indeed impossible, without some reference to the geological and physical characteristics of the land, particularly as a survey of Avon shows a strong correlation between man-made scenery and physical regions. An over-view is therefore first given of the geology and physical geography of the county, and this is followed by a brief account of the general history of human

action on the landscape before entering into the main part of
the work, a series of studies of the individual regions of Avon
and of the urban areas of Bristol, Bath and Weston-super-
Mare.

I

FOUNDATIONS

The character of the landscape is rooted in the rocks, and we ignore this at the peril of losing our identity as part of the natural world. There is a terrible trend to uniformity and anonymity in the recent works of Man—one town gets very like another, one motorway like all the rest; even villages are losing their identity—and it is only by the grace of the rock-foundation that we know where we are. The Cotswolds and Mendips, the coastal plains and the hill and valley country, are not as they were a hundred years ago, but thanks to the rocks they will never be identical with each other, and no amount of plastic surgery will destroy the essential bone-structure of the face of the land. Even under the urban blanket the ancient pattern of hill and valley and plain give character to what might otherwise become a meaningless clutter. In building we create an uneasiness, a sense of unneighbourly intrusion, when we depart from the use of local materials; and when our roads and field-patterns ignore the subtle slopes engineered through countless years by the subtle forces of Nature, it is not surprising that we often find the results distasteful. To treat the natural world as our bond-servant rather than our partner is to entertain a concept loaded with psychological and economic dangers. Firstly, we need to understand what she provides.

Nearly all the rocks of Avon are sedimentary, laid down by wind or water, rag-bags of second-hand materials made up of particles worn away from existing land or derived from shells and skeletons of sea-creatures or, in the case of coal, from the corpses of vegetation. Rocks derived from land are of three main types, sandstones, clays and shales, while those from sea-creatures are limestones. Sandstones are of grains of quartz, which is very hard, but the rock is hard or soft according to the type of cement—silica, iron oxide or calcite (lime). Clays have very small grains, absorb water and become slippery when wet. Shales, or mudstones, are hardened clays

17

forming very thin layers which tend to break up when exposed to weather. Limestones vary from unconsolidated masses of shells to compact, crystalline rocks, although more frequently the crystals (calcite) occur as veins. Soil is a highly complex substance formed basically from weathered rock and decayed vegetation and is alive with bacteria and small creatures.

The layers, or strata, of sedimentary rock often show that they have been highly disturbed by great forces which have bent and cracked them. A crack in the strata along which they have moved either laterally or vertically, or both, is called a fault and results from the great mountain-building movements (orogenies) of the past, each lasting many million years.

There are two other major groups of rocks: igneous, such as granite, which is crystalline and formed by the cooling of molten minerals, and metamorphic, such as slate, which have changed their form as the result of great heat and pressure. These two are insignificant in Avon.

There are other rocks which form superficial deposits on top of the solid geology and may mask it completely. These include peat and alluvium (river mud), both found on the coastal moors of Avon, and various deposits left by the glaciers of the Ice Age, of which the main one in Avon is Head. This got its curious name from being first identified at the heads of valleys in the chalk and is a gravelly deposit formed at the end of the Ice Age when freeze/thaw split off small pieces of rock from the hillsides which sludged down, lubricated by rain and mud, to spread out on the lower ground. In Avon it is found principally at the foot of the Mendips.

The thickness of the strata and evidence from the extent of decay of radioactive minerals give an indication of the geological time-scale, and it is vast, to be measured in many millions of years. The Earth is about 4–5,000 million years old, but life-indicating fossils become abundant only (!) from 600 million years BP (Before Present-day), although it seems that some form of life has existed for about half the Earth's existence. Man has been on Earth for about a million years—in other words, if the life of the Earth were a day, Man would have appeared about one minute before midnight. The major divisions of geological time into Eras and Periods is given in the table, and the rocks within those periods relevant to Avon are described in the following account, which must, however, as far as events are concerned, be regarded as having a high degree of probability rather than absolute certainty.

Table 1   *Geological Time Scale*

Years ago Duration millions		Periods	Eras	Mountain-building	In Avon
1	1	Recent Pleistocene	QUATERNARY		
63	12 12 11 27	Pliocene Miocene Oligocene Eocene	TERTIARY (CENOZOIC)	ALPINE	
230	72 46 49	Cretaceous Jurassic Triassic	SECONDARY (MESOZOIC)		
600	50 65 60 20 75 75	Permian Carboniferous Devonian Silurian Ordovician Cambrian	PRIMARY (PALAEOZOIC)	HERCYNIAN (ARMORICAN) CALEDONIAN	
5,000		Pre-Cambrian			

The Earth was already some 5,000 million years old when a sea whose southern shore stretched across mid–Wales and the northern tip of Avon was receiving the waste worn from an ancient land and the debris of its own inhabitants. From this were formed layers of sandstone, shale and limestone which were then thrown into high mountains as the earth's early continents began to shift. From the chain in Central Wales huge quantities of rock waste were carried down and deposited on the southern margins in swampy deltas and lagoons where they consolidated into a gritty, water-resistant rock, the Old Red Sandstone.

Locally more grey than red, this rock is today largely blanketed by younger rocks, but it surfaces in places to form upland with poor soil which, when not grazed or cultivated, tends to be colonized by gorse and heather. It forms the core of the Portishead–Clevedon ridge, where it is carved into cliffs at Redcliffe Bay; it lines the northern edge of the Shirehampton–Failand plateau and is exposed where this is cut through by the

Avon Gorge; and it looms above the southern boundary of the county where it forms Blackdown ('the bleak hill'), the highest land on Mendip.

At the end of the deposition period, the Devonian, the new land began slowly to subside below a warm sea and became covered in new deposits. At first the sea was muddy and the sediments formed into limestone shale, but, as it deepened and cleared, it was invaded by a host of living creatures whose shells and skeletons sank over millions of years like a submarine snow-storm and accumulated to form the massive grey carboniferous limestone.

Conditions were not everywhere and at all times the same during this immensely long period, and a late emergence of the land, particularly in the north, produced material which was deposited to form a red sandstone grit whose most notable landscape feature is Brandon Hill in Bristol, whose steep slopes have maintained it as a public open space amid a sea of urban development. Miners called this barren sandstone 'the Farewell Rock' because it marked the bottom of the coal-measures which were formed on it during the Upper Carboniferous period. This was a time when the climate grew tropical and the seas gave way to great swamps, rich in vegetation which included giant ferns, huge horsetails and scale-trees (lycopods) which rose in some cases to over a hundred feet and branched like giant candelabras. The swamps were their homes and their graveyards, and it was the accumulation of their remains which gave us the coal-seams of today.

From time to time, with oscillations in the level of land and sea, the swamps were covered in shallow seas, lakes or river deltas, and so the coal-seams are interleaved with layers of sandstones, clays or limestones which also form the surface in the coal-measure areas. In particular there was laid down between the upper and lower coal-measures an almost barren series of sandstones, the Pennant, from 1–3,000 feet thick, which was derived from temporarily uplifted land.

And then slowly and inexorably over more millions of years came a thrust from the south which threw the Devonian and carboniferous rocks into great ripples, their crests running east-west in the south and slewing round to roughly north-south in the north, and cracked and displaced the thin seams of coal. During this and the following Triassic period the rocks were eroded and buried beneath their own waste material until only traces remained. The carboniferous limestone forms the Mendips and the cliffed coastal ridges at Worlebury (Weston-super-Mare), Sand Point and Clevedon–Portishead. Inland it appears as the Broadfield Down–Lulsgate plateau; as the Failand Ridge which continues beyond the Avon Gorge through Bristol's Durdham Downs almost to Filton; as a ridge west of Bristol from King's Weston to Henbury; and as the edge of a large elliptical basin north-east of Bristol, running from Almondsbury to the north of Cromhall and then bending southward through Wickwar to Chipping Sodbury where it has been quarried in a mile-long trench, now disused, beside the B4060. South of Chipping Sodbury it is cut through by the railway and then disappears, surfacing briefly at Wick, where it is quarried for road-metal. It also forms a low plateau between Olveston and Alveston. It is quarried for road-stone and has also been much used for building, particularly in the grey towns of Weston-super-Mare and Clevedon. Scenically it usually forms open, waterless uplands whose flanks are gashed by dry gorge-like valleys such as Burrington Combe in Mendip and Goblin Combe near Cleeve, both favourite beauty-spots. Soils are generally poor, and the areas are used chiefly for grazing.

The Pennant is mainly exposed to the east of Bristol from Rangeworthy in the north, through Frampton Cotterel, to Oldland and Hanham, and is cut into gorges by the Frome at Frenchay and the Avon at Hanham Mills. It has been much used for building in the villages and the eastern suburbs of Bristol. It has a rather sombre look, its colour varying from grey to dark red, and the surface tends to scale off with weathering, which makes its frequent choice for gravestones rather unfortunate.

Because of the folding, faulting and thinness of the seams, the coalfields of the area were always difficult to work, but mining was widespread in the south-east and there were pits by many villages, such as Pensford, Clutton and Timsbury as well as in the Radstock area, while there was considerable mining in the Kingswood region, now largely hidden by housing. A small coalfield at Nailsea was once important in supplying a local glassworks. The last pit in Avon, near Radstock, closed in 1974. Soils on the coal-measures are

-variable, ranging from rather wet clays in, for example, the
Coalpit Heath area, to well-drained sands.

Extensive erosion, in the arid Triassic, filled in the area to
form a plain, and these deposits still cover much of the land
east of the coastal moors. The chief rock is the red Keuper
marl, but on the fringes of the limestone uplands this merges
into the Dolomitic Conglomerate where the screes of fragments broken off the hillside consolidated into reddish, rather
lumpy rock. The conglomerate weathers into a good soil, and
the rock itself was used for building, as for example in West
Harptree and, rather far from its home, Temple Meads Station
at Bristol. The Triassic sandstones in Avon are, on the whole,
too soft for building but there are local exceptions, as in the
stone used for much of Chew Magna. Drying-out of salty
lakes gave rise in places to concentrations of celestine (strontium nitrate, used in fireworks) and gypsum (hydrate calcium
sulphate, used in plaster-board) which are both extracted near
Yate, and the iron oxide which reddens the rocks became
sufficiently concentrated in places to be worth mining as
ochre, its main producers, before recent closure, being at
Winford and Yate.

By the end of the Triassic most of the region had been worn
down and filled in to form a plain with low hills which
gradually subsided below a sea in which for the next 70 million
years layers of clays and limestones were laid down as the
waters advanced and withdrew and the land tilted and rippled.
This is the Jurassic period, which is divided, starting with the
first deposits, into the lias (the Upper Lias forms the Midford
Sands), inferior oolite and great oolite (whose base is fuller's
earth rock and clay, and whose top is the Forest Marble).
There were six further sets of deposits, but these do not occur
in Avon.

The lias rocks are mainly clays and limestones, the latter
being more strongly developed south of the Avon where its
whitish-grey stone was much used for building and gives a
distinctive appearance to the villages. In the main the limestone forms broad, gently undulating plateau-tops between
the valleys whose river have often cut down into the underlying Keuper marl. Lowland soils tend to be sticky clays,
upland ones stony and brown and capable of supporting crops
in a mixed farming economy. The middle lias includes the

hard Marlstone Rock which projects as a narrow shelf at the foot of the Cotswolds north of Bath and provides village-sites from Upton Cheyney through Old Sodbury to Hillesley, and these also relate to the spring-line formed with the overlying Cotswold Sands (Midford Sands further south) which form much of the scarp face.

Above the lias come inferior and great oolite, sandwiching between them fuller's earth clay and rock. There is considerable variety in the inferior (i.e. lower) oolite, but in general the upper layers are predominantly rubbly or sandy limestone, and the lower are oolitic limestone. The word 'oolite', meaning egg-stone, describes the granular structure resembling fish-roe. The grains were formed by the accretion of lime round tiny fragments of shell or sand as they rolled about in shallow water. When this structure is even, without many fossils, the rock can be cut into large blocks for building. Inferior oolite is not generally good building-material, but a notable exception is found in Dundry Hill south of Bristol which provided stone for several of the city churches, including St Mary Redcliffe.

The fuller's earth series consists of layers of clay separated by a limestone bed, and the upper clay forms a spring line at its junction with the oolite, as at Marshfield and Tormarton. When wet, the clay is slippery and can cause landslips such as have occurred around Bath. Commercial fuller's earth was important in the development of the wool industry, where it was used for extracting grease from the cloth in fulling or 'tucking' mills. Today it is mined in only one place, near South Stoke, south of Bath.

The limestones of the great oolite, which cap the Cotswolds and their extension south of Bath are notable for the development in the Bath area of a particularly fine building-material which contributes a great deal to the attractiveness of Bath itself. Used by the Romans, it subsequently fell into disfavour, and it was not until the eighteenth century that its status was restored, mainly through the strenuous advocacy of Ralph Allen, who had acquired the Bath quarries. It is admirable in colour and texture, makes fine ashlar blocks and carves well, but it also has disadvantages. In the first place, it must be handled with understanding. In the quarry or underground shaft it is soft and may be easily sawn, but it must then be left for several weeks in the open to harden and lose its 'quarry water'. At that stage it must be stacked the right way up, as it lay in the bed, and this position must be maintained when it is built into a wall or it will rapidly crack and decay. Even then it causes difficulties, for it is very susceptible to atmospheric attack, particularly by sulphur dioxide which converts the calcium carbonate into a soft sulphate. It also attracts soot which clings to it with such tenacity that new-built Bath, all white and glaring, rapidly became black, and a great deal of money has to be spent on cleaning it up. Bath stone is not now produced in Avon and is in any case too expensive for general use. The substitute, an artificial composition of stone fragments and cement, is tougher but lacks the visual quality of the original.

Upon the great oolite, and today forming the surface around Great Badminton and south of Bath at Hinton Charterhouse, was laid the Forest Marble, a series of beds of clays and shelly limestone, with occasional sands. Still to come was the rest of the Jurassic and the 70 million years of the Cretaceous with its greensand, clay and chalk, but although it is probable that these rocks once overlaid Avon, they have been long since stripped away following the distortion caused by the heaving-up of the Alps which started about 70 million years ago and took perhaps 20 million years to complete. In consequence Avon slowly lifted from the sea and tilted gently downwards to the east.

It is almost impossible to comprehend, it is indeed difficult to believe, the stupendous operation which was then carried out by weather, rivers and sea upon the emerging land—stripping off the Cretaceous cover, cutting back the oolites to the Cotswold scarp, leaving the outlier of Dundry behind like an off-shore island, reducing the lias to low hills and plateaus, exposing over large areas the underlying Keuper marls and exhuming the remnants of ancient Carboniferous landscape—to give us the basic physical and geological pattern which we see today. It also produced a river pattern.

The early drainage of this stage was probably north-eastward to the Thames, but as the Bristol Channel deepened and the Severn came into existence, a new set of streams flowed westward and as they cut back began to capture, cut off and divert the earlier ones. This is one explanation offered for the curious course of the Avon itself, a river which rises near Badminton, flows eastward towards the Thames, then turns southward along the great clay vale to Trowbridge, only to turn westward to Bradford-on-Avon and then return northward through the steep-sided narrow Limpley Stoke valley to Bathampton, where it resumes a westward course, looping its way through the south end of the Cotswolds before entering a broad plain between Bath and Bristol. Even then its variety is not ended, for it reaches Bristol through a gorge in the Pennant sandstone and leaves it through an even more spectacular one in the carboniferous limestone at Clifton before winding muddily through flat land to the Severn Sea at Avonmouth.

An alternative explanation for this crazy course which was put forward at the end of the last century and then abandoned has received a revival with the discovery of new evidence. It relates the Limpley Stoke valley and the Clifton Gorge to the Ice Age, suggesting that the former is an overflow channel from a lake in Wiltshire and the latter was formed by a diversion of the original course by a local advance of the Welsh ice. The whole question is by no means resolved, and more fieldwork needs to be done.

The idea that large areas of the now temperate world were once covered with huge sheets of ice was first put forward seriously in 1837 and was greeted with derision, particularly by those scholars who maintained that the evidence pointed towards not ice but water, a proof of the reality of Noah's Flood, an event which, had after all, the support of Holy Scripture. Since then the evidence for an Ice Age (or Ages) has become overwhelming, and it is the critics who are now derided. On the other hand the detailed events of the glacial advances and retreat and their influence and effects are constantly under revision as new evidence comes to light, and any broad statement must be regarded as imprecise and liable to modification.

Generally speaking, we may say that about a million years ago the climate of the northern hemisphere grew so cold that snows failed to melt and great sheets of ice accumulated in northern regions and on mountain areas further south, and fanned out southward into the sea and over the land. This appears to have happened at least four times, each glacial period being followed by a much longer inter-glacial when the climate grew warmer and the ice retreated as it melted at the margins. So lengthy were these inter-glacials, the second lasting about 200,000 years, that we have no way of knowing whether the Ice Age has ended or whether we are living in one of the pauses.

The Ice Age has left no dramatic legacy to Avon, apart, perhaps, from the Avon Gorge, but nevertheless it had important results. During the ice-advances huge quantities of water were locked up in the glaciers, and the level of the sea fell, to rise again when the ice melted. This not only alternately bared and drowned the coastal areas but also affected the work of the rivers. Thus a fall in late glacial times gave the Severn the power to erode a channel some 70 feet below the present level, and a rise in about 60,000 BC filled the channel with mud and spread an extensive layer of clay on the coastal regions. A relatively stable period then followed, with perhaps a slight lowering in sea-level, lasting for several thousand years during which vegetation established itself upon the clays, forming peat-bogs and in some places woodland, until in Roman times, around AD 250, the sea rose again, to five miles back from the coast covering the peat with 'Roman' clay and raising the level of the Avon so that the Roman baths in Bath suffered a backwash up their drains and the level of the hypocaust floors had to be raised 9 inches.

Bath also illustrates another feature which may have resulted (although the theory is questionable) from change in sea-level, for its ancient heart is situated on a river terrace formed when the Avon cut down and left part of its former floor slightly above flood-level as a dry site. The Avon terraces were also important as the homeland of prehistoric Palaeolithic near-men of the first inter-glacial, and many of their tools have been recovered from such sites, particularly in the gravel terraces below the Clifton Gorge.

The closing stages of the ice retreat produced deposits of Head which form no marked topographical features in Avon but by its gravelly nature and slightly higher elevation is used in places as village sites—Yatton, for example. Higher rainfall, and melting snow, increased stream-activity and was probably responsible for such dry valleys as Burrington Combe.

And now, a mere ten thousand years ago, the sculptured rock-body of Avon, clothed in forest and marshland, lay waiting for that tiny period of human activity which was to transform it into the still-changing landscape of today. Down the eastern edge ran the rolling Cotswolds hills, steep-edged to the west, broken into hill country in the south. Along the southern side lay whale-backed Mendip, and by the muddy Severn shore, broken here and there, but not often, by rocky promontories, stretched the swampy moors. And between them lay the crinkled, complicated heartland of hill and valley, plateau and plain, with its promise of future farm and factory, mine and quarry, city and village, a promise totally obscure to the first modern men who had lately arrived and established a hunting and collecting economy based on their homes in the limestone caves of Mendip.

II

BACKGROUND

The early work of Man in modifying the landscape has left only fragmentary evidence in Avon, and there is little now to be seen on the ground. The first major break-through in environmental control had come somewhere in the Middle East, probably about 4000 BC, with the domestication of animals and the cultivation of crops. By about 2500 BC people of this new culture, the Neolithic, had arrived in our area, and although they have left few remains apart from a number of long barrows, or burial-mounds, their coming marks the beginning of an ever-increasing and accelerating modification by Man of the natural scene.

The best example of a long barrow, with its interior stone chambers, is at Stoney Littleton (735572), and its location away from the higher Cotswolds and Mendip (where prehistoric sites cluster most thickly) gives some support to the hypothesis that prehistoric settlement spread further into the lower areas than was previously thought and that the concentration of evidence in the limestone and chalk uplands may in part be caused by the destruction of lowland evidence by its history of more intensive cultivation and occupation. Normally, for example, we associate the megalithic monuments of the succeeding Beaker (c188–c1600 BC) and Bronze Ages with the open downland sites of Avebury and Stonehenge, but it is interesting that the Avon example at Stanton Drew (598636) lies low in the valley of the Chew. It is argued that the valleys, heavily forested and their soils difficult to work, would have been avoided, but there is little improbability in the clearing of small patches, and there was the added advantage of game in the woods and fish in the streams. After all, this early ploughless agriculture was more like gardening, and a great deal of food would still have had to come from hunting and collecting.

With the Bronze Age (c1600–c600 BC) came a new race, a considerable increase in trade, and a new culture in which the

28

burial-mounds are round. Their ploughs simply scratched the surface and did not turn the soil, so cultivation was obtained by cross-ploughing, and for this the fields were roughly square. Once again the burial-remains are found mainly on Cotswold and Mendip, but there is a scatter remaining on lower ground, principally above Camerton. Development of trade may be associated with the few finds along the lower Avon at Sea Mills, Westbury-on-Trym and Saltford.

Increased ability to modify the environment came with the introduction of iron axe-heads and ploughshares. The Iron Age in Britain is conventionally divided into A (c600 BC onwards), B (c400 BC onwards) and C (c150 BC to AD 43), the last being a late take-over by invading Belgic warriors. It is probable that it was the latter who introduced a heavy plough better-suited to dealing with clay lowlands. The most striking remains in the present landscape are the banks and ditches of the hill-forts of B, particularly on Cotswold and Mendip, but there is some archaeological evidence of activity in the 'heartland' in the Chew Valley (notably Pagan's Hill—557626) and the limestone ridges of King's Weston (Bristol), Brean Down (Weston-super-Mare), Blaize Castle (Bristol) and Clevedon. Perhaps the most notable examples of environmental control are the Lake Villages of Mere and Glastonbury (Iron Age B), but these are outside our area, and, in any case, nothing remains to be seen on the ground. Some of the hillside terraces, or lynchets (Old English *hlinc*, a bank), particularly evident on the Cotswold scarp (e.g. at Hinton Hill, 7476), may have originated in the late Iron Age but are more likely to be medieval, an extension of farming into marginal land. It is probable that in the period some use was made of the lowland clays for potting and that there was a development of the Mendip lead-mining industry at Charterhouse-on-Mendip, just south of the Avon border.

Onto the native pattern of subsistence agriculture the Roman rule, from the first to fifth century AD, superimposed a pattern of roads, urban development, industry and large estates. The major road was the great Fosse Way, south of Bath, which persists as the A367 and to the north as a minor road along the county boundary. Across this ran another main route from the port of Abonae (Sea Mills) eastward past Aquae Sulis (Bath) towards Marlborough where it joined the road

from Silchester to London. Between Bath and Bristol it is
followed by the A431 for much of its length. Another road led
from Abonae to Glevum (Gloucester), and its northern part is
now the A38. Yet another road crossed the Avon by Trajectus
(Bitton) and headed south for the lead-mines at Charterhouse
from which there was a road down to the port of Clausentium
(Bitterne, near Southampton) and another probable one along
the north edge of Mendip to a small port at Uphill. From Bath
yet another road appears to have run southwards via Frome to
Poole, although only fragments have been positively
identified.

The only major urban development was the town of Aquae
Sulis, which was a spa, utilizing the hot springs for a
magnificent bathing-establishment flanked by a major temple.
All this is now well below present street-level, but excavation
at the end of the nineteenth century re-opened the main baths
to view and made them a tourist attraction. Minor urban
developments were at Sea Mills, Bitton, Gatcombe, Brean/
Uphill and Camerton. Gatcombe, at the foot of the Failand
ridge, which appears to have been occupied by native farming
communities, was established in the third century, perhaps as
a marketing centre for the quite considerable pottery industry
of the clay lowlands. Brean/Uphill was a small port, and the
Camerton settlement, which lies above the village by the Fosse
Way, had small iron-smelting and pewter industries. The
important lead and silver industries of Charterhouse lie outside
our area.

While small-scale subsistence native agriculture continued,
a new element, the large-scale capitalist, slave-worked, estate
or villa, was introduced, some producing mainly corn, others,
particularly on the lower land, occupied with animal husbandry. Location tended to be market-oriented and therefore
near settlements, roads (although not on them) or water-
courses. The buildings were sited, where possible, on a gentle,
well-drained, sunny slope with a water-supply. In Avon they
have been discovered mainly along the lower Avon valley and
to the south. Very few have been found to the north (exceptions are near Cromhall, 686897, and Tockington, 628857).
Today there is nothing to see. One villa lies at the bottom of
the Chew Valley Lake, another, at Keynsham, within a
cemetery. Quite a number of villas and other settlements were

abandoned in the second century when the coastal levels were
drowned by the sea.

For the ensuing Dark Ages when the Empire collapsed and
the Celtic kingdoms formed and warred against each other
and, vainly, against the invading Saxons, we have confusing
evidence about political and dynastic events but very little
about economy. Some of the hill-forts, such as Cadbury
Camp near Congresbury, were re-occupied; many deserted
villas were inhabited by squatters; the temple and baths at Bath
collapsed, and Abonae was abandoned. The Anglo-Saxon
Chronicle records that in AD 577 Cuthwine and Ceawlin
fought against the Britons and killed three kings, Conmail,
Condidan and Farinmail, at a place which is called Deorham
(probably Dyrham, north of Bath); and they captured three of
their cities, Gleawanceaster (Gloucester), Cirenceaster and
Bathanceaster (Bath). It does not follow that the cities were
anything but ruins.

Nearly all the settlement names are Saxon in origin,
although some may have a Norman personal name tacked on,
as at Compton Dando (d'Alno), and Newton St Loe
(Peasedown St John is a made-up nineteenth-century name),
but some may simply be a renaming of an existing settlement.
A prime need was, as it always had been, for water, and lines of
villages are found strung out in the valleys of streams such as
the Chew, the Cam and Wellow Brooks, the Avon itself and
the Frome. Others line the spring-lines of the scarps, as along
the Cotswold foot (e.g. Old Sodbury), the Mendips (e.g.
Blagdon), and along the Triassic scarp north of Bristol (e.g.
Almondsbury). In the swampy levels advantage was taken of
slight rises of ground, as at Yatton, Nailsea and Oldbury, and
similarly the few settlements along the coast are related to
outcrops of harder rock, as at Aust and Portishead. Generally
speaking, there is a greater density of settlement south of the
Avon than north, and the low, heavy country round the
Ladden Brook, the northern tributary of the Frome, has only
hamlets. Some would be daughter-settlements formed during
the five hundred years before the Norman Conquest, a time in
which the villagers would be clearing the land and extending
the farming area. Although many of the farmhouses would be
in the village, as many are today, there is only scanty evidence
of common open-field farming, and it seems likely that from

early times the new land was divided into individual holdings and outlying farms were established, and that the keeping of flocks and herds was important, as it was at the time of Domesday Book in 1086. Comparison of Saxon land-charters and Domesday Book suggests also that there was fairly close territorial agreement between 'vills' (parishes) and the 'members' of manors—indeed many of the Saxon manors were no larger than a parish, although by the Conquest there were some considerable landowners in the area—Bath Abbey, for example, and the Earl of Wessex.

Bath itself revived and in the eighth century was given a monastery which became important enough to be the scene of the coronation of King Edgar in 973. Bristol (Bricgstowe, the place on the bridge) is first heard of on a coin of the time of Ethelred the Unready (976–1016) but, unlike Bath, has no details given in Domesday Book, where it is included in the 'Barton of Bristol'. The Barton paid the large sum of 110 marks of silver which suggests that the town was of some importance (Bath paid £60 and one mark in gold). Westbury, to the west of Bristol, was the site of a Saxon monastery, but the present-day slight remains are of a fifteenth-century rebuilding of the College of Canons established in c1194.

One notable landscape feature of Saxon times was the great hunting-forest of Kingswood and Fillwood Chase which spread north and south of the Avon, but mainly north, between Bristol and Keynsham. There was a royal hunting-lodge at Pucklechurch, and it was there that King Edmund was stabbed to death in 946. Technically, a forest was any area which came under the separate forest laws and was not necessarily wooded, but the geography of the area is such that this would have been a forest in the general sense. As, how-ever, it was sitting on a coalfield and quite good agricultural land between two towns in a relatively densely populated area, squatting become so powerful an influence as to render impossible, as the centuries passed, any reversion to its original use.

Nearly all the present village-names can be identified in Domesday, although some cases have to rest on inspired guesswork. There were a few manors with large populations of working males (the only persons recorded)—Keynsham had 110, Congresbury had eighty, Chew Magna fifty-three,

but in general numbers were small, about twenty to thirty—
Marshfield, for example, had thirty-two but ten were serfs,
which was unusual as there was usually only one or two,
probably house-servants. Each manor had a certain amount of
arable land, for it had to be self-sufficient, but what is notable
is the large number of sheep, not only on the Cotswolds but
spread over the hill-and-valley country and absent only on the
marshy lowlands. Pigs were usual, rooting for food in the
forests, and goats also figure in some of the accounts. Very
occasionally a horse or two is mentioned, for they were
valuable animals; the ploughing and draft-work was done by
oxen (*animalia*).

Notable additions to the scene in the eleventh and twelfth
centuries were the new stone parish churches, and many today
still retain some odd bit of Norman work—a doorway, a
pillar, a font or an arch. The best remaining interior is at
Compton Martin, but the most impressive is the chapter
house of Bristol Cathedral, dating from the twelfth century
when it was built for the Augustinian abbey. Also in Bristol is
the Norman church of St James, with its unusual wheel-
window; this was part of a twelfth-century monastery,
founded in 1129 as a Benedictine cell of Tewkesbury. In the
middle of Bristol, All Saints', now containing an urban-
studies centre, has two Norman bays. Of the great Norman
abbey at Bath nothing survived the Tudor rebuilding except
some pier footings and one window arch.

The homes of the villagers would have been of wood won
from the forest, and nothing survives of them, or even of the
more substantial manor courts—all we have is a Norman back
at Saltford and a north wing at Horton Court. Nor is there
anything notable in the way of castles, as there would have
been if the one built at Bristol in the twelfth century by Robert
of Gloucester had survived, for it was twice the size of
Caernarvon, with a keep larger than the Tower of London.
Richmond Castle at East Harptree has only a scrap or two of
wall embedded in a bank; Culverhay at Englishcombe
shows, not too clearly, the mound, courtyard and ditch of a
small motte-and-bailey; Stowey, on the hill above Bishop
Sutton, has a few mounds in a field; and all that remains on
Worlebury Hill above Weston-super-Mare is the earthen ring
of Castle Batch. Thornbury Castle, which now contains a

restaurant, was an unfinished piece of ostentation by the ill-fated Duke of Buckingham.

The thirteenth century produced a spate of monastic building. Ringing Bristol were St Mark's Hospital (1220, College Green), a Dominican Friary (1229, Quakers Friars), a Franciscan Friary (1234, Lewin's Mead), a Carmelite house (1267, site of Colston Hall) and St Bartholomew's Hospital (1274, bottom of Christmas Steps), which was on the site of a Norman church. Of these there remain the church of St Mark's (the Lord Mayor's chapel, much altered), the gateway to St Bartholomew's (the Hospital was considerably altered when it became the Grammar School in 1532) and two ranges at Quakers Friars which survived as guildhalls, one of which now contains the City planning exhibition. Part of the land was given to the Quakers, who in 1670 built a meeting-house there, although the present building is of 1747. The Templars had already been established in Bristol in about 1150, and the oval plan of their original church is now outlined in the bombed shell of the later building with its leaning tower and eighteenth-century Classical west doorway. Similarly the Augustinian abbey at Keynsham was early, having been founded in 1170.

Down on the edge of the marshes east of Weston-super-Mare, a small Augustinian priory was founded in 1230 at Worspring (today called Woodspring). Recently rescued from oblivion by the Landmark Trust, it has the remains of its church and a hall to be seen. Of the nunnery at Barrow Gurney established in about 1212 very little remains—part of a chapel and a tithe barn. At Hinton Charterhouse bits of a Carthusian monastery are still visible.

The monastic buildings were, of course, an addition to the landscape, but the extent to which monastic activities affected the economy and land-use is uncertain. The Bristol Augustinians seem to have done some work in draining and developing the marshlands by the Frome, and at Worspring work on draining and improving was done. The Carmelites brought in Bristol's first piped water-supply—to a single conduit by St John's gate. Certainly Bath Abbey was concerned in developing the wool industry and in organizing the farming of their lands about the city, an activity which sometimes brought them into conflict with those citizens who were also farmers.

There is evidence that in the thirteenth century the Abbey was operating a three-field and common grazing system but that enclosures were already being made. This conflicts with the previous suggestion that enclosure was very early in the region, and indeed there are open-field clues elsewhere in old names such as 'Eastfield', 'Westfield', 'Little Great Acres' and 'Tynings' (implying sub-division of older open fields), and the extent to which enclosure was original, the extent to which open fields were established and the rate at which they were sub-divided, must at present be left an open question.

Throughout the medieval period Bath flourished as a woollen-manufacturing centre, a market town and a national health centre but did not expand outside its walls. Bristol was the great *entrepôt* for the region, with a considerable coasting trade as well as connections with Ireland, Gascony, Spain and Portugal, and an increasing relationship with the North Atlantic fisheries. Wine in and cloth out was the main trade, but there were many other trade-goods—woad, leather, corn, fish, timber, iron and salt, for example, but no longer was there the Irish slave-trade against which the Bishop of Worcester had fulminated successfully in the eleventh century. For all this activity the anchorages of the Avon were insufficient, and in 1240 Bristol embarked on a major engineering project which affected the future pattern and lay-out of the city. This was a diversion of the Frome along a new cut, nearly half a mile long and about 40 yards wide, through marshland bought from St Augustine's. A new stone bridge, with houses and a chapel, replaced old Bristol Bridge, and a wall was built to enclose Redcliff on the far side of the Avon. Redcliff was the main manufacturing area of the town, and Bristol was important for such industries as cloth-making, leather, glass and soap, industries which sustained it through the considerable fluctuations in fortune of its shipping trade. There was, however, little suburban building before the seventeenth century in spite of the extensive area which formed the 'City and County of Bristol' under the great charter of Edward III granted in 1373. And so considerable has been the rebuilding and so devastating the wartime bombing that no secular buildings remain from the Charter year.

In the countryside there is little now to see of medieval secular building, although there is one attractive example in the nucleus of Clevedon Court, and another, built about 1470, makes up half of Congresbury vicarage. Many more survive from the wave of building and rebuilding in Tudor and Jacobean times, including a clutch of Courts, as at Iron Acton, Portishead, Clevedon, Nailsea, Siston, Barrow Gurney, Cold Ashton and (part of) Long Ashton, a number of farms and some other buildings such as Chew Magna Church House. It is probable that many of the small village houses with stone-mullioned windows date from this period, but they could be later, as vernacular building was slow to adapt to new fashions. Two other features of Tudor times, the enclosure of land for sheep-walks and the selling-off of monastic land, seem to have had little landscape-effect in the Avon area, although the suppression of the monasteries was important in providing building-land in Bath and Bristol.

Following the upheavals of the Civil War there came in the late-seventeenth and eighteenth centuries a period of prosperity. Bath and Bristol burst out of their city walls; manufacturing increasingly moved from cottage to town; new methods made agriculture more productive, while increasing population swelled the demand for food; mining in the Bristol and Somerset coalfields increased, as did calamine- (zinc-) mining on Mendip, feeding the growing brass industry of the lower Avon valley; and into the countryside came a new feature, the landscaped parks of the great country houses at Dyrham, Dodington and Great Badminton.

There was a considerable improvement in communications, with the construction of locks on the Avon between Bath and Bristol and the development of the turnpike trusts for the main roads. Many of the villages got new houses in the prevailing Classical style, but the major building developments were in the cities. Bath saw the creation of what were virtually two new towns in green field sites adjacent to the ancient city, an assemblage of streets, squares and crescents of high architectural order which makes it today a city of world interest and particularly sensitive to environmental change. Bristol, booming with the highly lucrative slave-trade and its attendant traffic in chocolate, sugar, cotton and tobacco, raw materials for its rapidly expanding industries, was busy adding its own Georgian suburbs and became, in size and trade, the second city in the land.

It did not hold the position long, partly because it was not well situated to develop any of the great coal-based growth-industries of the nineteenth century, partly because navigation of the Avon was difficult for the new large ships, and in some cases impossible, and partly because dock charges were very high. In spite of major works concluded in 1809 whereby the loop of the Avon within the city was converted to a Floating Harbour by locking it off from a newly made channel, the New Cut, and topping it up from a canal, the Feeder, its position was awkward, and it was not until the development of docks at Avonmouth at the end of the century that trade was considerably improved. The city docks are now closed.

A very big expansion took place, however, from the beginning of the last quarter of the century, and the growing city swallowed up large areas of countryside and engulfed whole villages, expanding its boundaries time and again. A similar, but smaller, expansion took place in Bath, although its annual influx of visitors for the 'season' had greatly diminished. One factor in this development was the influence of the railways, which after 1840 added new features of cutting, embankments, bridges and tunnel-entrances to the rural scene, as well as helping to increase the service function of the cities and the expansion of Clevedon and Weston-super-Mare as seaside resorts. They also affected agriculture, particularly in increasing accessibility to markets for milk and market-garden produce at a time when wheat, due to increasing supplies from abroad, was becoming a less profitable crop for local farmers. One result was the increase of grassland, a feature which became even more marked between the First and Second World Wars.

This change-over to pastoral farming continued as a trend between the wars, and the increasing use of farm-machinery, which had started with steam-power at the end of the nineteenth century, was cutting the demand for agricultural labour, a process which has accelerated since the Second World War and would have depopulated the villages if the bus and, more especially, the private car had not made them homes for commuters and caused most of them, particularly in the north Bristol fringe, to expand considerably. Between the wars a new feature was the introduction of council house estates, some of them rehousing people from slum-clearance

areas in the inner city, and since 1945 Bristol has extended
southward with municipal housing. Another tendency, again
accelerated since 1945, was the development of light industrial
estates peripheral to the town, or in adjoining villages and
linked to the major roads. Inter-war housing was also tending
to creep along the main roads and might have produced a
continuous belt from Bristol to Bath if it had not been for the
Ribbon Development Act. This modern housing, both
private and municipal, in town and in village, was characterized by a new feature, the small semi-detached house and the
bungalow.

Two industrial areas of particular importance, both origin-
ating just before the First World War, were Filton, with its
aero-works, and Severnside, with its heavy smelting and
chemical-works. Inner city congestion caused some firms to
move out, starting with Fry's, who migrated in 1922 to a green
field site near Keynsham which they called Somerdale; more
recently Wills have moved their tobacco factory to a new
building on the southern edge of the city, as have Harvey's
wine and spirit firm who now do not even import through
Bristol. Outside Bath and Bristol, the main manufacturing
areas today are around Radstock, Midsomer Norton and
Paulton, on the defunct coalfield, and at Weston-super-Mare,
where it was post-war policy to develop a broader-based
economy and where factories and houses were built to entice
firms from Birmingham.

Since the Second World War the Avon region has been one
of economic and population growth, although it has lacked the
government support available for more ailing areas, and it is,
literally, an attractive area, a generally pleasant place to live in.
Through lack of appropriate natural resources, it escaped the
worst landscape manifestations of the Industrial Revolution; it
has now, by conscious effort, to ensure that it maintains its
environmental quality against the pressures of the modern
age.

III

THE COAST AND MOORS

A moor to most of us probably signifies a bleak upland with
Cathy and Heathcliffe being blown passionately about—
unless of course our thoughts turn to the Moor of Venice, and
it might come as something as a surprise to find that in Avon,
as in adjacent Somerset, the moors are a flat and often melancholy area of clay or peat stretching inland from the chocolate
waters of the Severn shore. It is not, however, unreasonable,
for the Old English *mor* simply signified a tract of open waste
ground. The suggestion that Weston-super-Mare is really
'Weston-super-Mora' (Marsh) might seem reasonable but is
unlikely to be true, being founded on the evidence of one early
map, where it is probably a mistake. 'Weston-super-Mud' is a
local version which would hardly endear the user to the
Tourist Board. One further linguistic point to be made is that
the drainage channels which pattern the land between the
rambling rivers are called *rhines* (Old English *ryne*—
"probably", says the OED) which locally are pronounced
'reens'.

Unlike the East Anglian fens, the moors have few wide
vistas, for the lines of sight are generally blocked by nearby
hedges and bends in the road which resulted from the par-
celling-out of the land when drainage and enclosure, much of
it as late as the nineteenth century, transformed the poor
grazing-grounds and bits of arable into good summer pasture
and dotted the landscape with isolated dairy-farms. As it was
predominantly cattle-country, many hedgerows were put in,
and even where ditches provided adequate barriers, their
borders were often planted, partly to help to secure the banks.
Drainage, enclosure and rationalization of holdings went hand
in hand, for as long as the land was farmed in scattered strips, it
was impossible to achieve a co-ordinated farming policy. Back
in 1679 a report on Portbury noted "inconveniences" which
were detailed as "divisions of their lands into so many prells

39

[parcels] . . . not only in the common mead and corn fields but in very manie of their inclosed grounds . . . by reason thereof litigatious spirits may be troublesome and it seems of late have been. Not only land of different tenants, but of different lords are intermingled."

Rights of common, extinguished by enclosure, were, as on Mendip, attached to occupation of Auster (ancient) tenements, and the 'parcels' were usually fixed. In one area, however, East and West Dolemeads, which overlapped the boundaries of Puxton, Congresbury and Wick St Lawrence, there is record of a system of allocation by annual lottery. Each commoner was allocated a symbol, such as a pole-axe, a dung-pick or a shell, which was carved on an apple, and as each plot was visited in turn, one of the apples was drawn out of a bag to determine who was to have the plot for the year—a method very appropriate to a largely illiterate population. One part of Meads, known as 'the Out let', was then put up for auction to defray the expenses, most of which were incurred in the concluding 'revel'. For the auction an inch of candle was lit, and the last bid before the light went out determined the tenant for the year. The system ceased when the moors were enclosed in 1811.

Much of the moorland lies below the level of high tide and has been subject to intermittent and sometimes disastrous flooding. A notable example was the great flood of January 1607 when, according to a contemporary account, people "got up into trees" only to find that "the trees had their rootes unfastened by the selfe-same destroyer that disjoynted barnes and houses" so that "their last refuge was patently to die". The event is recorded on a board inside the church at Kingston St Michael (where a drainage-ditch surrounds the building like a moat), which states that "the sea banks broke" and the water rose to five feet within the church. Even recently, in 1977, the sea broke through the defences at Severn Beach and caused local flooding.

Flood problems were exacerbated by the embankment of the rivers, for once the streams overflowed, the water could not make its way back. Preventive measure adopted in the nineteenth century and generally successful were the construction of flood-gates or sluices at the mouth of rivers to keep out the tides, the building of pumping-stations and the strengthening of sea-walls. The flood-gates, however, created some additional problems: they stopped navigation of the streams, increased the build-up of mud, and were ineffectual when high tides coincided with heavy rainfall. Even today a wet winter will turn many fields into shallow, shining lakes.

Drainage of the clay belt has a long history, and it was mainly on the inner party moors that later schemes applied. There is often a distinct contrast between the irregular fields of the early drainage and the rectangular pattern of the later works, but sometimes one has been superimposed on the other, as in the pattern around the Congresbury Yeo. This had been drained in the eighteenth century, but the results were unsatisfactory, and a new scheme, commissioned from John Rennie, was carried out following a Drainage Act of 1819. A new channel was cut for the lower stretch of the river, and a sluice put at the mouth; another cut, the Hewish Rhine, was made and actually taken under the Yeo in a culvert, and many of the old rhines were widened and deepened. Another scheme, in the Gordano valley in 1810, cleared the drainage to the sea by dismantling the Portishead tide-mill.

Enclosure and drainage were also important in the development of the nineteenth-century seaside resorts as they provided flat land for building and parks at Clevedon, at Portishead, where a pleasure-ground was made on Rodmoor (although not laid out until 1910), and particularly at Weston-super-Mare, where in 1808 William Cox and Richard Parsley bought the local Auster tenements from the Lord of the Manor, Hugh Smyth-Pigott to whom Parsley was steward. This enabled them to petition successfully for an Enclosure Act in 1815 for some thousand acres, the heart of the present town. Part of the moor was sold to defray expenses, and that area, from Regent Street to the present bus-station, was the site of the first urban development, a tight-knit grid of small terraced houses quite unlike the grander buildings which were to form much of the later building. Meanwhile in 1826 the old rough dyke was replaced by a solid sea-wall from Knightstone to Regent Street, although its southward extension along the whole front had to wait for the Sea Front Improvements of the 1880s. Rights to the sands were still vested in the Lord of the

Manor and were not transferred to the town until the beginning of the twentieth century.

Settlement on the moor is in the form of individual farmhouses, a handful of hamlets and one village, Yatton, where the Keuper marl extends a finger into the heart of the alluvium. On the hamlets the most remarkable feature is the church at Puxton set on a winding road by reedy rhines. Its tower leans amazingly, and the interior has an atmosphere of rustic antiquity which comes from a remarkable collection of massive old benches, high box-pews and Jacobean pulpit, reader's desk and altar-rails. The ends of the rood-beam can be seen, cut off and flush with the walls, and there is the lower part of a stone chancel-screen. Above the south porch door is the date 1557 which may refer to a restoration. Curiously, tiny Puxton was chosen, with Worle, to give its name to a railway station which is nearly three miles away at St George, named after a chapel which no longer exists. St George is close to the interchange between the Weston-super-Mare road and the M5, and, because of its location by a main road near to Weston, it consists mainly of inter-war housing. The main line still goes through, and there is a level-crossing and a Co-op milk-depot, but the station has disappeared.

The 'Yat' in Yatton come from the Old English *geat*, meaning gate, and probably refers to its location as an entry-point from higher ground into the moors. Originally a single street, with some extra building after the railway came, the village is now considerably enlarged with post-war housing estates and the inevitable shopping precinct. The newer houses are in brick whereas the old are mainly in carboniferous limestone which outcrops nearby in Cadbury Hill. At the north end of the village are the railway station, Railway Inn, Methodist chapel, disused cattle-market and large furniture-works, while at the south end is the church. This is an imposing building with a truncated spire which is copied in miniature in the very successful modern addition of vestibule, lavatories (a welcome addition to any church), meeting-room and carpeted passage which leads to the old, ogee-arched north door. The south door has a large, beautiful porch with exterior panelled tracery and an impressive ogee arch spearing upwards into a descending figure; inside the porch is a delicate lierne vault. The lower part of the tower is Early English in style; the transepts are Decorated, and most of the rest is Perpendicular. The Newton chapel has notable tombs, including a big wall-tomb of Sir John Newton (1488) and his wife, Isabel de Cheddre (1498), who had the chapel built. Sir John's head rests on the family emblem, a wheatsheaf, his wife's more comfortably on a cushion, and this is repeated with the grim-looking Sir Richard Newton and his slender second wife on their big alabaster tomb-chest. The Newtons lived at Court Wyke, long since demolished. By the church the Old Rectory has an impressive fifteenth-century front with gables, buttresses and stone-mullioned windows, some with tracery. Just outside the village, on the slopes of Cadbury Hill with its Iron Age fort, is Cadbury House, a large pseudo-medieval affair of 1874 with gables, turrets and mullions, which has been turned into a country club.

Back at the coast the only extensive stretches of sand are to be found in Weston Bay, fine for donkey-riding, playing ball-games and building castles, although any child digging industriously downwards will soon come to the clay beneath. For most of the rest the coastal clays drop a few feet to stretches of oozy mud and are broken in only a few precious places by the rocky feet of low promontories—Worlebury, Middle Hope, the Clevedon–Portishead ridge and the little Triassic cliff at Aust, springboard for the Severn Bridge.

Worlebury, quarry-gashed and camp-crowned, carries on its southern flanks the rising tide of Weston's urban expansion with Italianate and 'Jacobethan' houses and crescents to the west, tidy inter-war semis and bungalows in the centre, and a tight rash of post-war housing estates to the east, nibbling away at the woods which Smyth-Pigott planted in the 1820s to beautify the bare hillside and make an amenity which the Town Council seemed extraordinarily reluctant to acquire. In 1909 they could have had them for £1,000 but refused; in 1914 they offered no bid when the woods were auctioned; in 1943 they were offered 396 acres for £10,000 and refused, and when a few years later they had a change of heart, it cost them £30,000 to acquire 300 acres. As the Weston-super-Mare History and Conservation Study Group remarked in 1976 in their excellent *All Quiet on the Weston Front?*, "What is noteworthy about this episode is not that the woods were more or less saved but that they should ever have been at risk."

Clinging to the hillside on the north-east is the little village of Kewstoke, whose church has a Norman south doorway and in the porch information about the 'Becket reliquary' (of which more later), and on the south-east is Worle, which has spread vastly since the War. The main street is chiefly of carboniferous limestone houses, but new shops and a shopping centre in light grey brick have been inserted. The war-memorial has a good shingled clock-tower which adds a touch of interest. The church, slightly up the hill, has a Norman doorway and stalls with misericords (literally 'pity of heart'), the little ledges under hinged seats which propped up the weary when standing. On these appear twice the initials of Richard Springer, Prior of Woodspring and Vicar of Worle from 1499 to 1516.

A couple of miles to the north of Worlebury stretches the parallel limestone ridge of Middle Hope, which, because of its relative inaccessibility, has been untouched by 'development' (although there was an unsuccessful project in the 1920s to build a 'bungalow town') and which in 1968 became a property of the National Trust. Wild and windy, with fine views and real, if miniature, cliffs, it is perhaps the most attractive natural feature of the whole coast and forms a splendid backing to the remains of the Priory of Woodpsring (originally 'Worspring', 'wooded copse'). This was a small house of Augustinian canons which belonged, as did St Augustine's in Bristol and Keynsham, to the Order headed by the abbey of St Victor in Paris, and it was founded in the early-thirteenth century by Robert de Courtenay, grandson of Reginald FitzUrse, one of the knights who struck down Thomas à Becket before the altar of Canterbury Cathedral in 1172. The Priory was dedicated to St Thomas, along with God and the Blessed Virgin Mary, and Becket's martyrdom is depicted on its seal, but, as de Courtenay wrote that he was founding the house in order to expedite the salvation of all his family, including ancestors and descendants, it may be an over-simplification to look on the act as simply one of expiation for the sins of his grandfather.

Worspring may well have had a relic of the saint, one of the small vessels of 'Canterbury water'—water mixed with a tiny portion of the saint's blood, for in 1849 there was discovered, walled up in nearby Kewstoke church, a three-inch wooden cylinder with a dark smear inside which was identified as human blood, and it is possible that this was a sacred relic hidden at the dissolution of the Priory in 1536. It was sent to the Taunton museum.

After its dissolution the Priory passed through various hands and became incorporated into a farm, until in 1968 it was acquired by the Landmark Trust, a remarkable private organization set up in 1965 "for the purpose of preserving small buildings, structures or sites of historic interest, architectural merit or amenity value, and where possible finding suitable uses for them; and for protecting and promoting the enjoyment of places of historic interest or natural beauty". (Their fascinating collection of properties ranges from follies to farmhouses and includes mills and mines, the island of Lundy and the High Street at Stourbridge; many can be rented for holidays.) Much of the monastery has disappeared, but there still remains the little church (minus its chancel), the infirmary and the gatehouse arch. The large monastic barn is used by the farm and is not accessible to the public. A full account of the Priory and its remains by D. J. Tomalin was published by the Trust in 1974.

From Woodspring Bay, overlooked appropriately by St Thomas's Head, the coast sweeps north-eastward to the last and longest of the carboniferous limestone ridges. Stretching from Clevedon to Portishead the plateau-top, much of it enhanced by downs and woodland, presents a cliff face to the sea and a steep slope south-eastward to the flat-bottomed Gordano valley which lies between it and the Tickenham ridge, the western end of the Failand plateau. The middle of the valley is covered with up to 15 feet of peat which forms fen and carr (woodland of alder, birch and willow) and includes the ten-acre Weston Moor Nature Reserve which was leased from Portishead in 1974 by the Somerset Trust for Nature Conservancy; approached by footpath, its entry is restricted in the bird-breeding season. There are interesting contrasts in vegetation between Weston Big Wood on one side of the valley and Norton's Wood on the other, for the former, designated 'a Site of Special Scientific Interest' by the Nature Conservancy, is on limestone and the latter on Pennant sandstone which develops an acidic soil. The M5 has been chiselled into the slope of the hills on the southern side of the

Gordano valley over which it gives splendid views, and from the service station can be seen the tower of Portbury church.

Portbury is one of the villages which lie along the edge of the valley, avoiding the once marshy bottom, and it was for long the centre of the Portbury Hundred. The manor belonged to the Berkeleys, with a short break in the Tudor period, from the time of Robert Fitzharding in the twelfth century until 1613, when it passed by marriage to the famous Coke family of Norfolk, who sold it in about 1785 to James Gordon who had made a fortune in the sugar-plantations of Antigua. The Gordons, whose arms are on the church pulpit, did a great deal for the valley, draining the marshes and erecting farmhouses, but the line died out locally, and in 1870 the manor was sold to Sir Greville Smythe of Ashton Court.

The church is of interest, and details of the phases of its building by the Berkeleys are in a pamphlet on sale inside, although the dates do not agree well with those in Pevsner's *Buildings of England*. Entrance through the Norman doorway inside the big south porch takes the visitor into a church whose aisles are so wide as to make the body almost square. Of particular interest are the carved corbels supporting the roof over the aisles and nave, the plentiful supply of stone seating along the walls and around the pillars (which is why the weak go to the wall), the curious ribbed vault of the vestry, and the charming little brass of 1621 on the north wall. In the village are the derelict remains of a priory with its tower, originally Tudor but much restored by the Gordons. It was a cell of the Augustinian Abbey of Bromore in Hampshire.

To the east of Portbury is Easton-in-Gordano which has spread with post-war building to join physically with Pill, from which it was separated as a new parish in 1863. The new developments are by no means unpleasant. Opposite Easton church, for example, a successful attempt has been made to build modern houses in the local idiom. The church itself had a fourteenth-century tower, but its body is a second rebuilding of 1871, retaining at its west-end interior a curious pattern of mouldings and abutments on the tower wall. A painted *Memento Mori* tablet of 1699 records Captain Samuel Sturmey's gift to the church of a copy of his *Marinors or Artistes Magazine*, a treatise on seamanship and navigation, which any "ingenious person" could borrow on depositing a surety of £3.

He also presented the church with a couple of astronomical 'Dials' which have since disappeared.

Pill (the name signifies a creek) was for centuries the home of the pilots who took ships up the winding Avon to Bristol docks and is situated where a steep-sided valley contains a tidal, muddy creek which here joins the river. The creek is crossed by a red-brick viaduct for the Portishead railway (1867) and is mostly filled in, forming a base for a modern, pleasant development of shops and homes. What remains is a haven for little yachts. The somewhat inappropriately named Marine Parade offers views of Avonmouth and the M5 bridge as it humps over the Avon.

South-west from Portbury along the minor road to Clevedon is Clapton-in-Gordano. 'Clapton' probably means 'hill place", and 'Gordano' probably refers to the shape of the whole valley as a 'gore'. The Court and church lie some distance from the roadside village, and it is probable that the latter developed on a new site during the time when it was connected with coal-mining. The Court has a fine three-storeyed porch tower. The church opposite is perched on a steep little hill below the line of the M5 and is of red sandstone with the interior walls plastered and grooved in imitation of ashlar. A Norman doorway leads into the nave, which has no aisles but a north chapel of about 1300 and probably originally detached. In the chapel is an ornate tomb with statues of Henry Winter, in armour, and his wife Katharine, kneeling face-to-face and praying ostentatiously over a prayer-desk under which sits a child with a skull in his lap. Beneath is recorded the death of their son Edmund in 1672; the hasty inscription overruns its panel.

On the far side of the valley are Walton-in-Gordano and Weston-in-Gordano, both very small. Walton is on the outskirts of Clevedon, and its old church, of which only the tower stump remains, is now within the latter's bounds—the new church in the village was built in 1839. Walton Castle, on the hill above, was built for Lord Poulett in about 1615–20 as a hunting-lodge and is a fine example of an early Gothic folly. It has an octagonal tower with an octagonal staircase-tower, all surrounded by an octagonal wall with round towers. To its east is a raised circle which was probably a Bronze Age cattle-pound of about 500 BC.

At the west end of Clevedon is a slightly detached upland forming Wains Hill, which overlooks the mouth of the Yeo as it wanders into Clevedon Pill, and Church Hill, which rises steeply above Salt House Fields with their park and lake. On it stands the ancient part-Norman Old Church of St Lawrence to which in 1833 was carried for burial the body of young Arthur Hallam, nephew of Sir Charles Elton of Clevedon Court. Hallam, who died in Vienna, had been Tennyson's dearest friend in their student days at Cambridge, and the poet was desolated by his loss.

> And the stately ships go on
> To the haven under the hill;
> But O for the touch of a vanish'd hand,
> And the sound of a voice that is still.

That was an immediate reaction, but it was not until seventeen years later, in the year that he became Poet Laureate, that Tennyson wrote 'In Memoriam' and visited the tomb of his friend. It was, he said, "a kind of consecration to go there". The poem, like *Hamlet*, is "full of quotations", of which perhaps the best known is—

> 'Tis better to have loved and lost,
> Than never to have loved at all.

Our Victorian forbears were easily moved to tears, and no doubt the lines sound sentimental, but that is because they are quoted outside the context of a long and complex work. 'In Memoriam' is basically an attempt to re-establish a personal faith when faith itself was being assailed not only by the shock of a particular bereavement but more generally by new and prevalent scientific dogmas, new and degrading ways of work, and a dismal economic creed—all, it seemed, in league to reduce the stature, dignity and freedom of mankind and to drain the world of colour and spirit. Was Man, indeed, no more than Super-Ape?

> I trust I have not wasted breath;
> I think we are not wholly brain,
> Magnetic mockeries; not in vain,
> Like Paul, with beasts, I fought with Death.

Not only cunning casts in clay,
Let Science prove we are, and then
What matters Science unto Men,
At least to me? I would not stay.

It is in such times of culture-shock that relief is widely sought
in a retreat to a semi-mythical past invested wishfully with lost
virtues, passions, and certainties, and to the Victorians this
increasingly meant medieval England, a merrie hotch-potch
of spires and knights and ladyes fayre and chivalry, of barge-
boards and gables and gargoyles, of Gothic lettering and ye
olde thisse and thatte, and England to herself being True.
It was *The Idylls of the King* and *Westward Ho!* (for Eliza-
bethans were also Romantic) and *The Last of the Barons*, and it
begat the Albert Memorial, Manchester Town Hall, Temple
Meads Station—and much of Clevedon and Weston-super-
Mare.

Although Gothic got into a great deal of Victorian design,
from fish-knives to furniture, it was not without rivals. Italy,
too, was Romantic, and its disadvantage of not being British
was to some extent overcome when Albert designed Osborne
House for the Dear Queen in an Italianate style, thus making
widespread eaves, low-pitched roofs, round-headed windows
and four-sided towers almost patriotic. Venetian Gothic,
moreover, which washed into England on the thundering tide
of Ruskin's rhetoric, gave an unparalleled opportunity for
ostentation, the other, less pleasant, motive for much of the
exuberance of High Victorian architecture. Architecture, it
was understood, was ornament, and ornament was display, so
houses were loaded with mass-produced carvings in the way
that women were loaded with jewels, to display the wealth of
their owners, the warm men of business.

Behind this display the middle-class man wanted his house
to be, perhaps more than his wife, comfortable and efficient,
and these Victorian villas are solid, well-founded buildings.
They are also large and difficult to run without servants, so
many today have been split into flats or made into hotels and
institutions. Contemporary technology, such as gas-heating
and lighting, was a source of pride, although it would be
anachronistically tricked out in ancient styles, as witness the
many Gothic lamp-standards and 'gasoliers'. Sir Arthur

Hallam Elton introduced street-lighting by gas into Clevedon in 1864, and, although he deplored this modern intrusion into the daytime scene, he invited admiration of its romantic effect in the darkness when "the dark valley sparkles with the scattered lights". He was also Chairman of the company which, backed by the Clevedon Bank and a local consortium of enthusiasts, brought technology in iron to the building of the Clevedon Pier, a remarkably elegant structure of 1869 which used rails which Brunel had intended for the South Wales Railway. (Regrettably, the centre section was destroyed by a storm in 1970, and although great efforts have been made to raise funds for restoration, its future is still uncertain.) Sir Arthur was a remarkable man, and much of the lay-out and development of Victorian Clevedon resulted directly from his activities. He was also a man of conscience, resigning his seat as MP for Bath (1857–9) because he disapproved of the Crimean War, building and maintaining a Cottage Hospital, setting up a lending-library and sponsoring educational provision. He added two new churches to the town, All Saints' in 1860 and St John's in 1878, which was designed by William Butterfield. St. John's is a quiet building and not typical of the aggressive style of one of the most remarkable of Victorian High Church architects, best known perhaps for his polychromatic All Saints', Margaret Street, London, and Keble College, Oxford.

Today it is still the romantic appeal of dramatic, though small-scale, scenery, fine views, winding walks, little parks, many trees, fine villas, elegant Regency houses of the earlier development along the shore, and the alternations of rocks and pebbles along the coast, which constitute Clevedon's main attraction, and the topography of the site has prevented the large-scale development of the more gimcrack and 'popular' features of the bigger seaside resorts. Until the railway came to Weston-super-Mare, Clevedon was larger and more popular than its rival; today the town's guide-book looks to the new and accessible motorway to bring increased custom—it is to be hoped that it will not destroy the place. So far it has managed to handle a certain amount of modern residential development for Bristol commuters and some industrial growth, such as the large Hales' bakery, without serious environmental injury.

Clevedon Manor is situated, unusually, some two miles away from the parish church, probably because the founder wanted a dry way to Bristol along the edge of the Failand ridge, and the house incorporates its own fourteenth-century chapel, whose unique window of reticulated tracery is one of the most attractive features of the building. Inside, the chapel, which is on the first floor, has a window on to the medieval Great Hall whose later modifications include a Tudor fireplace and an eighteenth-century plaster ceiling but which still retains on one side its Screens Passage with three fourteenth-century arches into what were the buttery, kitchen and pantry, later converted into a dining-room, a staircase (nineteenth-century) and a Justice Room which now holds a display of Nailsea glass but previously served as a waiting-room for the court which the Lord of the Manor, as Justice of the Peace, held in the Great Hall. At an angle to the Justice Room is a room, now a museum, which was probably added in about 1300 as a Hall to the oldest part of the building, a thirteenth-century three-storey rectangular tower. The west wing, which suffered several rebuildings, was demolished in the 1950s when the house was taken over by the National Trust. Behind the house rise pleasant garden terraces. The house and gardens are open on Wednesdays, Thursdays, Saturdays and Bank Holidays, from April to September.

It is a most pleasant place to visit, not only for the interest of its architecture, portraits, collections of glass and gardens but also for its atmosphere. It is small, unostentatious, domestic and calm (in spite of the busy buzzing from the nearby motorway), and in some undefinable way it breathes the spirit of a home long-loved. Of its long line of owners the most remarkable were the Eltons, who came on the scene in 1709 when Abraham Elton, a prosperous merchant of Bristol, bought the house and much land in Cleveland, Tickenham and Failand. In 1717 he was created a baronet. His great-grandson, the Reverend Sir Abraham Elton, who had the property from 1790 to 1842, gave Clevedon its opportunity to expand when he enclosed its common lands, but he was best known for his strenuous opposition to Methodism, his championing of Hannah More in the great Blagdon dispute and his unsuccessful dash to Bristol in an attempt to prevent his son from marrying the daughter of a Dissenter. His second wife, who he married when he was seventy, did much to develop Clevedon, in particular commissioning the mock-Jacobean house called Mount Elton. The Reverend's son, Sir Charles Abraham Elton, was a poet and friend of leading literary figures, including Coleridge, who earlier had spent his honeymoon in a cottage rented from the Reverend, and Thackeray, who often visited the Court and two of whose sketches are exhibited there. Tennyson stayed at the Court in 1850.

The next owner, Sir Arthur Hallam Elton, was important, as we have seen, in developing Clevedon, but his son, Sir Edmund Henry Elton, who had the property from 1883 to 1930, although deeply involved as chairman of the Urban District Council and Captain of the Fire Brigade, was most famous as 'the Potter Baronet', whose Elton Ware, of which there is a fine display at the house, had an international reputation, particularly in America where it was marketed by Tiffany's. Examples of his work can be seen on the 1898 clock-tower in Clevedon which he designed for Queen Victoria's Jubilee. Many more details of the house and its owners are given in the excellent booklet by Arthur and Margaret Ann Elton which is on sale there.

Twentieth-century housing, not at all unpleasant, is a much more marked feature of Portishead, where it climbs the hill and fills in the gaps of a complicated settlement structure which has four focal-points: the old village, the docks, the bay and the plateau. The original settlement, with its church and sixteenth-century manor house, lies on the leeward side of the hill, facing east, and is mainly Victorian with modern housing above and below. The single dock lies to the north and is dominated by the big red-brick cuboid bulk of the two electricity-generating stations with their four tall chimneys. Much of the old pill has been filled in with ash from their coal-fired boilers. Over the hill the old cliff line was first developed with a line of Victorian villas and then filled in below with inter-war housing down to Rodmoor, which was laid out as a pleasant park before the First World War and is bounded by an Esplanade constructed by the City of Bristol. The foreshore of mud has been colonized by marsh plants and is not attractive, but an open-air heated swimming-pool has been built into the side of the low headland of Battery Point whose fort was dismantled after the First World War. Development further west is mostly of inter- and post-war housing but also includes the Nautical School founded in 1909 largely by Bristol initiative.

The influence of Bristol was important. Whereas the development of Clevedon was due largely to the energetic efforts of the Eltons as Lords of the Manor, and that of Weston-super-Mare to private enterprise and the Improvement Commissioners, that of Portishead was much influenced by Bristol Corporation, who had become major landowners. This was particularly the case after Bristol bought out the Portishead Dock Company in 1884, but the City had in fact been Lord of the Manor since 1616 when it acquired parts of it for £950 from John Hall, a wealthy clothier of Bradford-on-Avon. The Corporation bought the rest three years later for £500. At the beginning of the nineteenth century it was the City which promoted the Enclosure Act, and it was as early as 1830 that it built a neo-Jacobean hotel on the wooded hill overlooking the creek. A suitably Romantic drawing of the hotel hangs in the bar today, and there is still an attractiveness about the spot—providing you keep your back to the power-station.

The marshland between Portishead and the mouth of the Avon belongs to the Port of Bristol Authority and contains the trapezoidal West Dock, re-christened 'the Royal Portbury Dock' when it was officially opened by the Queen in 1978. It is a dreary, featureless area compared with the Severnside industry over the river at Avonmouth which, however it may be criticized environmentally, has a certain weird grandeur about it when seen from a distance. (Both these areas will be considered further in the Bristol section.) At the northern end of the Severnside complex, towards Severn Beach, the land belongs to ICI, and there has been some housing development within smelling-distance of the works. Beyond this stretches nearly ten miles of lowland moor, quietly agricultural with individual farms and tiny hamlets, interrupted by three major feats of engineering, the Severn Tunnel (1886), the Severn Bridge (1966) and the Oldbury Nuclear Power Station (1965).

The idea of a bridge over the Severn pre-dates the railway tunnel, for it was in 1823 that the Postmaster General appointed Thomas Telford to advise him on how to improve the mail-coach route to Milford Haven. In the following year Telford proposed a suspension bridge at the Beachley–Aust crossing near the site of the Aust Ferry, the Old Passage, which he described as "one of the most forbidding places at which an important ferry was ever established—a succession of violent cataracts formed in a rocky channel exposed to the rush of a tide which has scarcely equal on any other coast". Telford's proposal came to nothing, nor was there any more success with later proposals put forward for railway bridges. Instead, the GWR put out a branch to an alternative ferry near Pilning, the New Passage, where the white hotel building still stands facing an oozy, muddy shore with patches of gravel and stone and affording fine views of the Welsh shore and, somewhat ironically, of the Severn Bridge. The New Passage was little better than the Old, and so it was decided to take the railway on under the Severn in a tunnel 4½ miles long and so difficult to construct that it took from 1874 to 1886.

Later proposals for a road-bridge near the tunnel site, over English Stones, a reef in the river, got as far as Parliament but were thrown out by a Select Committee in 1936. In 1943 Mr E. C. Boyce, County Surveyor for Gloucestershire, advocated building a bridge from Aust; in 1945 the Ministry of Transport agreed to take on the scheme, and in 1947 the Order fixing the line was confirmed. Work was then postponed in favour of building the Forth Bridge, which is of similar construction, although experience in building it enabled modifications to be made to the Severn structure. Work began on the Severn bridge in 1961, and it was opened by the Queen in 1966. A Welsh observer noted that tolls were to be taken on the English side!

It had cost £8 million. The main span is 3,240 feet; the total length is about a mile; the towers are 400 feet high; the cables are 20 inches thick, and the bridge was lighter for its length and loading than any that had ever been built before. It was hailed as a triumph of British engineering and is very beautiful, but it has not yet been considered wise to open all four lanes at peak traffic times.

A few miles north the 175-acre side for a nuclear power-station was chosen mainly because 13 feet below the sediments lay a band of Keuper marl which afforded firm foundations for the heavy plant and because out from the shore stretched a rock shelf which facilitated the construction of a 380-acre reservoir. This reservoir is surrounded by a concrete wall which retains five feet of water at ebb tide and provides 416 million gallons of water for cooling, fed to the plant by an underground pump-house. Spoil from reservoir construction was used to raise ground-level inland by 12 feet, a necessary precaution against flooding in an area which was below high-water.

The two reactors are of the AGR type (Advanced Gas-cooled Reactor). The gas is carbon dioxide which carries away the heat from the chain-reaction in the uranium dioxide fuel-rods and carries it to the boilers where it turns water into steam. Steam-power then drives the generators to produce electricity at 16,500 volts, which is then transformed up to 132,000 volts (130 kV) and fed into the National Grid at the sub-station near Iron Acton, from which it is either distributed by the South West Electricity Board or transformed to 275 kV to feed the Supergrid.

Work began on site in January 1961, and the station was opened in June 1965 by Anthony Wedgewood Benn, Minister for Technology and MP for Bristol East. Seen from the road, the buildings have the appearance of some technologically up-dated castle with two great drum-towers linked by a windowed curtain-wall. The tower walls are glass at the bottom and clad above in vertical strips of blue and light-grey sheeting. They hold the reactors. The service building which links them is in reinforced concrete. South of this lie the steel-framed buildings for the turbines, administration, stores and switch-gear, and the area around has been landscaped and planted with trees. In spite of its bulk—the towers are 60 feet high—the complex is quietly absorbed by the surrounding countryside.

The bridge and the power-station are remarkable enough, but there is the possibility, albeit an extremely faint one at present, of a stupendous and expensive feat of engineering which would transform the whole coast. Proposed in the 1920s, shelved, revived from time to time and today subject to Government sponsored research, this is the Severn Barrage, a proposal to turn the lower Severn and upper Bristol Channel into a lake, possibly by a dam below Weston-super-Mare, and thereby turn the tidal flow, the second highest in the world, to

the production of electricity. The environmental conse-
quences, which are being investigated by the Bristol
University Sabrina Project ('Sabrina' being the Roman name
for the Severn), would be considerable, particularly with the
permanent drowning of the off-shore mudflats and the loss of
tidal scour, and arguments for and against the scheme in its
environmental, engineering and financial aspects are strongly
held and as yet unresolved.

IV

WESTON-SUPER-MARE

Weston had 43,000 inhabitants in 1971 and from being the second largest settlement in Somerset became the third largest in Avon, yet in 1811 it had a population of only 163. By 1841 this had increased to 2,105, and in that year the arrival of the railway gave an impetus to development which by 1901 had resulted in a population of 19,845. This phenomenal growth, which was generated by the attraction of the town as a holiday resort, has left a splendid legacy of Victorian building of remarkable interest and quality, but it is worth noting that since then the population has doubled in size and that the town's functional structure has increased in complexity. The range and nature of its shops and services indicate that it plays an important part as a service-centre for the surrounding area, and that the extent and nature of its new housing is related to its developing industrial sector and to commuting and retirement, while its provision for visitors shows a clear division between trippers and stayers, although it is note-worthy that, unlike many other seaside places, there is no proliferation of large hotels. That is a circumstance to be welcomed in a town whose charm depends a good deal on a small-scale solidity which achieves decorativeness without undue ostentation and where the intrusion into the Victorian fabric of anything either gimcrack or gargantuan can be visually shocking.

The characteristics of Weston which attracted well-to-do citizens of nearby Bristol and Bath at the beginning of the nineteenth century were Romantic scenes, Salubrious air and, rather surprisingly in view of the muddy water and huge tidal-range, Sea Bathing. In 1805 the *Gentleman's Magazine* reported that "the village is much frequented of late in the summer and autumn for the benefit of sea air and bathing; several good lodging houses have been lately erected for the reception of company" and added the further attraction that the view from Worlebury Camp was "at once wild, grand, awful, and terrific". It might also have mentioned the splendid sunsets, much loved by local painters, which still occur as the low-level light refracts through the industrial haze of South Wales. The first Guide in 1822 also stressed the advantages in Weston of the "uncommon salubrity of its invigorating breezes", and another of 1829 noted with satisfaction that, of a hundred patients sent by an eminent Bath physician to Weston to breath the air, only four failed to benefit.

The early spa development centred on Knightstone, a small island just by the shore at the north of the bay. In 1820 it was bought as a speculation by two Bristol businessmen, Howe and Taylor, but the first major development came after 1833 when the Reverend Thomas Pruen acquired it and erected baths, lodging-houses, a reading-room and a causeway. The biggest development, however, was by Dr Fox, famous for a new and humanitarian treatment of lunatics in his new hospital at Brislington, Bristol, who acquired the property in 1837. Today Knightstone, with a theatre and public swimming-bath built respectively in 1903 and 1904, has been much re-modelled, but one of the old bath-houses, now a sauna, is recognizable by its Classical style. Meanwhile new residential building was focussed on two areas, the Knightstone end and half-way down the bay on the new enclosures between what are now Regent Street and Carlton Street, and in 1826 the two were connected by an esplanade. The northern area acquired a terrace or two and several large houses, but the southern part was developed as streets of two-storey houses which soon changed from their original use as apartments and became working-class accommodation. Later its position between the station and the front led to a rapid development of small cafés and shops which masked the earlier simplicity and has made the area meet for post-war 'development'. Between the two areas lay Weston's first hotels, the present Royal, built in 1805 and remodelled in 1845, and the Imperial of 1819.

In 1841 the proposal to build the Bristol and Exeter railway-line through Weston was resisted, and all the town got was a spur along which for ten years coaches were drawn by horses to a terminus which lay on the site of the present Alexandra Parade. In 1866 a new station, still a terminus, was constructed behind the present site of the Odeon, and finally in 1884 a loop-line was constructed through a third new station, on the then edge of the town. It cost the GWR £110,000.

In spite of the disadvantage of remaining for so long off the direct line, Weston entered into a building-boom which was energetically assisted by the local Commissioners, who had obtained their Improvement Act the year after the railway arrived. Development filled in the front between the two old centres and spread along the lower slopes of the hill, and the Guide of 1855 noted that "as if by magic, there have sprung up Oriel Terrace, the Crescent (both 1847), Greenfield Place, Prince's Buildings, Manilla Crescent (1850), and Wellington Terrace (1849) fronting the hill; together with an almost equal number of streets and houses, of less note in different parts of the town". The houses of "less note" may have been those in the fascinating area of working-class streets built in the 1850s behind the High Street and including Meadow Street, Orchard Place, Palmer Street, Orchard Street and Alfred Street—the latter extended in the 1860s to join the Boulevard. It is a region which retains much vitality, particularly as an area of small shops and cafés. Among the bigger developments particularly notable are Oriel Terrace in a restrained Jacobean style, coping well with its rise up the hill, and Royal Crescent (1847) with its striking depressed giant arches. Higher up the hill were hung the big villas such as Combe Bank (Italianate), Combe Lodge (Gothic) and the huge pink Italianate pile of the Villa Rosa (1847), demolished recently to make way for flats.

The culminating work of that period was the construction in 1860 of Weston's noblest street, the Boulevard, as a link for the estate developments of Christchurch and Montpelier which in 1854 had started on the hill slope above. This is High Victorian Gothic, all gables and bays and beams and carvings, yet remarkably restrained in style and scale, except for the two marvellously wild mock-medieval buildings at the west end, one of which houses the offices of the local newspaper. This late Gothic or 'Jacobethan' was to stamp its impression on Weston housing for the rest of the century, and very fine it looks.

Until 1861 southward expansion had been blocked by the White Cross Estate which Parsley had acquired for himself out of the enclosed lands, but in that year it was acquired for the town and included in the District bounds by a Provisional

Order. Starting with the ambitious scheme of Ellenborough Park, the area became covered with substantial houses down to Clarence Park, whose site was presented to the town in 1883 by Mrs Davies in memory of her father, 'Lawyer Davies', the first Clerk to the Commissioners, and one of the purchasers of the White Cross Estate. In 1872 the lands to the south were also sold off for building. All this development from Regent Street southwards was set back behind coastal dunes, but in the 1880s they were levelled and grassed over, forming the Beach Lawns, and the Esplanade was carried on to the new Sanatorium of 1868. A subsequent scheme in 1885 to turn the bay into a lake by building an embankment from Knightstone to the Sanatorium was rejected by Parliament as being over-ambitious. It would probably have created a mud-trap as effectively as did the later Marine Lake to the north of Knightstone.

Public buildings, many of them by a competent local architect, Hans Price, were a feature in the last quarter of the century. The Town Hall, which had been built in 1858–9, was extended in 1897 by Price; the Albert Memorial Museum and Night School was built in 1894 near Emmanuel Church (1847); and in 1865 came the first hospital building by Price in Burlington Street behind the 1928 extension which faces onto the Boulevard, where it is flanked by the neo-Baroque Museum and Library of 1900. The Museum has recently been moved to a new home in a most imaginative conversion of the 1912 Gas Workshops and showroom and has been developed into an extremely attractive and informative set of exhibitions. Education is represented by two of Price's most striking works, the old Board School (1897) in Walliscote Road and the School of Science and Art (1893), which became the Technical College and has been recently extended into a large concrete-and-glass Brutalist building singularly inappropriate in scale and style for its position. Considerable rebuilding took place in High Street with, for example, Osterley Buildings (1875), Somerset House (1899), another Price design, and a new Post Office of 1899, and the street began to develop as the main shopping area.

At the north end of High Street stood the house and grounds of the summer residence of the Smyth-Pigotts who in 1889 sold them to the Improvement Commissioners. The grounds were made into Grove Park, and the house became a library which was destroyed by incendiaries during the war. The surviving coach-house was used as a gardener's cottage and today provides a home for the Charter Trustees and the civic plate and regalia. Recent intrusions of a car-park and a cubic lavatory have not improved the setting, but the grounds are still fine and contain the remains of statues which Smyth-Pigott bought from Walpole's Gothic fantasy at Strawberry Hill.

Towards the end of the nineteenth century it was evident that Weston had come a long way from the days when its main customers were solid, well-to-do businessmen who came for the sea air and fine views, and the town joined its rivals in the race to capture the mass market. The focal-point of attraction was the stretch of sea-front at the end of Regent Street, which was the spot selected by the Improvement Commissioners in 1894 as the site for the 'Regent Street Pier'. An earlier pier had been built in 1864–7, but this sturdy, practical structure, which joined Birnbeck Island to the northern headland, was mainly for steamer-traffic and was in any case sited in a 'superior', off-centre area, where, said the 1891 Guide, the tourist might feel rather out of place! There is a proposal (1977) to re-develop it as a hotel. In 1904 the new Grand Pier, as it was then called, was opened, resplendent with fancy ironwork, numerous amusements and a big theatre which could hold two thousand people. It was twice as long as the present structure, for a fire in 1930 and damage in wartime necessitated an extensive rebuilding in which, unfortunately, it lost its air of fairy-tale extravaganza. Backing it, the Regent Street area became crammed with souvenir-shops, cafés, pubs and ice-cream parlours and attracted to itself a cinema and a waxworks—the cinema is now closed.

A little further north along the front lay an open space which belonged to Weston's first hotel, renamed 'The Royal' after the future Edward VII had stayed there with his tutors, but then called 'Rogers's'. Rogers's Field was acquired by the Council in 1924 after arbitration which awarded the claimants £2,640, and in 1925 a local businessman, councillor and philanthropist, Henry Butt JP, who became in 1937 the Charter Mayor, presented the Council with a cheque for the sum and the costs of arbitration.

In 1927 the Winter Gardens, which had been laid out on the

field at a cost of about £16,000, were opened, with a fine balustrading, presented by Butt, facing onto High Street, and the Pavilion blocking the seaward view, a low, domed structure which has continued to spread. At about the same time, the Council countered the unattractiveness of bathing in the muddy coastal waters, available only at high tide, by spending £50,000 on a swimming-pool on the sands.

Important as these changes were in the coastal belt, the most striking feature of inter-war development was the tide of housing which spread inexorably inland over the moors and along the hill to accommodate a residential population which increased by over eighteen thousand, nearly as much as the whole increase in the second half of the nineteenth century. This building was mainly in brick, often covered in pebble-dash, and the houses and bungalows followed the typical contemporary style of porch, gable and bay. Housing-patterns were also changing in the older parts, with large houses being converted to hotels, shops or flats or being pulled down to make space for re-development.

The whole process of expansion and re-development has continued since the war, including demolition of small streets to make way for a graceless shopping precinct and the development of Council estates segregated from the rest of the town by the railway-line, but the most important new element in the economy of the town has been the growth of light industry in the south-east corner on the Oldmixon Industrial Estate. This was a deliberate act of policy on the part of the Borough Council, who in 1958 inaugurated a scheme to take advantage of the 1952 Town Development Act by which grants were made available to help in the provision of housing for 'overspill' population from overcrowded areas when an agreement had been made between the two local authorities concerned. Weston therefore approached its nearest congested neighbour, Birmingham, where many workers already knew the place as a holiday resort, and arrangements were made whereby factory buildings and housing would be provided for any 'Brummies' who cared to come. In the event only a small proportion of the total work-force came from Birmingham, but although this hardly fulfilled the intentions of the Act, it provided Weston with what it wanted, a movement of firms into the area at a time when the Board of Trade was not inclined to grant Industrial Development Certificates for new industry outside the Development Areas.

Despite this necessary diversification, the holiday trade remains the mainstay of Weston's economy, and the main attractions are still the donkeys, broad, firm sands, lawns and parks, sea breezes, the clutter of cafés, souvenir-shops and ice-cream purveyors, and the cinema, theatres, Pavilion and piers, although there is some doubt as to whether they are quite the money-spinners they once were. The proliferation of hotels, mostly medium-sized the increasing number of holiday flatlets, and the ranks of bed-and-breakfast boards lining the entry-roads, are testimony to the huge seasonal influx of holidaymakers—although of only a part, for a high proportion of visitors are day-trippers. The consequence of this daily invasion is Weston's greatest curse, a huge tide of motor vehicles which surges into the town, swirls round the streets, overflows onto part of the beach and at peak hours ponds back the incoming stream to create frustrating lines of cars creeping along the entry-roads.

The problem is no worse than in most popular seaside resorts, but it is a pity that Weston did not adopt a more imaginative and radical approach to the problem instead of relying on the conventional and demonstrably feeble strategies of creating one-way streets, which confuse the visitors and irritate the residents, and of cramming into open spaces which could have been better used as areas of environmental amenity. The highway authority is now the County of Avon, and it remains to be seen what policy they will adopt following a survey which (in 1977) is still in progress. One possibility, which would be to create car-parks peripheral to the holiday area of the town and combine them with an efficient public transport system, would create problems for hotels and residents and would meet with great opposition from motorists and therefore from holiday tradesmen who would suspect a falling-off in custom. It would be a risky operation, requiring much initial capital-expenditure, but there would be very great environmental benefits from pedestrianization of the central area on a far larger scale than the present shutting-off of High Street. And it is, after all, environment quality which brings in the holidaymaker.

V

THE NORTHERN HEARTLAND

Geologically this area is of some complexity, lying between the coastal clays and the Cotswold limestones and running across the upturned edges of the variety of rocks which form the Bristol coalfield. Physically, however, it is a region of gentle relief which relates more to the river pattern than the rocks and divides into a western and southern part draining southward to the Avon through the Ladden Brook, Frome and Boyd Brook, and an eastern part draining northward to the Little Avon.

Much is still rural, but in the southern section, along the traffic-lanes out of Bristol, the landscape has been heavily overlaid with urban sprawl where comparatively small Victorian developments have been surrounded and infilled with a mass of post-war building which in general exhibits no regional identity. The post-war growth-rate of places such as Yate, Frampton Cotterell and Thornbury has been phenomenal, a rate which had the blessing of the South West Economic Planning Council who recommended that expansion for the region should be concentrated in that area in spite of much of its being in the Bristol Green Belt. They classified the area as 'Pleasant', which was one grade up from their lowest category of 'Unpleasant', and noted that this made it attractive for development—failing to add, however, that such development might destroy the attractiveness which brought it about.

The Severnside Study of 1971 suggested the development of a new town north of Bristol, but with declining birthrate this idea has been abandoned, although the Planning Council forecast the considerable growth by the year 2001 of 21,000 (23 per cent) for the Bristol–Severnside Region, which covers an area only a little larger than Avon, and considered that the major concentration should be in south Gloucestershire (i.e. north Avon). This is therefore a region under pressure and will

The Severn Bridge with a toll-barrier and service-area at the Aust end. Beyond, a second bridge carries the M4 over the Wye estuary.

Royal Portbury Dock, the Avon estuary and Avonmouth.

Weston-super-Mare: the sweep of Weston Bay up to wooded Worlebury, with (from bottom) the New Pier, Knightstone Pavilion and the old Pier joining Birnbeck Island to the mainland.

Clevedon Bay, with the promenade and pier.

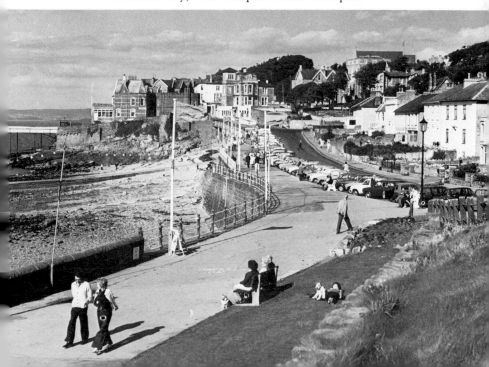

Chipping Sodbury from the air. Note the long, narrow burgage plots running back from the wide main street; also the off-centre position of the church.

Frenchay, from above, with the church and common and the
wooded Frome valley to the south.

Tilley Manor, West Harptree – slightly overwhelmed by ornament.

Horton Court. On the left is the Norman hall (c1140) and beyond that the roof of the church.

Worcester Lodge, Badminton. Designed about 1746 by William Kent, it shows the Beaufort arms on the pediment.

Dyrham Park: the approach down the Cotswold scarp, with the orangery on the left.

Chipping Sodbury. To the right, seventeenth-century buildings, some with original mullioned windows, some with sash. To the left, a nineteenth-century building with parapet and cornice. (The bay windows are modern.)

Marshfield: the east end of the High Street.

need inspired environmental planning if it is not to become a landscape in distress.

In fact, what is virtually a new town has developed at Yate, but without the overall planning of a statutory New Town where care is taken, admittedly not always successfully, to find a balance between residence, services and employment. It was built under normal planning provision but is largely housing, a dormitory town for Bristol, and it is under-provided with services, particularly sports and entertainment facilities. It has a fairly large pedestrianized shopping centre, established in 1965 and rather unfortunately sited between two busy roads. Yate was made the subject of a television programme in 1978 whose gloomy view of the situation evoked strong reaction from satisfied residents and left the outsider uncertain about the truth of the matter.

The extreme western edge of the region is marked by a small but significant step of about 15 metres where the Keuper marl surfaces from its cloak of alluvium and forms a gently-sloping shelf in which patches of conglomerate afford sites for villages such as Almondsbury, Olveston and Thornbury. The marl spreads more widely in the north and has a little lias-capped outlier at Aust which gives a foothold for the Severn Bridge. Behind it runs a steeper, higher step of carboniferous lime-stone, which provided much of the building-material for the older houses, and is followed from upper Almondsbury to Alveston by the A38, along the line of the old Roman road from Abonae (Sea Mills) to Glevum (Gloucester).

The influence of the A38 has given Almondsbury a modern ribbon-development to the east of the old nucleus, which is lower down and has an interesting church with a fine lead-covered broach spire and a Norman doorway in the porch. Most of the church interior is Early English, heavily restored in the nineteenth century. Points of interest are the big six-teenth-century tomb of the Veele family with inscriptions in Greek, Latin and English ("All Flesh Ys Grass"), another multi-lingual (Hebrew, Greek, English) inscription on the eighteenth-century wooden Classical porchway, and chancel windows to Charles Richardson (1814–96) and his wife. Richardson originated the Severn Tunnel scheme and previously worked with Brunel on the Thames tunnel and the Bristol end of the GWR. Up on the main road is a dominant brick Cottage Hospital with tower and cupola, designed by the Bristol architect G. E. Ponting in 1891. To the east is the Almondsbury Interchange where the M4 and M5 cross and link, the first four-level motorway interchange in Britain.

The M4 then heads north-west for the Severn Bridge and cuts through the shelf on which stand Olveston, a compact village whose fourteenth and seventeenth-century church was 'enlarged and re-pewed' in 1841, and the hamlet of Tockington with its charming village green and pleasant three-storey manor house rebuilt in 1712 by a mayor of Bristol. Further north-east is Alveston, which means 'Alwin's stone' and is not to be confused with Olveston which signifies 'Alf's place'. It is bigger and has a hotel and many new housing estates. Expansion began in late-Victorian times, and it was given a church in 1885. The remains of the old church, St Helen's, with a tower, part of the nave with Norman doorway, and a churchyard, stand silently at Rudgeway, about a mile to the south just off the A38. Behind them is the large sixteenth- to seventeenth-century Old Church Farmhouse.

About a mile north-east of Alveston is the pleasant, busy little town of Thornbury ('the thorny burh') set on a low hill. The original settlement was probably on the lower ground by the church but was developed up the hill as a new town in 1243–62 by Richard de Clare, Earl of Gloucester, who advertised it by promising that any who took up houses would have the same liberties and free customs as he had already granted to Tewkesbury. In medieval times it had a flourishing cloth-industry but this died out—Leland reported in the sixteenth century that "There hathe bene good clothing in Thornebyry, but now Idelnes much reynithe there"—and the town survived mainly as a market centre. The medieval lay-out consists of High Street, running down to Castle Street and the church and castle, and the parallel Back Street and St Mary's Street, with links across. High Street is broad, with a dog-leg at the top which gives a focus and sense of closure, but it tends to be choked with traffic.

There are many good Georgian and earlier houses in the main street but also a variety of Victorian revival styles such as the Registry Office (1839) with Georgian pediment, Doric pilasters and Egyptian door-frame; a neo-Georgian fire-station, dated 1930; a neo-Gothic Methodist chapel; a neo-Renaissance bank, and a neo-Gothic fountain of 1888. The eighteenth-century 'White Lion' has a rather splendid beast over its portico, and in St Mary's Street the Church Institute has a fine carved wooden porch dated 1679.

The castle, now a good, if somewhat expensive, restaurant, is an impressive Tudor building which Edward Stafford, Duke of Buckingham, failed to complete before he was executed in 1521. It was partly restored in 1720 and completed in 1854 by Anthony Salvin who had already built a complete castle at Peckforton in Shropshire. When Henry VIII and Anne Boleyn visited it in 1535, Bristol sent them ten fat oxen, forty sheep and a gilt cup.

The nearby church is Perpendicular and has a fine tower. In the south aisle the third Duke is commemorated by the Stafford Chapel where may be seen his badge, the Stafford Knot.

East of Thornbury and beyond the M5, the limestone ridge begins near Cromhall to trend southward and runs past Wickwar to Chipping Sodbury, where it is exposed in the railway-cutting and then dies away under the lias clays and limestones. Both Wickwar and Chipping Sodbury may be classified as medieval New Towns: the former became a borough when a market was granted in about 1285, and the latter was created by William Crassus, Lord of Sodbury, who granted it a market in about 1218. Both had water-power available: Wickwar lies on a plateau above the deeply-incised Little Avon, and Chipping Sodbury is bounded on the north by the Frome.

Wickwar, like Thornbury, once had a cloth-industry, but the town was never very prosperous, and cloth-making had died out by the eighteenth century when brewing and malting had become the main industries. The attractive High Street is wide, with plastered houses, a little Town Hall (c1795) with a clock, and at the bottom end the old grammar school of 1684. The street is an extension of the original settlement which is now represented by a heavily restored church (but with a fine eighteenth-century chandelier) and terraces which are all that remain of the sixteenth-century Poole House.

Chipping (i.e. Market) Sodbury is a larger place, much swollen by post-war building to the west where it almost joins to Yate. When it was originally planned, the main road was diverted to form the High Street, but fortunately for the peace of the place it has since been restored to its old line. The main street, which is wide enough for cars to park without marring the scene too seriously, is lined for the most part with gabled and stone-mullioned seventeenth-century houses, with occasional Victorian Gothic as in the police station, and a pleasantly piebald effect from a mixture of Pennant sandstone and lias limestone. A little clock-tower about half-way down was erected in 1871 as a memorial to Colonel Blathwayte of Dyrham Park who served in the Waterloo campaign. It was later altered to accommodate public lavatories and in 1948 was surrounded with an arcade. Tudor House in Hatter's Lane is a restored fifteenth-century building, plastered, with an over-sailing storey. As often happened with these wide market streets, buildings began to appear down the centre, but they have long since disappeared. The market, originally for corn and general provisions, became a live cattle-market in 1837. In 1954 it closed, and the business was transferred to Yate.

There is a great deal of interesting information about the town in *The Sodburys* by P. A. Couzens. (It may now be out of print but can be consulted in the local library.) He was not happy about recent development: "The pleasant little town we of the fading generation knew," he wrote, "has preceded us into the limbo of the soon to be forgotten past. Of history there can be none for the sprawling, characterless monstrosity that is rapidly despoiling the countryside." It is, perhaps, just possible that the heart of the town has been saved by the by-pass and that the dwellers in the neat new houses of the estates may, too, come to look upon it with affection.

From Chipping Sodbury and Yate the Frome (the word means 'brisk'), having started in Dodington Park where 'Capability' Brown formed it into cascades and lakes, continues westward until near Iron Acton it turns southward through Frampton (Frome-ton) Cotterell, Winterbourne and Frenchay (Frome-shaw) to join the Avon in Bristol. With its large catchment area and its restricted flow through the city, the Frome was a frequent source of flooding in Bristol until the 1960s when a 16-foot-diameter storm-water culvert was constructed from Eastville to the Avon about a mile north of the Suspension Bridge.

To the north and west of Iron Acton the area drained by the Ladden Brook is still largely rural, a region of dairy farms and small hamlets, whose most remarkable, and not altogether happy, feature is the extraordinary pattern of no less than seven pylon-carried electricity power-lines radiating from the distribution-centre north of Latteridge. The southern section, developed mainly on Pennant sandstone, has however, been transformed by post-war building and is separated only briefly from the low lias plateau to the west over which Horfield, Filton and Patchway have spread themselves and which at Filton provides level land for the BAC runways.

Iron Acton ('the oak settlement with iron mines') is a small linear village, not over-expanded, lying just off the B4508. It has a pleasant, large-porched church with a nice wooden pulpit and sounding-board dated 1624. A stair in the wall once led to a rood-screen but now contains a modern wooden cross. The fine churchyard cross is fifteenth-century and probably a memorial to one of the Poyntz family. Acton Court to the north is a sixteenth-century house with a large courtyard but is very decrepit. In medieval times there was iron-mining at Acton, Pucklechurch and Wick, the last being recorded in Domesday Book as raising ninety blooms of iron, but the workings died out. There was a revival at Frampton Cotterell between 1862 and 1874, most of the output going to South Wales, and there are flooded remains of the large pits and signs of the tramway which linked them with the Thornbury–Iron Acton line. Frampton was once also noted for the making of felt hats, but this stopped in 1880, and today the place consists mainly of post-war residence.

Frenchay, on the edge of the deep valley which the Frome has cut into the Pennant, still retains much of its village atmosphere. It has a large village green where W. G. Grace once played cricket, overlooked by a small red church of 1834. There is a large but not obtrusive hospital in the grounds of Frenchay Park (1780, enlarged 1804), and scattered buildings which include the Quaker Meeting House of 1808, recently restored and gay in white with orange shutters. There are pleasant walks along the river and beyond in the grounds of Oldbury Court which was bought by Bristol Corporation in 1937, the house destroyed and the grounds laid out as a park.

Below Frenchay the narrow Frome valley was for long a

scene of industry. There were at least a dozen mills in the nineteenth century, none of which is now working. Frenchay Upper Mill, for example, was used in the 1790s for iron-working, producing mainly farm tools, and became the works of the Frenchay Iron Company in 1814. In 1885 it was turned into tea-rooms which closed in 1956. From Frenchay Bridge to Eastville Park the valley has been turned into a secluded, wooded and pleasant walkway beside the river, but of the original six mills all that remain are some weirs, odd bits of masonry and, in a section called Snuff Mills Park, a recon-structed iron under-shot wheel turning lazily behind an openwork iron grille. The mills were originally for producing grist (corn), but some were lately converted to grinding snuff, although it is believed that that was not the case of the one in Snuff Mills Park. There were no mill-ponds in that section as the river itself provided sufficient quantity and head of water. A useful guide to the area is published by the Open Space and Amenities Committee, City of Bristol, and titled *Nature Trail: Frome Valley*.

West of Frenchay the M32 runs southward from the M4 down into Bristol where it ends abruptly in a roundabout, to the confusion of the uninitiated. For most of its length it is running along the edge of a fat finger of countryside which pokes southward into the urban fabric of Bristol and which flattens out at its northern end where we find the little hamlet of Harry Stoke and the village of Stoke Gifford. Harry ('hoary') Stoke is just a few houses, but down by the A4174 are the scars and tips of an adit coal-mine hopefully opened after the war and sadly closed in 1963. East of this is the new Bristol Polytechnic and a large motel, west is a new Co-op 'super-store', all as low and flat as the country around. Stoke Gifford has Bristol's post-war Parkway station, a small brick box with a large car-park, handy for the motorway, but the village lies on a slight hill beyond. It used to be owned by the Beaufort family, and at the side of the small green the large village school of 1863 bears the Beaufort arms, and a large pair of semi-detached houses next to it bear a ducal coronet. The church is curious, with an ogee arch to the south porch and a south aisle separated from the nave by rectangular fluted piers. The vestry was originally a private room with a fireplace where Lady Beaufort could attend service in comfort.

Westward again is Filton, continuous with Bristol though not administratively part of it, and north of that are the three large blobs of building which make up Patchway. 'Filton' probably means 'Hay (filithe) Farm', but there is little sign of rural occupation, and industry and housing line the A38 as it pursues its dangerous way to Gloucester. By the main road is St Peter's Church, which was re-oriented in 1961 when a new nave was built at right angles to the body of the old church. There is much inter-war and post-war housing and the industry which brought it into being—British Aircraft Corporation, Rolls Royce Engines and Filton Airfield with its huge hangars.

The aircraft industry started in Filton in 1910 largely because there were suitable premises available in the bus-depot and because the man responsible, Sir George White, was chairman of the tram and bus companies. George White was a remarkable man and a self-made millionaire. Born in Bristol in 1854, he joined a firm of lawyers as office boy when he was fourteen, became secretary to the new Tramways Company when he was twenty, went into business on his own as a stockbroker, and continued to supervise the development of the city transport system, changing from horse-drawn trams to electric trams and adding motorbuses and taxis. As chairman of the Imperial Tramways he introduced tramway systems into Middlesbrough, Dublin and London. In 1904 he became a millionaire and a baronet and began taking holidays in the south of France where he came into contact with the infant French aviation industry. He started his aviation company with his own money and in 1910 exhibited his first successful aeroplane, the Bristol Boxkite, on Bristol's Durdham Downs. The next year he was fulfilling an export order to Russia for eight planes. The First World War brought a boom in the business, particularly with the Bristol Fighter, of which over 4,500 were built, but in 1916 Sir George, over-working to the end, collapsed and died.

Sir George White's British and Colonial Aircraft Company became in 1919 the Bristol Aeroplane Company and between the wars developed an important engine division at Patchway which provided the Mercury engines for the Bristol Blenheim in World War II. Today the firm, no longer a family affair, is part of British Aerospace.

In 1945 the runway of the airfield was lengthened to accommodate the giant Bristol Brabazon, removing the village of Charlton in the process, and giant hangars, used subsequently for Britannia and Concorde, were erected in 1949. After six years the Brabazons were dismantled as uneconomic, but the hangars, in their size, proportions and simplicity of line, have fair claim to being among the most remarkable pieces of architecture in Avon.

Patchway is mostly modern housing, apart from the big Rolls Royce Engine factory, but is now developing as a distribution centre for goods, including Marks and Spencer foods, owing to its nearness to the M4/M5 intersection, an indication that motorways and giant vehicles have lost road transport the advantage it once had over the railways of door-to-door delivery without break of bulk.

Over to the east, beyond the Frome-Ladden basin, is a broad belt, some three to four miles wide, leading to the Cotswold scarp. It is mainly of lias clays but spills over onto coal-measures in the south-west and is drained mainly northward to the Little Avon, which, with its tributaries, is associated with Falfield, Tortworth, Charfield and Wickwar. East of Wickwar, by Inglestone Common, is a lowland clay area of extensive wood and coppice with appropriate names such as 'Wetmoor'. Tortworth, the most northerly of the villages, is a tiny place notable for an ancient Spanish chestnut in a field by the church. In 1800 a fence was put round the tree with a plaque recording that it was then "supposed to be six hundred years old" and adding a piece of enjoyable bad verse:

> May Man still Guard thy Venerable form
> From the Rude Blast and Tempestuous Storm.
> Still mayest thou Flourish through succeeding time
> And Last Long Last the Wonder of the Clime.

The ancient and decayed trunk is now surrounded by at least seventeen mature offspring. The nearby mansion, designed in 1849–52 for Earl Ducie, was described as "excrutiatingly uncomfortable" in spite of having 'WELCOME' inscribed over the archway. In the churchyard is a rather nice Jacobean-style monument with seats, erected in 1895 to the memory of Julia, Countess Ducie.

Charfield lies along the B4058 as it runs down into the Little

Avon valley and is mainly red brick, in both the old area and the pleasant new housing estates. The church of St James is 1881 neo–Gothic with a touch of Arts and Crafts in its imitation half-timbering; its effect is pleasant, as is that of the school opposite, founded and endowed by the rector in 1853. To the north is Charfield Mills, a big block of 1829.

The remaining sub-region of the Northern Heartland is the south-east, drained by the Boyd and the Oldland Brook. The former rises just south of Chipping Sodbury and passes through Codrington, which is tiny, Doynton, whose church retains some original herringbone brickwork, Wick, with large limestone quarries, and Bitton (Boyd-ton). The section for about a mile above Bitton is called, for no very apparent reason, 'the Golden Valley', pleasant and secluded but not very remarkable. Bitton has more to offer than the Victorian houses along the A431, for to the south is the secluded heart of the old village in a deeply rural setting. This southern group includes the school (1830), the old vicarage (1778 and 1823), the almshouses (nineteenth-century), the grange (mainly rebuilt in the eighteenth century) and the church.

The church is very large and fine, with some Early English lancet windows and a hundred-foot high Perpendicular tower (1370–77) with crocketed buttresses. Some Saxon work remains above the neo–Norman arch of 1847. The fine hammerbeam roof to the nave dates from 1867 and was made of cedar from a ship wrecked in the Bristol Channel. Much of the Victorian restoration was by the Ellacombes, father and son, who successively held the living for ninety-nine years. The son was very active in establishing new churches in the area and was also an authority on gardening. In St Catherine's Chapel are monuments to members of the de Button (Bitton), Newton and Whittock families who successively occupied Barr's Court, and in the nave is a hatchment in the name of Henry Creswick of Hanham Hall (died 1806). The Newtons and the Creswicks we have met in connection with Keynsham and shall meet again.

On a low hill between the Boyd and the Oldland Brook lie Pucklechurch and Siston. This was once part of the royal hunting forest of Kingswood, of which more later, and it was at Pucklechurch that the Saxon King Edmund, "lord of the English, protector of men, the beloved performer of mightier deeds, defender of warriors" (according to the Anglo Saxon Chronicle), was stabbed to death in about AD 946. King Edmund's Palace is marked on the map, but there is nothing there but cowsheds. The village is pleasant, although the B4465 rather spoils the little green by the church. The latter is mainly thirteenth-century with two interesting stellate tomb-recesses and an ogee arch which was brought in out of the weather in 1888. There are seventeenth- and eighteenth-century wall-monuments. In the village are some quite good seventeenth-century houses in grey lias limestone, and on the western edge are two large, stone-gabled and mullioned houses, one dated 1678. There is a good deal of modern development, some of which does not sit too well with the old part, and a trading estate, signposted from the M4, which shares grounds with a barbed-wire-enclosed Remand Centre and utilizes World War II barrage-balloon hangars.

The Oldland Brook, which drains the coalfield area, rises near Mangotsfield and passes Warmley, Oldland (mostly post-war estates) and Willsbridge, where it is crossed by the A431. The valley was used in 1832 for the pioneer Avon and Gloucester Tramroad which connected the collieries of the Coalpit Heath area to wharfs on the Avon opposite Keynsham and which was abandoned in 1865 except for a short southern section which was closed in 1904. Something remains of the wharfs (ST 666693 and 662698) and the entrance to Willsbridge tunnel can still be seen (ST 666707). The brook was dammed for power at Willsbridge, where there was an iron-foundry, and at Warmley.

The Warmley dam was built for a remarkable integrated brassworks set up by William Champion in the 1740s, and the supply to the millpond was augmented by pumping with a Newcomen engine which cost the company £2,000. This 'fire-engine' was supplied by the engineer Joseph Hornblower of Birmingham who also erected one at Radstock, the first steam-pump on the Somerset coalfield. "As to Champion," he wrote, "I think there are few mortals queerer, I hope I shall have done with him soon." Difficult the brass-maker may have been, but he came from a gifted family and was himself something of an inventive genius.

The customary method of making brass was to feed the furnace with powdered calamine (zinc carbonate) and broken copper, but the alloy was variable in quality and rather soft. In 1723 William's father. Nehemia, had patented a method of granulating the copper by passing molten metal through holes into running water, and in 1738 William himself patented what was probably the first means of smelting calamine on a large scale to produce pure zinc, or spelter. The problem was that the metal vaporized at furnace-temperature, and this he solved by passing the vapour through iron tubes immersed in water. The combination of granulated copper and pure zinc enabled a superior brass to be made, although the old calamine process also continued to be used until the middle of the nineteenth century.

William set up a spelter-factory in Bristol at Baber's Tower, just off Old Market, but it was soon reported as a 'nuisance', and for that and other reasons he looked round for a rural site where he could incorporate a spelter-works with a brass-refinery and a brassware-manufactory. He moved to Warmley, and in 1761 his company's inventory included twenty-five houses, one large spelter-works, two horse-mills, twenty-two furnaces, fifteen brass-furnaces, one large wire-mill, three rolling-mills and the fire-engine. It was probably the most up-to-date works in the country, a good example of vertical integration, employed some two thousand people and continued to grow. More furnaces, another steam-engine and a pin-factory were built at Warmley, and works were erected at Kingswood, Bitton, Kelston and St Augustine's Back in Bristol. For this expansion the company needed a large injection of capital, but when Champion applied for a Charter of Incorporation which would enable him to raise another £400,000, he was defeated by the opposition of other local companies and went bankrupt. The works were auctioned and never recovered their former glory, although some work continued into the nineteenth century.*

Not much remains. Champion's house, a pleasant four-square Palladian mansion with a triangular pediment, rusticated ground floor and brick coach-house, is now Council offices, and the plaque on it commemorates not William Champion but Miss Haskins, who there wrote the passage

* For details of the brass-making industry in Bristol and the lower Avon valley see Joan Day, *Bristol Brass*, 1973.

beginning "I said to the man who stood at the gate of the year", quoted by George VI in his Empire broadcast of 1939. Visible from the main road is a building, possibly the old pin-factory, with a clock-tower, which was renovated and opened in 1973 as an arts and social centre for young people. Behind is a circular tower which is probably the remains of of the company's windmill, but the millpond beyond, once decorated by a statue of Neptune, has been filled in and covered with caravans. Further along a kind of castellated gatehouse perched on an arch over the stream has been converted for residence. It is built of blocks of the dark-coloured slag from the copper-smelting, a material which is used in other places around Bristol, particularly for capping walls. The 'castle' at Arno's Court by the A4 going into Bristol is in this material, for it was built as a 'Gothick' folly by William Reeves who had interests in the copper-smelting industry. There is a good deal of modern industry today at Warmley, and the nineteenth-century housing in Pennant is swamped in acres of modern estates, mainly all red brick and white paint.

Of the once extensive works of the Bristol coalfield very little is left to be seen. Interest in industrial archaeology, which is well served in the area by the recording work co-ordinated by Dr Buchanan at Bath University and by the activities of the Bristol Museum staff, has arrived too late to do much more than list the limited remains. The mines were generally small and the spoil-tips unimpressive; moreover, much of the old workings has been engulfed and obliterated by the tide of urban expansion. California Pit (ST 665715) which was linked with the Avon and Gloucester Tramway still has the incline and the remains of an engine-house, and Siston Common Pit (ST 680738) by the main road from Warmley to Staple Hill has left derelict buildings and colliery workers' cottages. Hanham Colliery (ST 638721) in Memorial Road is now the site of a new factory, but one or two old buildings and some spoil-tips are visible.

More impressive is the quantity of Methodist chapels in the area, the result of Wesley's campaign which brought hope of a reward in Heaven for people who could hope for none on Earth, and a sense of worth and dignity in the eyes of the Lord to a class who had none in the eyes of Man. The work of the 'field preachers' and of Wesley and Whitfield is commemorated on Hanham Mount by an electric beacon, a cross of paving-stones, a replica of Wesley's pulpit and a stone font. It is not, perhaps, easy to find, but is worth seeking out and has, in addition, a fine view.

There was, of course, money to be made by owning mines, and one of the local success-stories of the latter part of the nineteenth century was that of Handel Cossham, who was born in Thornbury in 1842, became a clerk in the Yate colliery, married into the business and finished up as the greatest coal-owner in the Bristol district. In 1882 and again in 1884 he was Mayor of Bath, having moved to the opulent Victorian suburb of Weston Park, and in 1885 he became MP for Bristol East. He helped to found schools in Yate, Pucklechurch and Thornbury, but he is probably best remembered for the Cossham Memorial Hospital in Bristol, opened in 1907.

Today the main extractive industry is quarrying carboniferous limestone, mostly for road-metal, and in places the quarries with all the paraphernalia for crushing, sorting and loading are a distinctive feature of the landscape. Examples are to be found at Wick, north of Wickwar by the B4509 and between the A38 and M5 near Thornbury, with a rail connection via Iron Acton to the main line near Yate. At Yate and Wickwar are deposits of celestine (strontium nitrate), which is used in fireworks, and the area once provided most of the world's output. Production ceased in 1974 but has recently been re-opened.

The reddish-grey Pennant sandstone which as a building stone gives a somewhat sombre air to much of the Victorian development of Bristol's suburbs and coalfield villages, and the light grey lias limestone which takes its place in other villages around, are no longer used, and the old quarries are now mainly found as shallow, grass-grown depressions. In some places clay was dug, and there is a large clay-quarry, recently closed, at the south of Siston Common. More lasting has been the digging of brick-clays in the west at Cattybrook. The Cattybrook Works, reached by a brick road from the little village of Over, was founded in 1865 by Charles Richardson, whose commemorative window at Almondsbury we have already noted. He used some thirty million of their bricks to line the Severn Tunnel, and deep red, blue, buff or yellow Cattybrook bricks went to make many of the late-Victorian buildings of Bristol such as the old Wills tobacco-factory, Foster's Almshouses and the Fish Market in Baldwin Street.

Of the vanished past perhaps the most remarkable and certainly the most extensive was the royal hunting forest of Kingswood which, with Fillwood Chase, the Keynsham forest, had already suffered considerably encroachment by Stuart times. In 1615 John Norden, the cartographer, reported to James I that "for want of the boundaries and perambulations of the same chace I could by noe examination find the extent". He had heard that at one time the deer "raunging out of the forest over the river of Avon freely and without disturaunce fed as far as Dundry hilles" but that "time and discontinuance of use have forgotten the names, altered the bounds and lost the lands formerly belonging unto His Majestie's Chace of Fillwoode". A map of 1610 shows that the forest had shrunk to a tilted square with sides about two miles long, between Siston Common on the east and the present Bristol suburb of St George, an area which is now completely urban. Norden reported that parts had been enclosed by Sir Hugh Smythe of Ashton Court and that it was also probable that Bristleton (Brislington) Heath had been part of the Royal Forest but that "there are or have been coale mines within the same, which the confining lords have taken and inclosed much the same Common and take the profittes both of the land and mines." He reckoned that, if James claimed the forest, sold off the timber and leased the land, he could clear £5,487. The Stuarts certainly raised money in this fashion, and in 1670 Charles II leased rights of chase to Sir Baynham Throckmorton for £850. The rights were not worth having, as Francis Creswick of Hanham found when he and two others unwisely formed a syndicate to buy them from Throckmorton's daughters, for, as he wrote in 1718, " 'Tis true we have gotten a Decree from the King's right of Chase at great expense and not one farthing the better for it, nor will anybody ever, for 'tis now utterly destroyed and not possibly to be restored."

The Creswicks, who had made their money as merchants in Bristol, were a cantankerous lot and were nearly always going to law, particularly with their near neighbours, the Newtons of Barrs Court, and eventually with each other. This last happened in the 1830s when the younger son, Humphrey, bought Hanham Court from the elder son, Henry, and then would or could not pay. Henry had him imprisoned for debt. Fourteen years later a London gentleman, Thomas White, paid off the debt and took possession of the house and manor. And that was the end of the Creswicks at Hanham.

The name of Kingswood is now given to a District of Avon and its western fringe, which is virtually a suburb of Bristol, as are Hanham to its south and Mangotsfield to the north. Urban Kingswood is split in two by the A420, which is here lined with Victorian shops into which has been inserted a new shopping precinct. It is a mainly Victorian suburb in greyish Pennant, with infill and extension by modern housing, and a good deal of industry tucked away. Buildings of historical interest testify to the Nonconformist influence—Whitfield's first Tabernacle (built 1741, enlarged 1802)—in Park Road, the 1851 Congregational church behind and the 1843 Wesleyan chapel in Blackhorse Road. The school which Wesley founded was moved to a new building in Bath in 1852.

Things have certainly changed a great deal since the Kingswood miners banded together to pull down toll-gates and to smash the locks on the Avon in an attempt to free the passage of their coal, or the wild day in October 1738 when they refused to take a cut in wages from 1s 4d (about 7p) to one shilling (5p) a day and came out on strike. They jammed the roads with carts and pack-horses, wrecked the local inn, stopped coaches and demanded money, rioted through the streets and even persuaded the 'Civilized Colliers' of Brislington across the river to join them. It took a regiment to put them down, and in the Corporation accounts for the following year is entered "Recovered from the colliers who were prosecuted for rioting October 1738, the sum of £51".

VI

COTSWOLD COUNTRY

This land of plateau and scarp at one time made up most of the Hundred of Grumbold's Ash, although who Grumbold was and where his Ash was located are quite unknown, and it is even uncertain what hundred things made up the area. Hundreds (engagingly known as 'wapentakes' in the east and north) were divisions of the Saxon shires and had their own courts which, although functionally superseded by the work of Justices of the Peace, continued in some places to operate in a minor way up to Victorian times. In the eighteenth century, for example, the Duke of Beaufort was still holding a half-yearly court for the Hundred of Grumbold's Ash at which constables were elected and cases of petty debt were tried.

Long after the Hundreds had ceased to be of administrative significance they continued to appear on maps and to be used in regional descriptions. The 1841 census, for instance, classified its information under parishes, hamlets, tithings and hundreds, and the Victoria County Histories of Gloucestershire and Somerset both group their parish accounts by Hundreds. Over the centuries the boundaries of many became altered, and a map of 1750 shows that the Grumbold's Ash of Domesday (1086) had expanded to swallow up its southern neighbour, Edredstane, except for a portion which contained Marshfield and had curiously become a detached part of the Hundred of Thornbury.

The region was once known as the Southwolds, a name which was particularly appropriate, for although the area belongs physically and geologically to the sweep of Jurassic limestone hills which make up the Cotswolds, it is rarely recognized as such and has a building-stone less golden and a scarp less dramatic than in the more famous region to the north. This is not, however, to deny the Southwolds their own particular charm or to dispute their official classification under the rather clumsy title of 'Area of Outstanding Natural

Beauty'; indeed, there is good reason for maintaining that a drive along the A46 from Bath towards Stroud is one of the most visually pleasant in Avon.

From the Bristol Avon to the Little Avon runs the west-ward-facing scarp, a low green wall of grass and woodland patches, rising to about 200 metres and generally remarkably straight except in the few places where it is trenched by small streams whose valleys afford a route to the broad swell of the plateau. The B4465 uses such a valley and is paralleled by the M4 which has, however, because of its greater width, to be accommodated in man-made cuttings. At the foot of the scarp a narrow dissected shelf forms a distinctive ribbon which widens towards the south. It has a pleasant and secret atmosphere with narrow, sunken, hedged-lined roads, greenfields and frequent trees, and here and there glimpses westward to the Severn and the hills of Wales. Car-drivers, however, will probably be too intent on navigating the twisting roads to take much notice of the scenery. The villages, or rather hamlets, of the shelf include Dyrham and Dodington with their great houses and parks open to the public, Old and Little Sodbury, Horton, with its Norman hall, and secluded Hawkesbury with its noble church.

Old Sodbury (the name probably means 'Soppa's burgh') is on a loop off the A432, and its towered church stands on a knoll with fine views along the scarp and to Chipping Sodbury. There are Norman arches to the nave and two small Norman windows at the west end, while the chancel and transepts have thirteenth-century pointed arches. On tombs lie two knights, one fourteenth-century and, unusually, in wood, the other of about 1240, in stone, cross-legged and overwhelmed by his shield. Back on the main road the Dog Inn has a Tudor doorway, and opposite is a monument of 1897 consisting of a short Ionic column topped with a crown. Above the village the round battlemented tower is an air-shaft for the railway tunnel.

At Little Sodbury the church of St Adeline was built in 1859 with materials partly from the previous church which stood behind the manor where from 1521 to 1523 William Tyndale served as chaplain to the Walshe family. It is said that this was the time when he resolved to produce what was to be the first English version of the Bible made by direct translation from

Greek and Hebrew texts, a resolution which led to his death at the stake in 1535. The story is told in an enthusiastic pamphlet on sale in the church. The manor house, which is private, was extensively rebuilt in about 1919 for Baron de Tuyll, son of the Dowager Duchess of Beaufort, but still contains a late-fifteenth-century hall and seventeenth- and eighteenth-century work.

Further north is Horton and about a mile further on from that small linear village Horton Court and the little church of St James, mainly Perpendicular, with a nicely ribbed vault to the south porch, a Norman font, a Jacobean pulpit and monuments to Baron de Tuyll (1913) and eighteenth-century Pastons. The manor was conveyed in 1539 by Sir Nicholas Poyntz of Iron Acton to Thomas White, who in 1541 granted it to Robert Ellyot, Mayor of Bristol. The income was to be used for relieving Severn shipping of tolls at Bristol, and the manor remained Corporation property until 1921. Horton Court is mainly the house built in 1521 for William Knight, who presented Henry VIII's divorce case against Catherine of Aragon to the Pope and subsequently, in spite of the failure of the mission, became Bishop of Bath and Wells. One wing, however, is a Norman hall of about 1140, restored in 1884. Detached by about 20 yards from the house is an ambulatory which is presumed to have been modelled on a loggia seen by Knight when he was in Rome. The house belongs to the National Trust and is open free on Wednesdays and Saturdays from 2 p.m. to 6 p.m. from April to October.

Horton is linked with Hawkesbury in the sad little story of Miss Jenkins. She lived at Hawkesbury Manor and fell in love with young Paston of Horton Manor, but her family were Protestant and his Catholic so the match was forbidden. Sadly they parted, and Miss Jenkins, leaning from an upstairs window to wave a last farewell, overbalanced and fell to her death. The old manor house was pulled down over a century and a half ago, and hardly anything now remains of Hawkesbury except for a deep and wooded valley and a fine large church where you can buy a pamphlet which tells the tale of Miss Jenkins and much beside. The manor belonged to distant Tewkesbury Abbey from at least 972, but after the Dissolution it passed eventually in 1620 to the Jenkins family of Bristol (hence Miss Jenkins) who later became earls of

Liverpool, and the church has monuments to the first Earl, who died in 1808, and the second, who was Prime Minister at the time of Waterloo.

The church interior is large, light and handsome and is mainly Perpendicular, although the chancel is Early English and the north doorway Norman. In the chancel is the empty matrix of a brass which is presumed to be of the mitred bishop of Pershore, Thomas Upton (c1413). In the porch an old notice requests that dogs be left at home and pattens taken off. (Pattens were a kind of overshoe raised on an iron under-structure which kept the shoe out of the mud.)

At the extreme north of the scarp foot in Avon is the little village of Hillesley (probably 'Hild's clearing'), situated at the head of a steep valley which once provided water-power for cloth-making. In 1830 George Oldland of Hillesley patented a rotary machine for shearing cloth, but it did not make his fortune: others had had the same idea. The place is now a quiet rural village with a church of 1851 in Early English style which Vesey in *The Buildings of England* series calls "modest, learned and good"—one can see what he means although it sounds more applicable to a parson than to a church.

Most visited of the scarp-foot features are the two great but dissimilar houses of Dodington and Dyrham. After the Norman invasion the manor of Dodington was taken from the Saxon Alwin and given to the Bishop of Coutances, and by Domesday it had passed to his nephew, Roger de Berkeley. In the sixteenth century it was inherited by Nicholas Weeks who pulled down his castle at Dursley to build a house at Dodington. The expense ruined him, and he sold out to a local family, the Codringtons of nearby Codrington and Wapley, where lies buried John Codrington who fought at Agincourt and became standard-bearer to the King. In the Civil War the family was divided: John served as a lieutenant-general for the King; his brother Robert was for Parliament, while the other brother, Michael, was making a fortune in the West Indies. John was captured, and his estates were sequestered, but they were returned to him before his death. In 1721 William Codrington was created baronet, and it was his son who employed 'Capability' Brown to redesign the park much as we see it today, with clumps of trees, winding drives and two lakes separated by a waterfall with a little castellated Gothic

Cascade Building. William disinherited his son, another William, and after legal battles the estate passed to a cousin, Christopher Bethnell Codrington, for whom and with whom from 1796 to 1813 the architect James Wyatt designed and built the present mansion.

The house, in a Classical Roman style, is undeniably impressive, even if to some its interiors may seem vulgarly ostentatious in comparison with the satisfying austerity of the enormous six-pillared, pedimented portico. However, with its gilt and brass and marble, its enormous entrance hall and great staircase, and its profusion of plasterwork, it is undoubtedly a *tour de force* by the architect who had recently created for William Beckford the completely different Gothic fantasy of Fonthill Abbey. The ironwork of the staircase is in fact from Fonthill, although it was originally made in about 1760 for the house of Beckford's father. Linked to the house by a curved conservatory and gallery is St Mary's Church, which was re-built by Wyatt in the form of a Greek cross with a central dome.

There is a great deal to see and do at Dodington, which is why it is best to avoid going there on high days and holidays. For example, in the stables is a beautiful collection of carriages and coaches, and in the basement is a large collection of model soldiers; there are nature trails and an adventure playground with aerial walkway and miniature railway, but for some the most interesting 'extra' will be the collection in the Exhibition Hall which includes original plans and designs for the house, various charters of the property, maps and other details of the West Indian estates, and examples of anti-anti-slavery propaganda. The park and house are open to the public from Easter to the end of September from 11 a.m. to 6 p.m., the house opening at noon.

'Dyrham' means 'enclosure for deer', and it is appropriate that the Park has been re-stocked. The house, stables, orangery and church form a pleasant group on a human rather than a monumental scale. In the church, which has some good medieval tiles, is a vigorous monument to Sir George Wynter and his wife and eleven children. He bought the manor in 1571 from Sir Walter Denys who subsequently built Siston Court for himself. On Christmas Eve 1686 Mary Wynter married William Blathwayte, a rising London civil servant who became Clerk to the Privy Council for the reigns of Charles II,

James II, William and Mary, and Queen Anne, and was William's Secretary of State. Mary died after only five years of marriage (and four children), and she and her parents are commemorated in a fine wall monument.

William Blathwayte built successively (1692-4 and 1698-1704) what were virtually two new houses linked by the hall of the old manor. The first, designed by the French Huguenot Samuel Hauduroy, is a charming two-storeyed range with a raised garden terrace in front. The second, parallel and back-to-back with the first, was designed by William Talman who had been responsible for the east front of Chatsworth (1687-96) and had become Comptroller of the Office of Works in 1689, serving under Wren. It is rather grander, as befitted William's advance in fortune, but still not overpowering. It has two wings, one being a greenhouse and the other a matching arcade which dies away into the hillside. In front lie the gardens landscaped by George London, gardener to William III and Queen Anne, although not much remains of his design except the cascade, a stairway of water descending from a statue of Neptune up on the hill, and, to the west, gardens in the formal Dutch style. The house interiors are handsome and are particularly interesting for their Dutch associations. William was Commissioner for Trade and Plantations, which probably accounts for the use of American walnut in a staircase and some room-panelling. The house and park are now National Trust property and are open daily from 2 p.m. to 6 p.m. from April to September, and on Wednesdays, Saturdays and Sundays in October, November and March. Entry is between two fine lodges by the A46. Just north of Dyrham, on the side of Hinton Hill, is a striking collection of strip lynchets.

The southern end of the Southwolds, where the Bristol Avon has cut through, is heavily dissected leaving long fingers of upland such as Lansdown with its racecourse, Charmy Down with its disused war-time airfield, Banner Down with the Fosse Way along the top, and to the west the local landmark of tree-crowned Kelston Round Hill. The southern end of the Charmy Down ridge is cut off by Chilcombe Bottom to form Little Solsbury Hill. Tucked into the valley sides are the little villages and hamlets of Swainswick, St Catherine and Woolley, quiet and little-affected by the growth of nearby Bath.

Swainswick is a pleasant little linear village with some eighteenth-century houses and a barn of 1629. The church has a saddle-back tower and a fine late-Norman doorway. Inside is the tomb of the famous Puritan pamphleteer William Prynne (d. 1669), who variously and virulently attacked the King, the Bishops, the Stage and the Commonwealth, and from having supported Parliament against Charles I changed to sponsoring with equal vigour and sincerity the return of Charles II, to whom he presented Bath's loyal greetings as their newly-elected MP. In 1632 he had been fined, imprisoned and deprived of part of his ears; in 1637 the process was repeated, and he was branded 'SL' as a Seditious Libeller (he said it meant 'Stigmata Laudi'—'the mark of Archbishop Laud'). In 1650 he was again imprisoned, this time for "seditious writings and practisings against the Commonwealth."

The manor was acquired by Oriel College in 1529 and was rented by Prynne's father. The College, to the disgust of some of the village, has the Swainswick Sword which used to be in the old manor house, now a farm. The blade of the sword is nearly four feet long and carries the date 1423, although it has been suggested that this was a mistake for 1623, which would be more reasonable.

Perched on the opposite side of the Swainswick Brook and a little further north lies the little hamlet of Woolley, whose name is more likely to be connected with the stream (welle) than with sheep. Its church with a domed tower was built in 1761 by the Bath architect John Wood the younger. South-west of Swainswick, in the next valley, deep, pretty and wooded, are the church and court of St Catherine. The former was built, or enlarged, by Prior Cantlow of Bath towards the end of the fifteenth century, and his image appears below that of St John in the stained-glass window. The Court is mainly nineteenth-century neo-Tudor, but the north side is original. Almost a mile to the west on the road to Monkswood reservoir is Grey House, a late-seventeenth-century building with gables and mullions.

Another valley village is Weston, embedded in nineteenth-century villas and twentieth-century housing estates which join it to Bath, of which it is now administratively a part. The large parish extends up onto Lansdown, where we find fragments of the ancient St Lawrence's Chapel, established in the Middle Ages as part of a hospice for pilgrims travelling to Glastonbury. Opposite are Bath Racecourse and 'The Blathwayte Arms', which was originally 'The Star' and when it was rebuilt was renamed after the Blathwaytes of Dyrham who acquired much of Lansdown in 1690. Weston belonged to Bath Abbey, and the upland part was particularly important for grazing sheep. After the Dissolution it reverted to the Crown, which in 1628 sold it to the City of London. In the eighteenth century it was bought by Dr Oliver, famed for his invention of the Bath Oliver biscuit, who lived in Bath but has a memorial tablet in Weston church. Many details of Weston's past were researched by a local historian, Joan Hargood-Ashe, and it is unfortunate that her booklet *Looking Back at Weston* (1964) is now out of print.

The rolling plateau-top country, draining eastward through broad valleys, was more attractive to prehistoric settlers than the heavier, wetter, more densely-wooded lowlands, and the Cotswolds have many fine examples of Neolithic burial-mounds, the long barrows of the Cotswold–Severn group. 'Barrow' comes from the Old English '*beorg*', a hill or mound, and a Cotswold long barrow is typically an earth mound between 100 and 200 feet long, wider and higher at one end, covering a number of stone burial-chambers. It has been calculated that to build one, including the quarrying, would have occupied something like five thousand man-hours, and their construction argues a strong social organization. There are unfortunately no good examples in the Southwolds, and the visitor would need to go further north to visit Uley Barrow (Hetty Pegler's Tump) (ST 799011) or south to the best Avon example at Stoney Littleton (ST 735573), where a key and candle may be obtained from the farmhouse for a small fee. Round barrows, the burial-places of the succeeding Bronze Age people, are also found on the Southwolds but are better represented in Mendip.

From about 450 BC groups of immigrants with iron tools and weapons entered the area. Their most conspicuous monument in the present landscape is a line of walled camps or forts protected on one side by the steep scarp. The largest and most impressive is at Little Sodbury (ST 7682), approachable by a field path from the A46. In the entrance is a stone of more recent date marking the parish boundary between Little and

Old Sodbury. A smaller camp tops Little Solsbury Hill (ST 7667), north-east of Bath. It is National Trust property and has a plaque describing what is known of its history. Away from the Southwolds particularly fine camps are to be found at Dolebury (ST 450590) and Worlebury (3262). Their grouping suggests that they guarded three lines of approach—through the Southwold scarp to the Jurassic Way; along the rivers, especially the Avon; and through the Mendip passes—but this is conjectural, and their primary purpose may have been to serve as strongholds for local chieftains. Some of the camps, particularly if univallate (one-walled), were probably cattle-corrals, but others contained settlements of small wooden huts and these could have storage-pits for grain, for, with the introduction of more efficient ploughs, the economy changed from the primarily pastoral farming of the Bronze Age to an increasing concentration on arable.

Three successive Iron Age cultures are conventionally labelled A (Hallstatt), B (La Tène) and C (Belgic), although this is a dangerous over-simplification. The C culture was brought in the first century BC by powerful Belgic groups who established themselves as an aristocracy over the local people. They brought the general use of wheeled vehicles, and particularly of the war-chariot, a heavier plough and improved potters' wheel and the use of gold and silver coins. The tribe which established itself over Avon and the region around was known to the Romans as the Dobunni, and they issued a coinage with a distinctive three-tailed horse on one side and a curious branched symbol on the other. From this coinage we find that in about AD 40 the Dobunnic kingdom was split between a northern section centred at Bagenden near present Cirencester (the Roman Corinium) and a southern one whose capital is not known. When the Romans invaded in AD 43, the northern king, Boduoc, quickly came to terms, while his southern counterpart, Corio, resisted. One result of this was that whereas the northern Dobunni were allowed their own kingdom (although their capital was moved to the new town of Corinium Dobunnorum), the southern Dobunni were incorporated in a newly created Belgic canton with its headquarters at Winchester (Venta Belgarum).

Not long afterwards the Jurassic hills again showed their importance as a routeway when, from the south coast to the

Humber, they were followed by the remarkable diagonal Roman road which the Saxons later called 'the Fosse Way'. The date and exact purpose of the Fosse Way are matters of conjecture, but the weight of evidence seems to indicate that the road was not built as one project but resulted from the joining together of a number of sections of different dates. The short section in the Southwolds is marked by a minor road from Batheaston which climbs over Bannerdown and then forms the county boundary for some two miles. Before the formation of Avon, three counties, Somerset, Gloucestershire and Wiltshire met at the Fosse, and this place is marked by the Three Shire Stones (ST 796700). There were stones there in 1610, for they are marked on Speed's map, but they were replaced in 1736 and lettered S, G and W. In 1858 they were considered to be insufficiently impressive and were replaced by the present ones, which are therefore, in spite of their appearance, not prehistoric.

Roman rule resulted in the intrusion into the Celtic landscape of large agricultural estates, or villas, based on slave-labour and production for market rather than subsistence. Villa life continued into the Dark Ages after the withdrawal of Roman power, until superseded by the Saxon settlement which followed the Battle of Dyrham in 577. From then onward the story of Southwold farming is one in which emphasis fluctuates between corn and animal-products, chiefly wool. In the Middle Ages wool was the source of much wealth in the Cotswolds, but instead of turning over huge areas to grassy sheep-runs, it was more usual to include the sheep in a rotation system where they were 'folded' on temporary fallow or stubble. Where the open-field system was in use, there was a contrast between the Southwolds and the Vale, for while the latter changed from an early two-field system, with one field in fallow, to a three-field system which was more productive for crops, the Cotswold region tended to keep to the two fields which gave more land for grazing.

In the latter part of the fourteenth century cloth instead of raw wool began to be the principal export from England. The Cotswold region, with its wool-production, its water-power along the scarp, its access to fuller's earth in the hills and teazles in the vale, and its proximity to the great port of Bristol, was excellently placed to develop a cloth-making industry. The development was, however, in the central and northern parts, and the Southwolds had nothing to compare with, for example, the industry of the Stroud valley. Bath had an important cloth-industry, fostered by its monastery, but by Tudor times this was recorded as "much decayed". Nearby Twerton, just downstream and now part of Bath, had a flourishing cloth-industry which lasted into the twentieth century, and in the north there was a small industry at Hawkesbury, but generally speaking cloth-making developed mainly in the hills south of Bath, in the Vale and at Bristol.

In the eighteenth century corn was becoming important, and open fields were giving way to enclosures. Marshall, writing in 1789, reported that "thirty years ago" the Cotswolds were nearly all "in the open state" but were "at present" mainly enclosed, and Rudge, in his *History of the County of Gloucestershire* in 1803, commented that "within these last hundred years a total change has taken place in these hills . . . now with few exceptions the downs are converted into arable enclosured fields, and an easy communication is made with the different villages, through a country almost inaccessible to strangers, and sometimes travelled with difficulty by natives." The little local roads were, however, still narrow and winding until the Great Roads were turnpiked in 1726 (B4465), 1742 (A420), 1745 (present A46) and 1751 (B4040). It is to eighteenth-century enclosure that we owe much of the present scenery of large, rectangular, stone-walled fields.

Further change came in the nineteenth century with a modernization of agricultural practice. A six-fold rotation was adopted with turnips, barley, grasses (two years), wheat and oats or legumes, and the fertility of the rather poor stony soil was maintained by the folding of sheep, although the emphasis was then on cross-breeds for meat, and the old Cotswold breed was fast dying out. Cattle for milk and cheese were also on the increase, and today it is milk and grain (either for fodder or as a cash-crop) which are the bases of Southwold farming. In the spring the country is all green, but as the season progresses, there emerges a pleasing patchwork of greens and golds as the crops come to ripen, a scene to be savoured at speed as the visitor drives up the A46 or, better, at leisure by the walker along the Cotswold Way, a signposted stitching-together of ancient paths from Bath to Chipping Camden.

There are few villages on the uplands, and the largest, Marshfield, owes its importance to its situation on the main east-west road. The 'marsh' in its name may refer to local water but is more likely connected with the Old English '*mearc*', a boundary (from which we also get terms such as 'the Welsh Marches'). Until recently the long grey main street was the main road, and a toll-house still stands at the west end, opposite the almshouses of 1619, but the village now has a by-pass. At the east end is the Market, a small triangle near the large Perpendicular fifteenth-century church with a nice Jacobean pulpit, the seventeenth-century Manor House with an early-eighteenth-century front, and the seventeenth-century Home Farmhouse. 'The Lord Nelson' in the Square and 'The Catherine Wheel' in the High Street are both early-eighteenth-century with shell hoods. 'The Catherine Wheel's' windows have noticeably thick glazing bars. Next door, public lavatories have been incorporated in the ground floor of the old market house, or Tolzey, which bears a tablet recording the building of the house in 1692 by John and Mary Goselett, who also gave the town a mace. John died in 1692, Mary in 1698, and their memorials are in the church. Mary was the daughter of John Harington of Kelston, and her sisters are also buried in the church.

Most of the village buildings, mainly eighteenth-century, are of interest. One of the earliest is the seventeenth-century Hospice which has a gable with a two-storeyed bay window and a gabled two-storey porch. To the east has been added an unremarkable huddle of post-war housing. About a mile to the north Castle Farm (ST 772745) is a Folk Museum as well as a working farm and is open from June to September on Wednesdays, Saturdays and Sundays from 2 p.m. to 6 p.m. The early-nineteenth-century castellated block of farm buildings has a growing collection of agricultural and domestic bygones, and there is an ancient cruck longhouse. A well-known local feature of Marshfield is its Mummers' Play presented annually on Boxing Day in the High Street.

Marshfield never seems to have possessed more than a very rudimentary form of town government in spite of its economic importance. It ranked fourth in Gloucestershire, after Bristol, Gloucester and Cirencester, in the tax assessment of 1334, was important in the Middle Ages for the wool trade, and in the eighteenth century had important industries of malting and candle-making. The manor belonged to the Bishop of Wells at the time of Domesday but in 1106 passed to Bath Abbey and in 1170 to Keynsham Abbey, although, to complicate matters, the church itself belonged to Tewkesbury Abbey. The abbot of Keynsham granted it a fair in 1266, and this was confirmed in 1486. Mainly for livestock, it was held in the High Street until 1901, when it was moved to a meadow. It is now no longer held.

West of Marshfield on a minor road which links the A46 and A420 lies Cold Ashton, a small, attractive place with beautiful views over the St Catherine valley to the south. Manor house, rectory, church and school follow each other in procession along the north side. The first is an impressive early-seventeenth-century building showing a basically medieval form with Classical trimmings and lies behind a fine round-headed archway with Roman Doric pillars. The large rectory, with a pleasant garden, was built in the sixteenth century but much altered and enlarged in the nineteenth. Here died Sir Bevil Grenville from wounds received at the Battle of Lansdown in 1643. The church, almost hidden by trees, was rebuilt between 1508 and 1540 by the rector, Thomas Key, who embellished it with his rebus, a T twined in a key. He also installed a very beautiful oak pulpit with an elaborately pinnacled stone canopy. The Latin on his tomb records that he "did at his own cost build all this holy church". Other monuments include tablets to the Whittingtons who lived at Hamswell House in the parish and whose descendants sold the property as late as 1935. These rural Whittingtons were related to the famous Lord Mayor of London commemorated annually by leggy ladies in pantomime.

Just as the name 'Marshfield' probably conceals the Old English for 'a boundary', so does 'Tormarton' to the north near the M4 interchange; and just as Marshfield was a main-road town, so was Tormarton, for until 1800 it stood on part of the Bath–Cirencester turnpike. Today it is a scatter of grey houses, including such pleasant eighteenth-century buildings as the Old School, although the row of Gothic cottages in Back Street is nineteenth-century. Remains of the old manor house, with the de Rivers arms on a chimney stack facing the church, are incorporated in Manor Farmhouse. The lower stages of the fat little church tower are Norman; there is a Norman chancel arch and some Norman mouldings on the outside of the east wall which include an uncommon wheat-ear pattern. Memorials inside include one to prolific Gabriel and Katherine Russell who died in the 1660s, having produced twenty-one children. Across the road from the church Tormarton Court is eighteenth-century and was once the rectory.

Nationally, the best-known feature of the Southwolds is Badminton House and Park, first established by Edward Somerset, son of the impoverished Marquis of Worcester who was reputed to have spent over £700,000 in the service of Charles I. He successfully established himself by first renouncing the family Catholicism, then gaining the friendship of Oliver Cromwell and finally supporting the restoration of Charles II who in 1682 created him first Duke of Beaufort. His magnificent monument is in the church attached to the house, to which it was taken from St George's Chapel at Windsor when Queen Victoria wanted the space for a memorial to her father. The imposing house in its great park is open to the public on Wednesdays from the end of May to early September and at Spring Bank Holiday weekend. The three-day horse-trials are in early April.

The building history of the house is somewhat confused, but the central block, apart from the pediment and cupolas, dates from the original house of 1682, as do the Grinling Gibbons limewood carvings in the dining-room. The rest is mainly of the early-eighteenth century and is chiefly to the designs of William Kent, who was a friend of Lord Burlington and one of the leading figures in the Palladian movement. Kent was an innovator in landscape gardening, organizing the great park to provide a visual setting and pleasing vistas from the house. Medieval parks had been mainly for hunting and for the raising of horses—incidentally, until the eighteenth century deer and hare were the main quarry, and the Badminton Hunt is credited with starting in about 1760 the fashion for fox-hunting and breeding special hounds from staghounds and harriers. Another innovation was the game of badminton, first played about a century ago in the great hall of the house where it is said that the duke played tennis, found he was damaging his pictures and substituted a shuttlecock for the ball.

The park is dotted with buildings and follies, but the most magnificent is Kent's Worcester Lodge (c1746) at the end of the three-mile ride from the north entrance to the house. Attached to the house, the church of 1785 is of Classical design and littered with ducal monuments. The chancel and apse were added in 1875. The village of Great Badminton is not very remarkable but has a fine range of almshouses of c1714, proudly bearing the Beaufort badge in triplicate. Little Badminton has a pleasant village green with a dovecote and a small church, mainly Early English.

About a mile to the south, near Acton Turville, is Badminton railway station, now closed. It was opened in 1903 when the GWR constructed its last major line. The Severn Tunnel had opened in 1885, but there was no connection to London without going through Bristol, and a direct line would have to contend with the Southwolds. The problem was solved by digging the Badminton Tunnel, which is over 2½ miles long and ventilated with a line of castellated towers, such as the one at Old Sodbury. The importance of this line has been increased since the war by the establishment of the Parkway station near the M32 and A38 routes into Bristol. Acton Turville has an interesting toll-house with a fine clock, an old well with a nineteenth-century canopy, some early-nineteenth-century *cottages ornés* and a church which, although heavily restored in 1853, retains a very fine Early English bellcote and a re-inserted blocked Norman doorway.

There are two major monuments to men on the South-wolds. One, near Hawkesbury Upton, was erected in 1846 in memory of a member of the Beaufort family, General Lord Robert Edward Henry Somerset. It is a high stone tower in a commanding position and offers superb views after an exhausting climb to its balcony. The other is by the road which drops down the north end of Lansdown (St 722703) and was put there in 1720 by Lord Lansdown to commemorate his grandfather, Sir Bevil Grenville, who near there in 1643 received the wounds from which he shortly died at Cold Ashton. The battle that killed him was part of a chain of events in the telling of which it is necessary to range outside the region.

When the Civil War broke out in 1642, the Royalist cause was weak in the Avon area, and both Bath and Bristol were garrisoned for Parliament. In the winter of 1642–3, however, Cavalier hopes were revived by news that Sir Ralph Hopton, in a brilliant campaign, had defeated the Parliamentary forces in Cornwall and was marching back with a contingent of some four thousand Cornish pikemen and musketeers under the leadership of their beloved Bevil Grenville, grandson of Sir Richard Grenville of the famed *Revenge*. They were a formidable fighting force of great tenacity and courage and in June were joined at Chard by the Marquis of Hertford, Prince Maurice and the Earl of Caernarvon, with some fifteen hundred horse, 300 dragoons, and about fifteen cannon. Hertford took nominal command, Hopton acted as chief of staff, and Maurice was given charge of the cavalry. Meanwhile Sir William Waller, recently put in command of the western Parliamentary forces, was making preparations at Bath, and Alexander Popham was organizing the country levies for defence.

The Royalists seemed unstoppable. Rapidly they took Taunton and Bridgwater and moved eastwards to occupy Wells. It was from there that Hopton wrote to his old friend Waller proposing a conference to see if further bloodshed could be avoided without loss of honour. Waller's reply is famous both for its simple nobility and for its illustration of the agonizing situation of men of conscience in time of civil strife: "The great God who is the searcher of my heart," he wrote, "knows with what a sad sense I go upon this service, and with what a perfect hatred I detest this war without an enemy. . . . We are both upon the stage and must act such parts as are assigned to us in this tragedy. Let us do it in the way of honour and without personal animosity."

There was no meeting, and towards the end of June Hopton's forces moved out of Wells and headed for Bath. On 3rd July they were advancing up the Limpley Stoke valley towards Batheaston while Waller's army was drawn up on the heights of Claverton Down on the opposite side of the valley, watching the ambush they had laid in the woods. The ambush failed, beaten off by the Cornishmen, and Maurice's cavalry crossed the improvised bridge at Claverton and advanced up the hill. Waller promptly withdrew to Bath. It was by then evening, and the Royalists assembled at Batheaston, where in the morning light they found that Waller faced them from the eastern flanks of Lansdown in a position so strong that Hopton retired his forces northward to Marshfield.

The following morning, Wednesday 5th July, the Royalist army marched westward to attempt to take Bath from the north. Assembled on Freezing Hill, they looked over the deep valley and tangled country which separated them from the steep north-facing slope of Lansdown and saw with dismay that Waller had moved his men in the night and was occupying the brow of the opposing hill "in a situation well nigh impregnable". Hopton, ever a realist, decided on retreat and in the afternoon began his preparations. Two things caused him to change his mind: the first was the successful repulsion of a Parliamentary cavalry attack, the second a demand from the enraged Cornishmen for an order to "fetch those cannon". In the late afternoon the order was given, and in the face of murderous fire the Cornish pikemen, toiling time and again up the steep wooded hill, finally reached the brow and the guns—and held. "They stood," wrote Richard Atkyns, who was there, "as upon the eaves of a house for steepness, but as unmovable as a rock." Attack after attack was hurled at them in the gathering dusk. Grenville fell, mortally wounded. But still they stood, and as the light faded, Waller withdrew about a quarter of a mile to behind the stone walls which divided the fields.

In the short July night, while the Royalists got what sleep they could, their sentries watched the twinkling lights of what they took to be the camp fires of their opponents. At dawn they found they had been deceived, for the 'campfires' were lengths of lighted match hung over the walls, and Waller's men were back in fortified Bath, doubtless waiting reinforcements from nearby Bristol. The Royalists, physically and morally exhausted, were in no condition to embark on a siege. Grenville was dying, and early in the morning Hopton himself was severely wounded and temporarily blinded by the explosion of a powder-cart. And so the army drew itself together and plodded off back through Marshfield and Chippenham, pursued by Waller, to find themselves surrounded at Devizes.

Here Maurice and Hertford broke through, fetched cavalry

reinforcements from Oxford and on the grassy slopes of Roundway Down inflicted a crushing defeat on the Parliamentary forces. In a few days the Cornishmen were back at Bath, took it and marched on to Bristol where they were joined by Prince Rupert, who had arrived from Oxford with a strong force of cavalry, foot and cannon.

It was a mere eighteen days from the Battle of Lansdown and an extraordinary reversal of fortune which did little good for the morale of the lawyer Nathaniel Fiennes who was governing Bristol for Parliament. Yet the city was well provisioned, and her defences were strong. Not only did she have her city walls, her castle and the protection of the Frome and Avon but she had also a forward line of forts with connecting earthworks along the hills above the city.

The attack began at dawn on 26th July, the Cornish contingent advancing on the south side while Rupert's men attacked the line of forts to the north. The Cornish were repulsed, and the attack on the forts was thrown back time and again until, at a point between Brandon Hill Fort and what was later renamed the Royal Fort, Colonel Henry Washington, member of a family which was to produce the first American President, led his troops in an attack which broke through the defences and opened the way to the city walls. Washington's Breach is commemorated by a plaque on the wall of the University at the top of Park Street, a thoroughfare which did not then exist.

Within, the city confusion and conflicting council. Many citizens naturally wanted to preserve their property from bombardment, fire and looting; others were for carrying on the defence. The redoubtable Dorothy Hazard, a Puritan lady of great character, gathered a band of women to defend the Frome Gate, resolved to fight to the last. Fiennes himself was irresolute, concerned about the low supplies of powder and anxious to make the best of what seemed to him to be a very bad job. He called for a parley and accepted Rupert's terms by which the garrison would be allowed to march away under a safe-conduct of three days. So eager was Fiennes to be gone that he marched the defenders off before the agreed time and thus gave the Royalists a pretext for plunder.

For two years Bath and Bristol were held for the King. At Bath a local man, Sir Thomas Bridges of Keynsham, was

Governor, while at Bristol Prince Rupert was nominally Governor, with Hopton in charge of the garrison until he was later made field-marshal of the West. In March 1645 the fourteen-year old Prince of Wales, the future Charles II, was sent to Bristol to be set up with his own Council for the West.

In July 1645 the New Model Army under Fairfax and Cromwell arrived victorious in the West. The siege of Taunton was raised; Bridgwater was taken. On the 18th the army was at Wells, and on the 30th two regiments were sent to Bath, which quickly surrendered. Having marched into Dorest and taken Sherborne, Fairfax returned to mount an attack on Bristol, and by 23rd August the city was surrounded and the blockade complete. On 4th September Fairfax called on Rupert to surrender, but the Prince played for time, and on the 9th Fairfax lost patience and ordered an assault which began at 2 a.m. By early morning the attackers had broken through the line of forts, and at 8 a.m. Rupert surrendered the city on terms which allowed his forces to leave with their horses and swords but no firearms. He could not have hoped to hold the plague-ridden unhappy city, and at least he kept his men, but to his uncle, the King, the surrender seemed un-forgivable.

It was not until nine years later that Cromwell ordered that Bristol Castle be 'slighted'. The demolition was carried out with efficiency, and on the site grew up new houses and streets, the chief of which was inevitably named Castle Street, a busy part of Bristol life until it was demolished by a new destroyer, the air-raids of World War II. At the same time as the castle was pulled down, the Royal Fort was destroyed. On its site stands the elegant Royal Fort House of 1761, and opposite is the University physics building designed by Sir George Oakley and erected in 1929. Its castellated Gothic keep seems hardly appropriate either for housing modern labora-tories or for commemorating a Civil War blockhouse, but presumably Sir George had his own ideas about what a Royal Fort should look like.

A similar Romantic and unhistorical spirit inspired a lesser architect, Charles Dyer, when for the slopes up which the Cornishmen advanced at Lansdown he designed in 1836 'Battlefields House' (ST 725691), castellated, turreted and Gothic, with a roadside Tudor Lodge.

VII

THE AVON VALLEY

The Bristol Avon starts off insignificantly in the north-east of the county which borrowed its name and saunters unobtrusively over the border as if making for the Thames. At Malmesbury it appears to change its mind and heads southward along the great clay wall until at Bradford-on-Avon it turns west, parallel to its first course and then north to re-enter its home county south-east of Bath. From there it flows northward through one of the best bits of scenery in Avon, a narrow valley whose wooded sides rise steeply to Claverton and Bathampton Downs on the west and Kingsdown on the east. Clinging to the western hillside is the A36 Bath–Warminster road, and crammed into the valley bottom are the river, the Kennet and Avon Canal, opened in 1810, and the railway line constructed in 1848 to link the main GWR line through to Bradford-on-Avon.

Just inside the county border the canal changes sides and is carried over the river by the splendid Dundas Aqueduct from which can be seen the site of the inclined plane through Conkwell Wood which brought down the stone for its construction from the quarries above. At the northern end of the valley a tramway from the Bathampton Down quarries crossed the road by the so-called Dry Arch, now demolished, which stood where the A36 bends sharply westward for Bath. Remains of the stone blocks to which the rails were fastened can still be found in the path through the woods.

There is little room for building in the valley, and the only settlement is Claverton, a pleasant though not remarkable linear village on a loop off the main road. Here in the graveyard of the heavily restored church is the tomb of Ralph Allen who died in 1764, having made two fortunes, one out of organizing the cross-posts in the West and the other from Bath stone-quarries, and who built himself the magnificent Palladian mansion of Prior Park overlooking Bath. He bought

Claverton Manor in 1758, but all that is now left of its manor house is a set of balustraded terraces, for the building was pulled down, and in 1819–20 a fine new neo–Grecian mansion was built on the top of the hill, designed by Sir Jeffrey Wyattville, better known for his remodelling of Windsor Castle. This new Claverton Manor has now been cunningly reconstructed inside into rooms authentically furnished to reproduce different periods in American domestic history, while other rooms and galleries illustrate specific themes such as cowboys, Indians, the religious sect of Shakers and the village store. The American Museum, unique and fascinating, is open from March to October, Tuesdays to Sundays, 2 p.m. to 5p.m., and is normally approached from Bath through the main gate to the University.

About three miles south of Claverton the county boundary loops eastward to include a small section of the River Frome, and there is steeply sited Freshford. The village, which is a Conservation Area, is a charming collection of grey Bath-stone houses in a variety of styles from seventeenth-century gables to nineteenth-century-Italianate and Gothic, with converted industrial buildings and stables, and a small amount of new housing, all set among steep slopes, woods and open pasture. The nucleus round the stumpy church, mainly nineteenth-century, is on a hilltop between the Frome and a small tributary, but the rest is in clumps dotted along tangled roads.

Back at Claverton a twisting, narrow road leads down to the Claverton Pumping Station (ST 792644) which raised water from the Avon to the canal by channelling the river's power against two coupled 15 feet 6 inches breast-shot water-wheels which worked a pair of beam-pumps. It was designed by the canal's engineer, John Rennie (1761–1821), and has been restored. Visits can be arranged through the Kennet and Avon Canal Trust, who have done a great deal to restore the canal as an amenity.

At its northern end the valley opens up into a wide flood-plain which swings round to the west before constricting once again in its passage through Bath. On the bend the Avon is joined by the Bye (or Box) Brook whose valley carries eastward the London road, the A4, separating Bathford from Batheaston. With Bathampton on the west these form a trio of attractive villages which were strongly influenced by the architectural fashion of eighteenth-century Bath. Although overwhelmingly farming and residential, this area has some industry, notably paper-mills at Bathford and Harbutt's Plasticine at Bathampton.

The ford of Bathford was through the Bye Brook and was replaced by a bridge which is now preserved as an ancient monument. There are many handsome houses including Eagle House (c1750) near the church, Rock House (1730) and Titan Barrow (1748, by Wood of Bath), now called White-haven, in the High Street. The large church is an uninspired late-Victorian effort but has a nice Jacobean pulpit, some seventeenth-century monuments with attractively artless lettering, and a set of stocks in the porch. Down by the stream are the red-brick paper-mills, and up on the hill is Brown's Folly, an eye-catching tower erected in 1840 by Mr Wade Brown, a local quarry-owner.

At Bathampton is a pleasant group of canal-bridge, pub and church. The last is mainly nineteenth-century but of interest as the burial-place of Admiral Phillips, first Governor of New South Wales, in whose memory the south aisle has been fitted up as an Australian chapel. From Bathampton a toll-bridge crosses the Avon to Batheaston which is virtually part of Bath and has a good deal of new building, although there is some good eighteenth-century stuff, such as another Eagle House, built in 1727 by John Wood the Elder for himself, and Batheaston House on the main road, dated 1712. Batheaston Villa, eighteenth-century with a touch of Gothicry in its battlements, was where in 1775 Lady Miller started her highly popular and very foolish poetry contests.

As the river enters Bath, it turns southward, with a steep slope to the west and flat land to the east on which, in the late-eighteenth century, after the erection of Pulteney Bridge in 1770 to designs by Robert Adam, was developed the elegant suburb of Bathwick with its splendid Pulteney Street leading to the Sydney Hotel (now Holburne of Menstrie Museum) and Gardens (now a public park). South of Pulteney Street the low flat land is used as playing-fields, part of which has recently been taken for the erection of a Sports Centre. Further south again, where the canal joined the river, coming down a flight of locks (one of which has been filled in for road 'improvements' while the others have been restored), the nineteenth century saw the development of the working-class district of Dolemeads and in 1908 the red-brick terraces of the first bit of Council housing.

At Dolemeads the river again changes course, swinging westwards and creating the steep north-facing Beechen Cliff, which still fortunately retains much of its woodland but less happily has changed its grey nineteenth-century streets for a set of staring white modern cubes which have been likened locally, perhaps unkindly, to chicken-coops. Here at the foot of the hill the railway crosses the river by a skew-bridge and the road by means of the post-war Churchill Bridge which replaced the old Bath Bridge which lay a little further west.

Westward from the Churchill Bridge to the outskirts of the city at Newbridge, the river is lined with a miscellaneous collection of industrial building which includes a corset-factory, flour-mills, engineering-works, cabinet-making factories, a semi-dismantled gasworks, and the remains of gaunt nineteenth-century cloth-mills on the island at Twerton which was created by the eighteenth-century canalization of the river. It is a workaday stretch far removed from the tourist image of Bath.

At Newbridge the river begins to meander muddily over a wide plain of pasture until at Hanham Abbots it enters a long gorge-like section cut through the Pennant sandstone, and this plain section is notable for leisure activities, particularly fishing and boating at Newbridge, Saltford and Keynsham, where a marina was opened in 1975 and where lock-side pubs at Saltford and Hanham have taken on a new lease of life. Competition between the various river-users is strong, and its resolution is a headache for Avon planners. It is, to use the awful jargon, a 'honeypot', and one of the problems is that the flies (or bears? or bees?) travel by car.

Industry is too scattered to be dominant, but it would be impossible to ignore the red-brick bulk of Fry's factory below Keynsham, to which they moved in the 1920s from their cramped quarters in the middle of Bristol. Robinson's paper-works a little further east are also considerable and include the old offices with tottering clock-tower once part of the brass-works and the subject of considerable conservation contro-versy. Less obtrusive, because flatter, are the big sewage-works below Saltford, but they are a reminder of two important facts about the river: firstly that its chief function is to carry away effluent and storm-water, and secondly that its management is the responsibility not of the County but of the Wessex Water Authority, which was set up under the 1973 Water Act to be responsible for river-management, water-supply and sewerage over the whole drainage-basin of the river. Of the once prosperous brass-industries there are remains on the Avon at Saltford, Keynsham and Swineford.

The main settlement in this stretch is Keynsham which since the War has grown from some seven thousand inhabitants to over twenty thousand and has more supermarkets than Bath. The popular, and incorrect, derivation of the name is from St Keyna, who is said to have been a fifth-century Welsh princess of stubborn virtue who fled from her suitors, settled in the Avon valley and turned the local serpents into stone, thus creating the fossils known to geologists, who have a different mythology, as ammonites. The name, of which the earliest known form is 'Caeginehamme', probably means 'Caegin's meadow'.

The town is situated on a small plateau between the Chew and a brook draining the Vale of Stockwood and in medieval times was a single street with the church and the abbey at one end and the market at the other. The date of the foundation of the original priory is uncertain, but in 1166 it was refounded as an abbey by the Earl of Gloucester. After the Dissolution the buildings became a quarry for stone, and in about 1650 the Bridges family, who acquired the land and buildings in 1552, used much of what was left to build a mansion on the spot. This was demolished in 1776, and what remained of the abbey was "dug up to level the ground". After the railway came in 1840, there was an expansion of Keynsham with substantial stone houses, and the abbey area was developed with 'villas', involving destruction and removal of much material. Another transport development, the cutting of the by-pass in 1964–6 through the centre of the abbey, inspired a rescue-dig which enabled many features to be plotted and which revealed part of a stone staircase which is exposed on the side of the cutting. Some of the stonework is in a little museum by the entrance to Fry's where there are also remains from the big Roman villa found in Keynsham Cemetery and, outside, the foundations of a very small villa removed from their original site by the factory.

The large, fine parish church, which was not part of the Abbey, has a thirteenth-century chancel, but the rest was heavily reconstructed in 1861–3 except for the tower, which is seventeenth-century Gothic, replacing the original central one which was destroyed by a thunderstorm in 1632. Inside the church are two fine screens, a Carolean pulpit and various monuments to the Bridges family.

Of the few old buildings in the town the most notable are the almshouses on the Bristol Road which were founded by Sir Thomas Bridges in 1685. In Station Road is the late-seventeenth-century gateway of Keynsham House with Norman fragments, presumably from the Abbey, built into the back. Across the High Street Gothic Methodist faces Classical Baptist, offering an interesting contrast in nineteenth-century noncomformist styles.

Most of the High Street has been refaced or replaced to provide modern shops, and at the east end is a shopping precinct built in conjunction with a white, cracking, rectilinear Town Hall which is now the home of Wansdyke District Council and a good local library. Beyond bulks a cubical brown-brick 1976 development of flats, offices, shops and leisure centre, standing above the Chew valley, which here and beyond the A4 bridge has been turned into a pleasant park featuring some remains from the old brass-mills' water-power system. Also in the valley is the nineteenth-century Albert Mill which once used water-power to grind tropical woods for the extraction of dyes—a logwood-mill.

The majority of Keynsham is recent, starting with a modest inter-war development and then expanding at a tremendous rate since the post-war 'overspill' arrangement with Bristol. Housing has spread southward in two built-up areas separated by the Chew Valley; services have developed, and shopping is good. Other places may use their entrance-signs to boast of antiquities, but Keynsham's proudly announce 'Free Parking'—how long they can continue to do this remains to be seen.

Neighbouring Saltford has also expanded considerably since the War but the old settlement, sloping down to the river, still retains a village atmosphere. The church, in a

pleasant setting, is mainly a nineteenth-century reconstruction, including a gallery of 1851, but has a Jacobean pulpit and
a carved possibly thirteenth-century font. On the walls are
tablets to members of the Flower family whose eldest sons
were customarily christened with the unusual name of
Lamorock, and in the porch is a memorial to a pair of feet,
which belonged to Frances Flood, an itinerant Cornish-
woman, until she got smallpox in 1723 and they fell off.

> Though here beneath the mould they lie
> Corruption for to see
> Yet they shall one day reunite
> To all eternity.

Beside the church is the Norman manor house with at the back
a fine first-floor window with zigzag mouldings and on the
east gable a big carved beast. Down by the river are boating-
stations, and there is much fishing and sailing. The brass-
battery mills, where water-worked hammers beat brass plates
into big dishes, finally closed in 1925 and are not open to view.

The new broad bridge at Keynsham, built after the floods of
1968, replaces an older one which took its place in history in
1685 with the arrival of the army of the Duke of Monmouth,
pretender to the throne, some ten thousand strong, recruited
during his progress from Bridport through Taunton,
Bridgwater and Shepton Mallet to Pensford. It was never
exactly clear what Monmouth's intentions were, but it seemed
evident that he was making for Bristol, which was, as the Civil
War had shown, the key to the West and whose capture might
encourage the reluctant gentry to join his cause. The city was
most vulnerable to attack from the east, which would mean
crossing the Avon at Keynsham, and the King's troops had
therefore broken down the bridge. On 24th June it was
repaired by a detachment under Captain Tyler sent by
Monmouth from Pensford; troops of the Gloucestershire
Militia were driven off, and early in the morning of the next
day the rebel army arrived and assembled on Sydenham Mead
below the bridge. Here Francis Creswick, who we have
already met in connection with Kingswood Forest, noted and
later reported to the Duke of Beaufort who was in command at
Bristol, that the army consisted of over a thousand horses,
some eight thousand foot and eight cannon, and that although

some of the men were well armed, others were "indifferent" and some had nothing but "an old sword or a stick in their hands". For his presence at the Mead, Creswick was later imprisoned in Gloucester Gaol on a treason charge trumped up by his old enemy Sir John Newton of nearby Barr's Court, and it took half a dozen petitions, a deposition from the Duke of Beaufort and a confrontation with Lord Grey, commander of the rebel cavalry, to get him released. The next year James II visited him at Hanham Court.

Monmouth's slim chance of success was to press straight on to Bristol; instead, a night attack was decided on, and the troops withdrew to Keynsham, Monmouth himself occupying the house of Sir Thomas Bridges, who had vacated it to "avoid offence" and on meeting his friend Creswick had gone off to stay at Hanham. That night two small parties of the King's cavalry, neither knowing of the other's presence, converged on Keynsham. Captain Parker's horsemen had swum the Avon to get between the rebels and Bristol and had then doubled back into Keynsham where they met confused resistance. Into the mêlée charged a detachment under the command of Colonel Oglethorpe who had pursued the trail of the rebels from Pensford, and the King's men by their combined, if unco-ordinated, efforts extricated themselves and got away to the south. Casualties were few, the dead being estimated as four King's men and fourteen rebels, but the effect on morale was devastating, the attack on Bristol was abandoned, and on that night began the retreat which was to end in the massacre of Sedgemoor on 6th July. In the swift retribution of the Bloody Assizes, eleven Keynsham men were sentenced to be hanged.

Sydenham Mead was at that time a common meadow, as were most of the flat lands along the Avon, and the large field was divided into unenclosed strips allocated to each of the commoners. At the time of the enclosure of Saltford Mead, for example, in 1851, there were over seventy sub-divisions distributed among some twenty people. The present field-pattern along the river is mainly the result of nineteenth-century enclosures. Another legacy of the nineteenth century is the embankments, cuttings, bridges and tunnels of the Great Western Railway and Midland Railway, the former opening in 1840 and still in use, the latter in 1869, closing in 1966.

Valley-bottom farming stops abruptly at Hanham Lock, where the sandstone cliffs close in and there is pleasant walking through the woods. Hanham Abbots (which once belonged to Keynsham Abbey) is a hamlet on a road up from the lock and has a fourteenth-century church (restored in the nineteenth century), whose tower abuts directly on the Court, a building with elements from the sixteenth to nineteenth centuries and a large, probably fifteenth-century barn. Up on the top of the rise, by the main road, Manor Farm has an eighteenth-century barn surmounted by a statue of Ceres, locally known as 'Sally-on-the-Barn' and reputed to fly about the village at night.

Some two miles of pathway through the riverside woods leads to the industry-packed trench from Conham and Crew's Hole to Netham Lock from which the Feeder Canal of 1809 runs straight ahead, cutting off the southern loop of the river. It is a strange world down there, isolated from hill-top suburbia above, but it must have seemed even stranger in the eighteenth century when it was the smoky home of a zinc- and brass-industry based on water-transport and local coal, an industry to which a single chimneystack on the hillside above Crew's Hole still bears testimony. The bulkiest factory today is St Anne's Board Mills near where the Brislington Brook comes down the steep, narrow valley which holds St Anne's Wood and St Anne's Well. The well, which has a modern cover, was associated with the medieval chapel of St Anne which was visited by Henry VII in 1486; the wood is a narrow linear park and bird-sanctuary with an extraordinary remoteness from the busy traffic and modern housing of the plateau-top only a short distance away. The southward swing of the river from Netham Lock leaves a broad flat area which includes Temple Meads and St Philip's Marsh and became filled in the nineteenth century with a railway station and a spreading jumble of factories and warehouses, depots and railway sidings and clusters of houses. It is still a busy area and in the post-war period has acquired the brand-new big fruit and vegetable market below Totterdown bridge; gone, however, is the huge Great Western Cotton Factory at Barton Hill (ST 610727) which was built in the 1830s and once gave work to over a thousand people.

Behind Temple Meads Station the Feeder Canal rejoins the river and supplies water to the Floating Harbour, constructed between 1804 and 1809 by locking off the river and cutting a by-pass, the New Cut, to take the tidal flow. The New Cut rejoins the river just beyond the modern road-complex at Cumberland Basin and just before it trends northwards into the Avon Gorge, spanned by Brunel's Clifton Suspension Bridge. Beyond the gorge is the Horseshoe Bend, notoriously difficult to navigate and limiting the length of ships which could reach the City docks. Beyond that the river flows again through lowland to Avonmouth where its original mouth was converted into a dock and a new channel cut. All this, however, is part of the Bristol story.

The role of the river is changing, and all along its length is evidence of past economic activity—the once-busy canal now being renovated for leisure use, the silent brass-mills, the river locks now used by pleasure-craft instead of barges, the watermills abandoned, the Floating Harbour closed to shipping—but the continued presence of factories, the growing importance of leisure pastimes, and the concentration of traffic on the limited number of bridges, all indicate that the Avon has a decisive influence on the region through which it runs.

VIII

BATH

There has been a lot of bother about Bath in the last few years, both locally and nationally, starting with controversy over the Buchanan road-tunnel proposals and building up to accusations that the Corporation and its planners were allowing, even encouraging, the wholesale destruction of the smaller Georgian architecture of the city, replacing it with shoe-box buildings which were not only unneighbourly but not even good examples of modern architecture. The Beaufort Hotel, the Ballance Street flats and the Southgate shopping precinct have become the Wailing Walls of architectural journalists. Visitors may therefore be surprised to find that Bath is still beautiful, unique and very Georgian.

They should not, however, conclude that concern over the fate of this superb townscape is misplaced or unwarranted, for the glory of Bath lies not in its great set-pieces alone but in the whole Georgian assemblage of buildings, of whatever rank; and it is true moreover that there is no post-war building to which we can point with pride, except perhaps one, and that one is not innovatory but replicative. It houses the Spa offices and souvenir-shop and replaces the New Baths of 1889 which were a curious collection of pilaster, knobs and false storey in a crumbling stone which gave an unwarranted appearance of antiquity. For the new design the architect looked to the work of Thomas Baldwin in the 1790s which produced the surrounding complex of colonnades, Pump Room and Bath Street, and as a result the new building, by mirroring the scale, style and decoration of its neighbours, forms a mannerly and satisfying element in the total environment. Indeed, it is difficult to imagine any other form which would have done as well, especially when we consider the uncomfortable intrusion into the High Street of the flat face, unwieldy scale and black hat of the 'Harvey' block.

In some cases replication is the right thing. For example,

when part of the Francis Hotel in the south range of Queen Square was bombed, its replacement by anything except a copy of the original would have ruined the whole composition. In other cases, however, the Georgian style may be impracticable for modern purposes, and Bath's inter-war Georgian Post Office, Co-operative stores, cinema and electricity offices were not particularly suited to their functions. At its simplest, the problem is that the rules of Georgian architecture require windows in unsuitable places and rooms of unsuitable height. Shop-windows can also present difficulties, so that, for instance, Milsom Street is mainly Georgian in its upper storeys and modern plate-glass below. Another factor is that it is no longer economic to face buildings with Bath stone, and the reconstituted variety does not, some critics maintain, make a good neighbour to the real thing even if you like it as a material, which many do not. But Bath stone itself has disadvantages, for it is susceptible to weathering, and the cost of cleaning and repairing is considerable even when, as in the case of Bath, a certain amount of grant assistance is available.

These problems apply also to the streets of small houses, variously described as 'artisans' cottages' or 'Georgian slums' according to taste. Whether they are to be retained and internally modernized or removed and replaced by new buildings depends partly on fashion and partly on economics, neither of which is immutable. In contradiction to the policy accepted through most of the post-war period, it is now nationally more fashionable and, possibly, more economic to preserve and rehabilitate, a change which shows itself awkwardly in Morford Street where demolition of the bottom end has been followed by a cosmetic treatment for the top.

If we adopted the attitude of the Georgian architect/ developers, we would have no doubt. They had nothing but contempt for the architectural heritage of Bath and were determined to replace it with a style which, in their time, whatever its ancient origins, was revolutionary. The argument that they could do this because for the most part they were working on green field sites does not hold water, for the first intention of John Wood was to re-make the city itself, and although his schemes were at first rejected as 'chimerical', the power of the idea became so strong that by the end of the century there was hardly a medieval façade left unchanged except where there sits in the middle of it all, perfectly happily and neighbourly, a whacking great Gothic Abbey, knobs, angels and all.

But of course we cannot do it. What those proud and brilliant and obstinate men of the eighteenth century created is far too big, far too much of a piece, far too precious, for us to mess it about, and since we seem incapable either of building neo-Georgian in a way that looks anything but slightly wrong or of producing a new style which sits in happily with Georgian, then the more we stick to facsimile building or to refurbishing the originals the better. What we do behind the façades is another matter—the Georgians did not care, and the backs of their glorious crescents are a mess. Curiously, the Victorians, who are so often said to have been so tasteless, did not manage at all badly—look at the wings of the Guildhall, or the Pump Room concert-room, or the second block of the Mineral Water Hospital. Unfortunately none of these is functionally first-class.

It must be remembered, however, that Georgian Bath is a relatively small part of the city, and if we were capable of producing in a modern idiom something to catch the imagination and feed the spirit in the way that Wood and his successors did, there was opportunity for it to be done. Down by Avon Street, for example, beside the river, where there is a jumbly mess of post-war building and derelict space, was an opportunity to create a New Town, as Bathwick and Walcot were Georgian New Towns, which would show that we, in our own way and in our own idiom, and with our own materials, could create a townscape of first-rate quality. Was it lack of vision, lack of nerve or lack of money? Or was it lack of purpose? Do we know what the Bath of today is *for*?

This is the fundamental question. What is the function of the place? What is its economic base? Or, more crudely, 'Where's the money coming from?'

Georgian Bath was created by speculative builders aiming to cash in on the swelling demand for residence, especially for houses to be hired for the season. Wood had his historically imperfect dream of creating a Roman city with Circus, Forum and Imperial Gymnasium for Medicinal Exercises, but he knew perfectly well, for he was a shrewd operator, that, although his designs might provide such outward forms, what he had in fact to build were housing estates, and when he produced his publicity material, he was careful to stress the advantages of having a house in a city where there were cheap Provisions, Healthy Walks, Polite Society and Many Families of Distinction. The whole thing was done on credit with bank-loans raised against future profits from letting, so that when the Napoleonic Wars came and trade fell off, the Bath bank crashed, quite a few architects became bankrupt, and building came to a halt. It was risky business, but it produced a city. The very stone itself had not before been popular, and its use was partly the result of high-pressure salesmanship by Ralph Allen, who had acquired the quarries and whose famous tramway down what is now Ralph Allen Drive was advertised mainly for its merit in lowering the price of the stone by a quarter. It made Allen's second fortune—his first he had acquired as Postmaster.

The money for Georgian Bath, on which depended the livelihood not only of the builders but also of a whole host of people such as furniture-makers, carriage-builders, servants, shopkeepers and prostitutes, was therefore made outside the city and brought in, which meant that when the annual influx fell off in the nineteenth century a new form of city economy had to be found, for the people who were retiring in increasing numbers to live in Bath were smaller spenders. In general the main solution was to widen the market for the City's products, and this, with the help of improved communications, was done by the growth of industry, largely based on the old service crafts and the increasing development of Bath as a service and shopping centre for the surrounding area. In the last quarter of the century there was a revival of the oldest and most consistent service the town had offered, treatment with the mineral waters. The new wave of visitors did not, however, rent houses for the season but put up in hotels, and so the late Victorian period saw a spate of hotel-building in Bath and an extension of the treatment facilities. Another development was the increase in Corporation spending based on borrowing backed by the income from the rates.

The industrial and service elements continued to develop between the wars, and Bath enhanced its reputation in the field of health treatment, no longer based principally on the use of

The Dundas Aqueduct, which carried the Kennet and Avon Canal over the Avon. Doric pilasters, frieze with triglyphs and cornice with modillions, all in Bath stone, although there has been later patching in brick.

The River Avon near Saltford, with remains of annealing ovens of the old brass-mills.

Pulteney Bridge (Robert Adam, 1770), Bath. The big building was the Empire Hotel (1901) with, to its right, the spire of St Michael's and, to its left, the dome of the Guildhall. Left of the River are the Parade Gardens.

Rehabilitation: a Georgian group in Bath reconstituted within and redecorated without.

The Beaufort Hotel, Bath, with car-park below. The wall of boarding hides the site of an abandoned scheme for Law Courts. Pillars and pediments distinguish Camden Crescent on the hill.

Post-war building in Bath, from vaguely neo-Georgian to glass curtainwall.

(*Overleaf*) Bath from the air. See key on pp.210-11.

The interior of Bath's Pump Room.

The Great (Roman) Bath, in Bath. Everything above the stumps of the pillars is Victorian.

The Avon Gorge and Clifton Suspension Bridge – Clifton on the
right, Leigh Woods on the left.

The road-complex at the entry to Bristol Docks. The waterway on
the right is the New Cut of 1809, and on its right is Bedminster.
The main body of water is the Floating Harbour, and Queen Square
and the Centre lie to the left of the last bridge.

the mineral waters but on the concentration of specialist consultants and hospital facilities. The function of Bath as a spa, however, retained some significance. The most notable developments in building were the council housing estates on the periphery and a certain amount of planned development in the inner city chiefly in the Kingsmead-Southgate Street area. Meanwhile the splitting-up of Georgian houses into flats continued apace, as did the exodus of residents from the central part of the city. A considerable piece of planning for developing the south-east quarter of the city was frustrated by the outbreak of war. Three important planning actions were the restriction of surface-material to Bath stone or an artificial substitute, the listing of buildings of architectural interest and the preservation of the green-hill setting of Bath.

Since the Second World War the problem of the city's economy has remained unsolved. There has been a healthy development of industry by both expansion and innovation but there are severe site-limitations on further growth. There has been an increase in offices, services and shops, in educational facilities and in medicine—although it is possible that we may soon see the end of the use of the natural hot water. Bath has enlarged her hospitals and built a sports complex, a covered shopping centre, a new bus-station, several office blocks and a university. During the war the Admiralty moved in and has remained the biggest single employer of labour. Bath has an annual Festival of international repute. In common with other heritage towns she has experienced a major increase in her tourist industry, although it tends to be of the short-stay variety. None of these enterprises, save tourism, is likely to get much financial advantage from investing in the preservation of Georgian Bath. Who then is going to pay, particularly in time of economic depression? Should it be the nation, on the grounds that Bath is part of the national heritage? Elizabeth I ordered a national collection for the rehabilitation of the Abbey—is that a precedent? Should the money come from the ratepayers (most of whom do not live in Georgian houses) on the grounds that they reap the benefit in environmental terms? Can the money be got out of the tourists? This was the method the Corporation adopted to help to pay for their development of the Pump Room/Bath Street area in 1789 when they got Parliamentary permission to charge an extra toll at the turnpikes. Could more money be brought in by developing facilities for establishing Bath as a conference centre? Should gambling be re-introduced? For whom, then, are we building?

In the eighteenth century the money for development came from well-to-do clients who could pay well for the latest fashion in houses. Materials and labour for building were relatively cheap, and the low-wage servants required for running the one-family establishments were in plentiful supply. Moreover the well-heeled clients wanted to live centrally where public amenities were within sedan-chair ride. The workshops, the artisans, the poor, were provided with meaner, often jerry-built streets either on the periphery, as in Dolemeads down by the river, or in close proximity to the large set-pieces, and it is a sad thought that those slums are often aesthetically more pleasing than the physically better accommodation that has been provided in our own century. Food was bought at the markets, and shops were usually converted from houses. Public buildings were financed either out of the rates or by private speculation. The capital for the Upper Assembly Rooms, for example, was raised by a tontine subscription, a system where, when a subscriber died, his shares were distributed among the other investors until eventually one ancient person would hold the lot. Fortunes were made (and lost) in the property market. There were no planning restrictions, for, where Corporation property was involved, it was finance and not aesthetics which concerned the Council, but there was pattern of style, an agreement about rules of design, which meant that although there were considerable differences in detail and a changing spirit through the century, the overall effect of this piecemeal development by a number of separate architects produced a townscape which has a marvellous feeling of cohesion. It also has a consistency of scale, and that scale is a human one—there was, and is, no place for giganticism in Bath. In those days you put your money on your back and walked up and down to show it off, an activity which called for wide pavements in front of a solid but not ostentatious back-drop of buildings.

Or you did if you were well-off. If you were a house-servant, you shared, at a different level, in this life, wearing your livery and inhabiting, albeit in an attic, the house of your employer—"plunged", as Mr Smauker the footman said to

Sam Weller, "into the very vortex of society". But if you belonged to the poor, which Mr Smauker and his employer would believe to be your own fault, you would do a long day's work for little money and go back to a disease-ridden slum. Or else you would beg, hoping to be paid to remove your revolting presence. Or if you were a girl of, say, thirteen, there was always prostitution before venereal disease put an end to your physical charms.

That was the other world behind the lovely squares and terraces and crescents and circuses, behind the glittering public assemblies, and it was to that world the Victorian reformers, to their eternal credit, directed their energetic attention. They were environmentalists, in the sense that they believed that morality could be promoted by decent housing, and therefore the legislation which they drove through government was directed towards health, for improving the Sanitary Condition of the Labouring Poor. It was the motivating power of the early stages of town-planning and gave our cities, Bath no exception, acres of healthy, monotonous bye-law housing which, in the event, proved too expensive for the really poor and tended to be occupied by the lower-middle classes. And because sanitation necessitated a whole structure of water-supply and sewerage, the benefits extended to the better-off people, who were able to dispense with their chamber-pots and install water-closets. The rates went up, of course, and not everyone was happy about that. At the turn of the century some really low-cost housing was introduced, a Bath example being the rows of little red-brick terraces over the river in Dolemeads. The other example, Lampard's Buildings, has been demolished.

Between the two World Wars concern with sanitation continued, with further improvements in water-supply and sewerage, with health insurance and the 'panel' system, and with slum-clearance schemes, although there Bath came low on the list for Government assistance. The biggest change, however, came with the legislation which enabled the Corporation to build estates of houses to be let at a low rent. These appeared mainly on the fringes of the city, where land was available. Set out at a low density, they usually have ample gardens but recently have had to have a good deal of money spent on bringing them up to acceptable modern standards internally. There was increasing concern with visual aspects; controls were introduced, for example on ribbon development and advertisement hoardings; we have already seen that the green slopes around Bath were denied to the developers. A wider vision of the scope of planning was incorporated in the Town and Country Planning Act of 1932 under which Bath set up a committee whose major scheme, produced in 1939, was aborted by the war.

After the war the Town and Country Planning Act of 1947 set up a new national apparatus, and Bath became a Planning Authority. In those early euphoric and idealist days, planning-enthusiasts looked to a future when under their wise, benevolent and imaginative direction cities would create for themselves a superb new environment in which all citizens would be happy, healthy and, hopefully, good. That was not exactly what the government had asked them to do, but it seemed that the opportunity was there.

As things turned out, it was not, the basic reason being that there was not enough money to pay for adequate staffing or to finance proposed development. As time went on, the Planning Authorities found themselves more and more in the position of having to farm out development to private organizations and to try to get their dreams realized at second hand by imposing such restrictions and making such requirements as they could without losing developers' interest completely. This 'will-you-won't you' process incidentally, takes a long time. If they had tried it on John Wood, he would have gone elsewhere. Then, of course, there were two lots of planners, the professionals who were servants of the Council, and the amateurs who were their masters. Today there are four—one pair for Avon to prepare the master Structure Plan and another for Bath to prepare the Local Plans. Avon has just (July 1976) produced an Interim Development Plan "as work is continuing on the Avon Structure Plan which will set the guidelines on how the county shall develop in the years to come". The amateurs are obviously going to have opinions of their own, and to some extent these are going to be influenced by political affiliations and a desire for re-election—there is nothing sinister about this: if you want to serve the public, you have got to get elected by them. But at least the amateurs sought professional advice. Bath Corporation appointed a

Chief Planning Officer who was an authority on eighteenth-century architecture; they commissioned a traffic report from an eminent consultant; they obtained the services of a prestigious architect as a visiting adviser; they submitted schemes to the Fine Arts Commission; they bought and exhibited a large and expensive model of the city and published maps and drawings and pamphlets. There were discussions with the Bath Preservation Trust, itself beset by internal dissension. Judging by letters from councillors, they read the local paper, which contained a good deal of criticism of their actions. Perhaps they had too much advice.

The eighteenth-century architect/developers saw no need to consult anybody except themselves and the acknowledged experts—experts who spoke with one voice, but their aims were far more limited than those of the planners of today, their clientele was much more limited, and the kinds of things they had to build were much fewer. They were, in fact, not planners. Today the concern is not just with providing houses and public buildings for the richer classes but with meeting the whole socio-economic requirements of a region of which the city is only a part, and with attempting to resolve the conflicts between a multitude of competing interests—all this not just for today but for a future which, in the nature of things, is unknowable. It is, of course, an impossible task, and it is no wonder that it is beset with confusion, criticism and failure, but to do without it and to leave everything to market forces and the Invisible Hand seems likely, judging by nineteenth-century precedents, to lead to a degree of social injustice which is quite unacceptable in these days of the moral and political forces and tender social conscience of the privileged and voting-power among the under-privileged. On the other hand, some people maintain that planning simply increases the power of one class, a minority, over another, the majority, and are deeply suspicious of the motives of planners who do not, after all, live in Council houses or work in factories.

It has been argued that 'planning' is least onerous and most advantageous to those who are already well-off and powerful, and, by another writer, that "British town-planners are not altruistic because they serve (a) their own ends and (b) those of the existing power structure"—views which lead some critics to demand more planning, but by a different class, and others to propose abolition of all institutional planning—"Might planning turn out to be rather like Eysenck's view of psychoanalysis: an activity which, insofar as it gets credit, gets it for benefits that would happen anyway—minds can cure themselves, maybe people can plan for themselves?" A middle point of view, based to some extent on French theories, is that planners should provide information and advice but not issue directives.

Whatever attitude is adopted, it does seem that to concentrate solely on visual aspects of physical planning is to simplify the situation to the point of unreality. Such aspects will, however, concern some people deeply, and it is right that they should make their case. It then becomes the job of planners to resolve, to the best of their ability, the conflicts between such advocates and the other pressure-groups who are each concentrating on some individual concern. Which group is going to win, and why, is yet another question, and the losers will have many dark accusations to make.

For a city with a visual quality of Georgian Bath, there will inevitably be a very strong local and national preservationist lobby—the environment itself weaves its spells and argues its case—the very stones cry out. It would be a bold man indeed who voiced a secret thought that eighteenth-century streets, like eighteenth-century social life, might be a tiny bit boring, yet if there had been a few such inconoclasts, perhaps the modern additions to the place would have been more lively. In fact, Georgian Bath is not uniform but full of variety and surprise both in the details of individual buildings and in the transition from one small area to another, as in the sudden revelation of Lansdown Crescent at the end of a steep little road, of the Pump Room through the colonnade or of the little paved area of Margaret's Buildings with its unexpected entrance from Brock Street and the sudden surprise of Catharine Place at the other end. To lump together the solidity of Queen Square, the richness of the Circus, the stark simplicity of the Royal Crescent and the delicacy of Pulteney Bridge and call them all 'Georgian Architecture' is an absurdity of simplification. What holds it all together is a uniformity of material (all Bath stone), a single stylistic *spirit* (surface modelling, recessed windows, horizontal roof-line with roofs discreetly, but not completely, hidden) and a modular scale where repeating motifs divide long stretches into visually comfortable sections.

Judged by these criteria, none of the big rectangular, flat-faced blocks, with their staring windows, sawn-off roof-lines or big black hats, and their walls of plastic stone which stains horribly but will not weather, is fit to be intruded into the Georgian scene. Nor, for that matter, are the clumsy, ill-spaced details of neo-Georgian stores. A lot of people do not notice this and cannot understand what the fuss is about; others object violently out of nostalgia for a familiar past, feeling as if their youth has been murdered; others believe that it is beyond the wit of present-day architects to design a building suitable for the occasion and therefore would call a halt to any further substitution; others, often architects, maintain that the job could be done properly if only architects were not crippled by financial straitjackets and/or the timidity of their clients. To the contention that costs rule out anything but chunky box architecture, the answers are usually either a flat denial or else a demand that more money be spent. Adam Ferguson, for example (*The Sack of Bath*, 1973), writes that "If developers are not prepared to take a somewhat smaller profit in Bath than in, say, Middlesbrough, then they must be told to go to Middlesbrough and get on with it." He also maintains that "Those who live in and enjoy the beauties of an eighteenth-century town should not expect the amenities of Harlow New Town or Hemel Hempstead." Bath is apparently still for special people.

But if Bath is to be other than a ghost-town, its citizens must be able to find adequate work and to live in contemporary comfort. So planning needs to be concerned with factories and shops and offices and entertainment, and homes and schools and recreation and services. If Bath were very much smaller, it might just manage to exist on the tourist trade, with the inhabitants acting out the life of a past century, playing to eighteenth-century dancing in the Assembly Rooms, carrying people in sedan-chairs, staging the occasional hue and cry through the streets, ringing the Abbey bells to welcome arrivals and selling newspapers with reports of a great victory at Trafalgar—but that will not do for a city of over fifty thousand people, and there must be, as there has been in the past, as there was in Georgian days, change and adaptation.

Hopefully, however, the bother about Bath has helped in a change of concepts and ideas, a change which has influenced Government legislation and altered the possibilities for handling the local situation. In 1967 the Civic Amenities Act required planning-authorities to define Conservation Areas, and the following year Bath Council so designated six areas, totalling 432 acres. In 1973 this was extended to a total of 1,296 acres, and in 1975 nearly two thirds of the City became a single Conservation Area, which a Conservation Area Advisory Committee set up to meet bi-monthly. It has representatives from the City Council, Avon County Council, Bath Preservation Trust, Bath Group of Architects, Bath Environment Campaign, the Trades Council, the Chamber of Commerce, the Georgian Group, the Conservation Society and the Standing Conference of Women's Organization, and would probably be quite enough to send a latter-day John Wood to Middlesbrough!

The problems of a Conservation Area are not, of course, related only to buildings. One of the things which notoriously bedevils such places is the volume of modern traffic. It is a general problem, and it is of some significance that in the Avon interim development plan by far the largest section is devoted to parking (eighteen pages as against eight for education and six for residential development). Naturally, Bath Council took advice, and in 1965 appeared a Planning and Transport Study by Messrs Colin Buchanan and Partners which included proposals for pedestrianization of much of the central area, increased peripheral parking and a tunnel under the Georgian heart. In 1969 it became official policy, and it raised such a storm of controversy, directed mainly towards the tunnel and the large-scale approaches, that the Secretary of State intervened and proposed a Steering Committee with representatives from his Department, the City Council and the Preservation Trust in an attempt to resolve the conflict. They ordered that more studies should be made. Then came the change in local government, and Avon became responsible for traffic-management throughout the county. So they joined the Group and predictably called for more information. New plans were submitted in 1976, the tunnel scheme then having been abandoned, partly because of expense as it would cost up to £14 million pounds at a time when the money available for new road works from 1971 to 1986 was £8·5 million of which £3 million had already been spent. Before embarking on the full scheme, Avon decided to try out five experimental measures, first putting the proposals on display to test public reaction. As a result, one, the closing of Pulteney Bridge to most vehicles, was withdrawn; two relating to parking were modified, and two relating to traffic-flows were unaltered, the schemes to be introduced in September 1976. In the meantime Bath had already extended pedestrianization and modified its one-way system. It remains to be seen whether these com-paratively mild palliatives will be sufficient to reduce the problem to acceptable proportions.

Problems are nothing new to a city whose whole history demonstrates a habit of revival. Out of a swamp the Romans raised in the first century the gleaming city of Aquae Sulis, but after four centuries of busy life it collapsed, abandoned, back into the marsh. On top of it, some hundred years later, the Saxons began the building of Bathanceaster, with its monastery of St Peter and St Paul whose prestige became such, with its *mira fabrica*, that it was chosen in 973 as the place for the consecration by Archbishop Dunstan of Edgar of Wessex as King of all England.

And so began Bath II, which was to develop into a neat little medieval town with monastery, market, fair and woollen-industry. The walls were rebuilt, probably on the Roman footings; a new street pattern was developed between the houses and gardens, and a great new Norman Abbey church and monastic buildings dominated the centre and south-east of the city. The builder was Bishop Robert, who in 1157 got the Pope to acknowledge Bath as the diocesan seat so that the abbey church became a cathedral and the abbey was demoted to priory. It was not until 1243 that Wells was reinstated and the see became Bath *and* Wells.

Later bishops favoured Wells, and the fabric of the cathedral at Bath was so neglected that in 1499 Bishop Oliver King was moved to order its complete rebuilding on a smaller scale. He was said to have been inspired by a dream in which he saw "a vision of the Holy Trynite, with angels ascending and descending by a ladder, neer to the foote of which was a fayre Olive Tree, supporting the Crowne, and a voice that said— 'Let an OLIVE establish the Crowne, and let a KING restore the Churche',"" which is why he ordered the carvings on the west end which we see today, ladders, angels, olive crown and bishop's mitre; the statue of Henry VII is, however, Victorian. The church was a beautiful exercise in late Perpendicular Gothic, light, with its great windows, simple, entirely satisfactory in its urban setting, but it still lacked a roof to the nave when the monastery was dissolved in 1539 and the lands and buildings passed into lay hands.

It was the end of the second Bath, for not only did the city lose its monastic importance but its main source of income, the cloth industry, was in a recession from which it never recovered. "We are," wrote the Mayor in 1622, "a verie little poor Citie, our Clothmen much decayed, and many of their workmen amongst us relieved by the Citie." As he was reporting to the Government in relation to taxation, it is hardly surprising that he emphasized the slump in the economy, but the truth was that by his time Bath had already begun to find a new source of wealth in the entertainment of wealthy visitors who came for the sake of their health. There seems to have been something of a Jacobean building boom, and contemporaries wrote that the city had "wonderfully beautified itself in fine houses for victualling and lodging" and that there were "fair and goodly buildings for the receit of strangers". Thus rose Bath III, and although there was a severe setback during the Civil War, when the city became a garrison and hospital town first for the Royalists and then for Parliament, it soon got back to business afterwards and was well spoken-of by those shrewd observers Samuel Pepys (1668) and Celia Fiennes (1695). Today there is little evidence of the buildings of the time for they were largely obliterated by the creation of Bath IV—Georgian Bath, a city created out of chaos.

The cause of this chaos was the rapid development of a new function which attracted visitors in such numbers that the city was for a time neither physically nor socially able to cope. It arose from the selection by London society of Bath as a summer resort and gambling-centre where, as Goldsmith wrote, "they might have each other's company and win each other's money, as they had during the winter in town." Bath, with no Assembly Rooms, an inadequate Pump Room, limited accommodation, rapacious chairmen and surly servants, was overwhelmed by the sheer numbers and un-disciplined behaviour of the visitors and might never have seen its future Georgian glory if it had not been for a thirty-one-year-old Welshman, Richard 'Beau' Nash, who arrived in 1705 to try his luck at the tables, was given the unpaid job of Master of Ceremonies and within a few years had, with nothing more than the force of his personality, imposed order and decency on the turbulent society, provided Assembly Rooms and persuaded the Corporation to clean up the city and license the chairmen. The result was that Bath continued to retain its social attraction after the 1730s even though the gambling craze had died down, partly restrained by national legislation, and continued to expand physically.

The style of the new building was settled by John Wood the Elder when in his early twenties he designed Queen Square (1736) in the Classical, Palladian form, and although later in the century the style became more refined, lighter, more ornamental, particularly in the work of Thomas Baldwin (e.g. Guildhall, Pump Room, Bath Street, Pulteney Street), there is a strong family resemblance throughout. The later style was influenced by Adam and may be compared with his one con-tribution to Bath, Pulteney Bridge with its little shops. Stylistic change can also be seen by comparing the younger Wood's Royal Crescent (1774) with Palmer's Lansdown Crescent (1792), Baldwin's Somersetshire Buildings (1782) with the rest of Milsom Street (1760s) or the north side of Wood Street (above the shop fronts) and the south side (Northumberland Buildings, again Baldwin 1778).

The main spread of the Georgian town was northwards up the hill, but a more consciously grandiose scheme was started for Bathwick, east of the river, once Pulteney Bridge had been built for access. Georgian schemes for Bathwick were, however, frustrated by financial difficulties, and only the main axis of Laura Place and Pulteney Street pointing like a sword at the Sydney Hotel and Sydney Gardens was completed, the rest being added later on an *ad hoc* basis. Pulteney Street lies over the flood-plain of the river and was therefore built on a plat-form, a device used earlier by Wood for his Parades between the east side of the city and the Avon.

There were no grand individual houses; for those we have to go to what were then separate villages. Examples by Wood the

Elder are two Eagle houses, one (1727) in Batheaston, which he built for himself, and the other in Bathford, where he also built Titan Barrow (now Whitehaven). Batheaston also has Bailbrook House, probably by John Eveleigh, and in Widcombe is the elegant Manor House of about 1727. The biggest and finest is Prior Park on the southern hill rising to Combe Down. It was designed by the elder Wood for Ralph Allen, Bath's richest resident, but became a boarding-school in the mid-nineteenth century, when considerable alterations and additions were made at the east and west wings, including the addition of a large church and a rather fine Baroque staircase, which was added to lead up to the front door. In the grounds is the Palladian bridge, by Allen's Clerk of the Works, Jones, who took over the work after there had been some dispute with Wood.

Meanwhile the medieval city was undergoing a classical transformation piecemeal but so effectively that we have today very few examples of the old gables (e.g. Sally Lunn's house, Hetling House), stone mullions and bay-windows (Abbey Church House, which is a reconstruction). The medieval baths, which on the Dissolution passed to the city, were rebuilt, and in 1789 the Council obtained an Act for its one piece of town-planning to improve the 'ways' round the baths. The results are the Pump Room, colonnades, Bath Street with its quadrant ends and the serpentine-fronted Cross Bath. All this elegance was designed by the young City Architect, Thomas Baldwin, but he was dismissed by the Corporation over some matter connected with the accounts, and the work in the Pump Room and Cross Bath was completed by his successor, John Palmer.

By the end of the century, however, the economic underpinnings of Bath IV were becoming shaky. There was something of a sunset quality in the social life of the city during the Napoleonic Wars, and when peace returned, the old order had changed and Society began to find its pleasures elsewhere, either at the rapidly developing seaside places or on the Continent, a process which was accelerated after the 1840s by the expanding railway network and the newly-discovered Romantic attractions of mountain and lake in Cumbria, the Highlands and the Alps. A writer in 1840 described Bath with its "empty streets, deserted shops, tradesmen without customers, goods lacking buyers, the few amusements we have left desert", and although this was special pleading, there is sufficient evidence to show that there had been a considerable decline.

The answer was, as we have seen, to create Bath V, a modern city for residence, service and manufacturing, equipped for modern living with a new water-supply and main-drainage, with gas and electricity and tramcars, with new schools and new churches and new hospitals, with new parks and gardens and with acres of new suburban houses— indeed, the Victorians built more of Bath than the Georgians ever did and with a sounder economy in view. After all, said the 1888 Handbook to Bath, "the idea of many hundreds of gaily-dressed ladies and gentlemen sauntering through life, bathing, promenading and dancing within the city, and forming themselves in Watteau-like groups on the slopes of the hills, and all under the paternal despotism of an *Arbiter Elegantarium*, is not one which we can connect with stability."

Yet, curiously enough, in their search for stability the Victorians were constantly occupied with change: ripping up the streets to put in pipes, knocking down corners and building afresh, putting in new streets, massively renovating the abbey, digging out the Roman baths, erecting concert-halls and libraries and new markets, re-facing shop-fronts, planting trees where the Georgians had cobbles, putting in plate-glass where they had glazing-bars, building monster hotels in prominent places and pushing extra bridges across the river. Today many feel that things are even worse, for Bath V is still in transition, still seeking its identity, but in an age which, lacking both the inspired opportunism of the eighteenth century and the passionate energy of the nineteenth, is characterized by a state of nervous uncertainty which drives the decision-makers to huddle together for comfort in committees whose choices will almost inevitably fall upon mediocre proposals. Then there are the despairing who believe that planning is too important to be left to professionals and too difficult to be in the hands of amateurs; the cynical who maintain that the legislators are either too simple or too venal to be trusted with decision-making; the egalitarians who teach that everybody's opinion is as good as everybody else's except that the proletariat's opinions are rather better, and would put everything to a referendum; the anti-urbanites who would like all cities done away with as being inherently evil; the Corb-ites who want gleaming towers on little legs; the Jane Jacobites with romantic visions of the social warmth of (cleaned-up) slums; the Howard disciples who campaign for low density, low rise and lots of greenery, and the for-Betjeman's-sake-leave-it-alone brigade. And there are the people who could not care less as long the rates are kept down—and a lot of people in Planning Departments and Councils who are working extremely hard to try to do a good job and getting precious little thanks from anybody.

Who is right?

IX

BRISTOL

With nearly half a million inhabitants, a broad-based economy whose products range the alphabet from Aircraft to Zinc, with a university of high repute and a port of some significance, Bristol is by any standards a major city. It is the largest of the new Districts of England and contains nearly half the population and over half the rateable value of the County of Avon. By a charter of 1373 it was to be "a County by itself and called the County of Bristol for ever"; in the eighteenth century it was the second largest city in England, and in the post-war period it has been one of the major economic and population growth-areas of the country. It is hardly surprising, therefore, that it pressed strongly for Metropolitan County status under the re-organization of local government and was disgusted when this was refused. On the other hand, an administrative isolation for this major economic centre would have made nonsense of the city-region basis of the new system for it is to Bristol that a wide surrounding area looks for much of its employment and for the services which occupy some sixty per cent of the city's employment.

Yet despite its size and the variety of its industries, despite even the monstrous multiplication since the war of high-rise flats and offices and car-parks and hotels, Bristol still has something of a country air about it and something of a country pace, and this for several reasons. In the first place the city, though large, is not so big as to become isolated from the surrounding green hills and the long fingers of open land which they poke into the urban fabric. Secondly, its internal adaptation to an irregular pattern of hills and valleys forms it into a collection of urban villages, small areas of individual character. And thirdly, there is a great deal of vegetated open space within the city: there are no fewer than 264 parks and open spaces, covering nearly 4,000 acres and giving, as the City Guide is proud to calculate, 37·7 square yards per head of population. Some of these are welcome, if perhaps rather over-managed, little patches of flowerbeds, asphalt paths and shaven grass, but many are considerable and have the feeling of open countryside, as in the grassy expanse of Durdham Downs, the 115 acres of Oldbury Court Estate at Fishponds and the wooded grounds of Blaize Castle, Henbury.

Another important feature which breaks into the urban blanket is the deep penetration of water into the heart of the city, and it is unfortunate that it has been felt necessary to hide so much of it under roads—no wonder that Neptune's statue shakes its trident towards the land! It is indeed appropriate that the arms of Bristol show a junction of green land and blue water, with a golden ship sailing out of a silver castle, and that the other symbol of the City is a flower, the Scarlet Lychnis, otherwise known as 'the Nonsuch' or 'Flower of Bristowe'.

The elements which compose the special 'feel' of Bristol are distinct, and the boundaries between the 'soft' open spaces and the 'hard' built-up areas are firm. This is a strong relationship quite different from the weak amalgam of tower-blocks and 'landscaped' surrounds which characterizes some of the re-development of Bristol's inner city residential areas where the Corporation, faced with the problems of bomb-scars and a low standard of housing amenity and the urgent need to provide homes, adopted the then conventional wisdom of bringing in the bulldozers to clear the way for Anytown. It is, of course, easy to be wise after the event, to forget the heavy sociological and aesthetic criticism directed against the considerable inter-war 'house-and-garden' estates such as Knowle West, and to ignore the extent to which local authorities are constrained by government grant policy, where, for example, money in quantity was not available for rehabilitating whole areas of old property before 1968. It should also be remembered that life in low- or even medium-quality eighteenth- and nineteenth-century housing has problems of its own and that the image of cosy social life in the little streets may possibly be something of a middle-class myth.

Obtrusive as high-rise is within the traditional Bristol scene, it forms only a small part of post-war development. The major housing provision has continued to be in conventional suburban 'estates' particularly on the southern and western fringes of the city at, for example, Brislington and Shirehampton. Too much scorn has been poured on 'Subtopia' and too little appreciation expressed of the very real opportunities for pleasant living offered by a well-designed estate.

Road-transport has received a great deal of attention in post-war Bristol, as in other major cities, for it is on efficient communication that the economic and social life of a city depends. Bristol, whose chief planning-officer was a highways engineer, plumped for an orthodox solution to the problem of accommodating the motorcar. Basically this consisted of inner and outer circuit-roads, a complex of loops and flyover to Cumberland Basin at the western end of the city to sort out the traffic-streams entering and leaving, and an urban motorway, the M32 or Parkway, to link with the M4 to the north.

The Inner Circuit, with a radius of about half a mile, encloses the ancient heart of the city, the post-war Broadmead shopping complex and, south of the river, a rather nondescript, mainly industrial area. It is punctuated by a number of roundabouts of which the old Tramway Centre, now called simply 'the Centre', which suggests incorrectly that it is the city's focus, has been made into a large elongated example. Half-way along the eastern side of the loop is the £2½ million Old Market Street Underpass and south of that a 'temporary' overpass which has been there for several years. Strangers tend to find it very confusing, and it is possible that the signposting could be improved, especially at the Centre, but for drivers who know the lay-out, the circuit is fairly efficient. What is not easy is getting on to it, off it or across it, particularly in the rush-hours.

The Outer Circuit and the Parkway are not yet completed and have produced a good deal of controversy. As the District Plan Project Brief says somewhat sadly, "The Easton and Eastville area of the City suffered the blight of the Parkway and Outer Circuit Roads for many years. During this period, and then during the construction stage, the area in the immediate vicinity of the road line seems to have declined badly due to the uncertainty of the impact of the road," and notes that "Since this route [Parkway] was planned, there has been substantial change in Central Government attitudes towards environmental effects of highway construction." It is surprising how long it has taken for government, local and national, to realize that motorways form physical and social barriers and not very nice neighbours. And only recently, as traffic begins to pond back along inadequate exit-routes, is it being generally realized that motorways can create first-class traffic jams.

In 1976 Avon, who had become responsible for traffic planning, decided to commission a study, as required by the Department of the Environment, into the justification for a link between the Parkway and the A4 Bath road south of the river and in any case to go ahead with a new bridge at Hanham in the east of the city and use it to join the two Bristol–Bath roads, the A431 and A4 which would be made dual carriage-way, continuing the road in a southern loop (the line of the Outer Circuit) to join with the Bristol–Taunton road (A38). A ring-road was to be constructed northwards from the A38 to loop round the northern and eastern fringe of the built-up area down to the new Hanham bridge. On the other hand, the original proposal for a long section of the Outer Ring in the south-east was abandoned, as were several proposed improvements to radials. These decisions should be viewed in the context of Government requirements for drastic cuts in local spending. A proposal in the specially commissioned LUTS (Land Use and Transport Survey) for tolls on traffic bound for the central area was rejected. Proposals to introduce extensive bus-priority facilities, such as bus-lanes, were agreed, but it may be felt that a much more radical approach to the provision of public transport might have been adopted, although it is difficult to see how that could be done without a very heavy restriction on the entry of private vehicles into the central area, which was the purpose of the toll proposals. Government proposals in 1977 to cut allocations to local government in support of public transport will, if carried out, have an even more disastrous effect.

The Cumberland Basin interchange which feeds north-wards by the inter-war Avon side Portway to the M5 and southwards on one link to the Long Ashton By-Pass on the A370 to Weston-super-Mare and on another south-east to join the A38 Taunton road, was opened in 1965. With its 1¾ miles of elevated slip-roads, it is an ingenious solution to packing an interchange into a small area and is the central feature of a series of such interchanges, one to the north and two to the south,

within three-quarters of a mile. Unfortunately the limited
space makes for very short run-ins to the main stream and
requires quick lane-changes. Drivers have been known to go
round several times until in desperation they have left by the
wrong exit. Once again signposting is not, for the stranger, a
strong point in Bristol's traffic-system.

Two other aspects of post-war planning which have
affected the fabric of the city are central re-development and,
more recently, the designation of conservation areas. The
original commercial heart of the city, lying around Corn
Street, between the Frome and the Avon, was considerably
rebuilt in Victorian times and has had relatively few recent
alterations, but the area to the east was heavily bombed and
after the war lay desolate. The first major new feature was the
Broadmead shopping complex covering about 25 acres. Here
are all the usual large over-heated stores and other shops (with
household goods, clothing and footwear predominant) which
people expect to find in a down-town shopping trip. This
provision, and a useful pedestrian access to the gloomy bus-
station, makes it well patronized, but architecturally the
complex is a jumble of styles and sizes in which the few
buildings of any merit are devalued by their unneighbour-
liness. For many years this lack of cohesion was made even
worse by on-street parking and circulating traffic, but recently
the central part has been pedestrianized, and although the
streets are now unnecessarily wide, there is room for trees,
which help to give some character to the area, and for seats
which help to alleviate the weariness engendered by the long
distances to be walked. Indeed the place is now something of
an oasis in the middle of the unrelenting traffic of the inner
circuit and the towering unco-ordinated blocks of later office
development.

Fortunately there are some bits left over from the past. The
Arcade of 1824–5, a civilized little corridor of bow-fronted
shops where you can buy a variety of things from skating-
boots to screwdrivers, is next door to Wesley's New Room
(1739, enlarged 1748), the world's first Methodist church,
with a modern (1932) statue of the preacher on his horse; the
Room is open to visitors. Merchant Street is graced by the
delightful little court of the Merchant Taylors Almshouses;
Lloyd's Bank won a Civic Trust Award in 1960 for having

restored them and doing them up in green and white. Almost opposite is one of the entrances to Quakers Friars where an assembly of medieval and eighteenth-century buildings stand in a grassy surround among the functional but graceless service-entrance to shops.

Part of the land of the Dominican friary was bought by the Quakers who built a meeting-house there in 1670; the present one dates from 1747–9, its Classical forms contrasting but not clashing with the remains of the friary buildings. The medieval buildings were used for some time as halls for the Bakers' and the Cutlers' Guilds, now for a number of purposes including the Exhibition Room of the City Planning Department, open weekdays from 1 p.m. to 4.30 p.m. The Meeting House, in which William Penn married Hannah Callowhill in 1695, is now a registry office.

The Broadmead area lies in the flat bottom of the Frome valley, and immediately to the south the land rises sharply to a low plateau before descending to the Avon. This low hill was the site of medieval Bristol, divided between town and castle.

The medieval town occupied the western, broader part of the hill and was bordered on three sides by the Frome, which, until 1239, curved round to join the Avon near Bristol Bridge. A beautiful little town-plan drawn by a fifteenth-century Town Clerk, Robert Ricart, for his 'Mayor's Kalendar' shows a pattern of four streets leading from four gates in the wall and meeting at a High Cross. The medieval pattern persisted, and the streets are readily identifiable. Bristol Bridge led through St Nicholas Gate at High Street, which climbed the low hill to the High Cross and then continued as Broad Street down to St John's Gate, beyond which lay St John's Bridge and the Frome Gate. Both churches were built above their gate, but the Bristol Bridge entrance was so inconveniently narrow that in 1763 St Nicholas's was pulled down and rebuilt to one side in good Georgian Gothic. Gutted by war-time bombing, it has been outwardly restored and inwardly re-designed to form a fine ecclesiastical and historical museum which includes an excellent introduction to the growth and dvelopment of the city. The medieval crypt remains and is used at present as a brass-rubbing centre.

St John's, rebuilt in the fifteenth century, surmounts the only remaining medieval gate. An adjacent church of St

Laurence was destroyed in 1580. The gateway, which carries statues of Brennus and Belinus, legendary founders of Bristol, has its original main archway, with portcullis grooves, but the smaller flanking openings are a nineteenth-century addition. On the inside of the wall there used to be a conduit to which water was piped from the top of Park Street via the site of the Colston Hall, then occupied by a Carmelite monastery. It was moved outside in 1827 and came into its own again during the 1940 blitz when for a time it was the only source of water in that part of the city.

St Leonard's Gate, and the church from which it was named, has long since disappeared. It opened into Corn Street, which was continued after the High Cross by Wine Street to New Gate where later was built a prison, "White without and foul within". Near there was the church of St Mary-le-Port, of which the tower, obscured and overshadowed by modern offices, still stands, and beyond, between town and castle, was St Peter's, now only a shell, and St Peter's Hospital. The latter started life in the fourteenth century as the home of the Norton family and was rebuilt in 1612 by Robert Aldworth. It later became a sugar-refinery, then the Bristol Mint, and in 1668 was bought by the Incorporation for the Poor and turned into a workhouse. With its splendid half-timbering, magnificent plaster ceilings and impressive panelling and stone carving, its destruction in the blitz was perhaps Bristol's most serious architectural loss. Nearby stood St Edith's Well surmounted stumpily by St Peter's Cross. These were acquired by Richard Hoare in the eighteenth century and may be seen in the grounds of his house at Stourhead in Wiltshire. There also is the High Cross, presented to him, quite illegally, in 1762 by his friend the Dean of Bristol. The story of this Cross and its copies is a sad and complicated one.

Originally erected to celebrate the great Charter of 1373, this magnificent edifice stood at the heart of the city for over three centuries, high, noble and increasingly inconvenient to traffic. In 1733 it was moved to College Green, where residents complained so effectively that it was pulled down and, as we have seen, given away. Nearly a hundred years later Bristolians awoke to their loss, and the Dean led a fund-raising campaign to pay for a copy, which was installed in 1850, only to be moved in 1888 to the middle of the Green to make way for a statue of Queen Victoria. It was again taken down in 1950 to open up the view of the new Council House. Six years later the top part was rescued and erected in a corner of Berkeley Square where, largely unregarded, it still stands, the kings and queens sadly gazing at the moss in their laps.

Two of the churches in the heart of the city have disappeared: St Ewan's, was finally demolished in 1822 to make way for the Council House, and St Werburgh's was transferred stone by stone in 1879 to the expanding industrial suburb of Baptist Mills. The two remaining, Christchurch and All Saints', add a delicate distinction to the city skyline with their eighteenth-century towers, one bearing a spire, the other a domed lantern which was altered in 1807 and rebuilt in 1930. Inside, however, Christchurch, all white and gold and graceful, is a Georgian creation of 1786–90, whereas All Saints' has two heavy Norman west bays leading into a fifteenth century 'hall church'. All Saints' contains a fine monument to Colston, and Christchurch has two little bell-striking figures, the Quarter Jacks, standing above its ornate neo-Renaissance portal of 1883. The Jacks used to face Wine Street but in the eighteenth-century re-building of the church were removed and not restored until 1913. They are on loan from the Council at a rent of 12½p a year.

The most imposing church lies just outside the city walls to the south-west. This is St Stephen's whose fifteenth-century tower, splendidly crowned with pierced battlements and high pinnacles, still manages to impress in spite of being hemmed in by taller but less inspired buildings, and whose green little churchyard with trees and benches maintains an extraordinary atmosphere of peace so close to the feverish traffic of the Centre. It is a good place to read a book, eat sandwiches and buy coffee from the church room. It is also an appropriate spot for considering the function of the House of God amid the Temples of Mammon.

If we equate Mammon with commercial activity, then he must be the presiding deity of the central area, for its functions became increasingly commercial and administrative, and in the nineteenth century there was a great rebuilding which has left a wealth of Revival styles to be enjoyed in a very small area. Thus the severe Grecian of the Old Council House (Smirke, 1822–7) contrasts with but does not suffer from the richly ornamented Italian Renaissance of its neighbour, Lloyd's Bank (Gingell and Lysaght, 1854–5, with a later bay in the same style), while a little further down Broad Street the Renaissance façade of the Grand Hotel (Foster and Wood, 1869) looks across at the heavy Gothic of the Guildhall (1843–6) which was designed by R. S. Pope. His son added an even more spirited medieval Assize Court (1867–70) at the back, facing on to Small Street. Also Gothic, but in the style of a Loire *château*, faced in crisp terracotta, is a building which Alfred Waterhouse designed for the Prudential in 1899; it stands in Clare Street, an extension to Corn Street begun in 1766. The most extraordinary sight, however, is the Art Nouveau façade in ceramic tiles designed by W. J. Neatby in 1901 for Edward Everard's printing-works in Broad Street. This has been incorporated in the sober and successful design of a new building for the Legal and General Assurance Company (Alec French Partnership, 1973). Broad Street, incidentally, has two fragments of early history which are worth seeing, the beautiful shell hood of the former Taylor's Hall, down a side passage, and what is probably the oldest well in the city in the bar of the Grand Hotel.

The most distinguished building is the eighteenth-century Corn Exchange, designed by the elder John Wood of Bath and erected in 1740–43. It is severely Palladian in style with rusticated lower storey, pilasters and triangular pediment, and although Wood complained that the Corporation was interfering with his design, it is very much of a piece. The open, colonnaded piazza at the rear was given an elaborate upper storey and glazed roof in 1872, but this was replaced with a shallower one in 1949. Between the Exchange and the remnants of High Victorian architecture in Baldwin Street, including the polychromatic brick Fish Market, is a fascinating region of markets, warehouses, pubs and restaurants. Some of its attraction was lost in 1968 when the wholesale fruit and vegetable market was moved out to a million-pound site at St Phillips, but there is still a lively collection of market-stalls. Outside the Exchange, where it is set back from Corn Street, are the Bristol 'Nails', little baluster-like brass tables used in the old Exchange by merchants when conducting their business—hence the expression, say Bristolians, 'paying on the nail'; Bathonians, who have a Nail in their market, may care to dispute this.

If the western end of the plateau was the home of God and Mammon, the eastern end might be considered the domain of Mars, for there was the castle. The first, built by Bishop Geoffrey of Coutances, was of the motte-and-bailey type, but it was superseded by a massive keep and outworks erected in sandstone early in the twelfth century by Robert of Gloucester, bastard son of Henry I. Another major rebuilding took place in the time of John, who became Lord of Bristol by his marriage to Hawisa (Isabella) daughter of William of Gloucester. He seems to have made it his headquarters during the reign of his brother Richard and to have prepared it for defence in 1215–16 when he was facing the opposition of his barons and a French invasion. On his death in October 1216 it was at Bristol Castle that his young son Henry III, hastily crowned at Gloucester, held his first Council and re-issued Magna Carta. Other changes were made in the fourteenth century, but by 1480, when William Wyrcester made his careful survey of Bristol, much of the castle had fallen into decay. Some rebuilding was done during the Civil War, but in 1645 the castle's destruction was ordered by Act of Parliament, and subsequently the area was built over.

These streets and houses, which had become a busy shopping area, were devastated by bombing in 1940 and for over twenty years lay derelict, used mainly as 'temporary' car-parks. A proposal for building a museum on the site has been postponed, but at least there is now a grassed open space with a few trees and paths east of the carcass of St Peter's Church. It is worth visiting for the views of the industrial area across the river. In the far corner windowed housing has been put round the one piece of castle above ground, two vaulted rooms whose purpose is uncertain, although they may have been antechambers to the great hall.

A view is also obtainable of some of the visually unco-ordinated ring of densely packed high and bulky development which skirts the Broadmead area. Much of this is for offices, and it is alarming to note a prediction, based on present trends, that in Avon "at the very most only half of the 9 million square feet of office space that can be considered to be available in 1986 will actually be required". There are also multi-storey car-parks, but as a season-ticket costs over £100 it is not surprising that cars creep into every available side-street. As in

Broadmead, it is not so much that individual buildings are unsightly—some, like the purple home of the United Press (1974—RIBA Award 1975), are striking—but that they pay no attention to each other. One attempt to integrate is seen in the sweep of buildings of the St James's development (1975) which has a ground-level hole to let traffic through into Gloucester Road. Head-on it has a certain massive dignity, but once you can see the ends it begins to weaken for it is basically a patterned free-standing unconnected wall. It also has a clumsy parapet at one end which looks like a block of pale yellow cheese with triangular holes in it. At the other end the wall breaks back into the red-brick Georgian of Brunswick Square which it respects in scale but not in spirit.

It is possible, however, that the Square may be saved from further encroachment for the area around, including the stone-faced Portland Square with its pleasant ironwork round an oval tree-planted garden in the centre, is one of the thirteen Conservation Areas designated under the Civic Amenities Act in 1967, an Act whose intentions had already been anticipated in Bristol by the designation in 1964 of Corn Street and Queen Square as 'Areas of Special Control'.

Brunswick and Portland Squares (the Duke of Portland was High Steward of Bristol), together with King Square to the west, were started as eighteenth-century suburban developments on the then northern fringe of the city, and St Paul's Church in Portland Square was erected in 1789–94 to serve the new development. In 1834 a very large Congregational Chapel was built on the north side of Brunswick Square, but since the last war it has been a warehouse and is now empty, and there are proposals to turn it to community use and to open up the old Unitarian cemetery behind as a park.

Portland Square is in quite good condition, and several buildings have been renovated, but the area around is badly run-down and given over to warehousing, small factories and dereliction. Visually this could once again become an extremely attractive region, but it is likely to revive only if new economic life can be injected. The official Study puts its faith in office development, but in view of the trends noted above, this may be an over-optimistic view. Is it possible that it might again become a high-quality residential area?

The eighteenth-century "itch for building", as a contemporary called it, carried development even further north onto "Kingsdown, Delightful Spot!" This low hill forms the skyline to the north of the inner city and took its name from its function as an exercise-ground for the castle garrison. In the Civil War it was used for an outer line of defence, with forts and an earthen wall, and it was their removal which opened up the land for building. Originally occupied by prosperous middle-class people, it remained fashionable until after the First World War but then declined in prosperity and upkeep. It now exhibits in a small space three different attitudes to the development of such an area.

In 1958 the Corporation acquired the land and in 1965 started work on the south-facing slope. The City Architect's original plan was for four- to five-storey blocks, but the scheme was abandoned in favour of multi-storey flats, for, said the official *Civic News* in explanation, "The picturesque is seldom comfortable and rarely convenient." The development provided 347 'dwellings' in close proximity to work-places in the central area and was opened in 1967.

The second phase was the development of High Kingsdown, and there, too, the policy was one of complete replacement. This time the proposal for high blocks came first, but opinions had changed, and the Corporation finally settled for a private development which was low-level and high-density with brick walls and pedestrian walkways which created a tiny secret city with clearly defined edges. It is particularly pleasant where plants are softening the rather stark outlines of the walls, and to the visitor it seems a remarkably imaginative and successful attempt to create a modern townscape in which privacy is combined with accessibility in a satisfying visual context, although to some it may seem over-secretive.

In between these two developments lie the remains of the Georgian suburb, unusual in that streets tend to be one-sided with house frontages on one side facing back gardens on the other. There has been a good deal of renovation by private householders but no overall sprucing-up, and in 1970 a Kingsdown Conservation Group was formed to encourage the designation of Kingsdown as a Conservation Area and to promote improvements. The designation has been made and a City Planning Department Study published, which lays stress on control of new building, restriction of change of use from residence, discouragement of multiple occupation, retention of traditional features such as pennant-paving, and possible closing to traffic of some small streets. On the whole, however, it seems to look to the good-will and energy of the inhabitants to achieve the all-over up-grading required. At present it requires some imagination to see how this area, as compared for instance with Portland Square, will look when renovated, but there seem good possibilities of an environment which will earn both pride and affection from its inhabitants.

If we think of the urban fabric of Bristol as a patchwork quilt draped over hills and valleys, plateaux and plains, then the Conservation Areas may be considered as individual patches selected because of their intrinsic interest and beauty to be renovated rather than replaced, a piecemeal approach which, as was suggested at the beginning of this chapter, is more appropriate to Bristol than to the much smaller city of Bath which, with its greater uniformity of style, calls for, and has at last obtained, conservation treatment over a very large area. Because of the criteria adopted for their selection, the Bristol Conservation Areas make a useful basis for the study, by examples, of the growth and development of the city.

Two such areas are near Kingsdown, one to the west at the end of the hill and stretching down towards the city's heart, the other extending immediately southward, both strung along ancient radial routes through what was once open country. The southern one climbs up from Christmas Steps, an ancient thoroughfare which was 'improved' in the seventeenth century: "This Streete was Steppered Done and Finished September 1699 . . . Named Queene Streete" proclaims a plaque near the top. At the bottom end is the old gateway of St Bartholomew's Hospital, a small, mixed community founded in the thirteenth century and never very prosperous. The buildings housed the newly-founded Grammar School from the Dissolution until 1767 when the Grammar changed buildings with the City School (Queen Elizabeth's Hospital), founded in 1590 by the Will of John Carr, a Bristol and London soapmaker. In the nineteenth century both schools moved to newly-built premises,

appropriately Gothic for the Grammar (1879) and Tudor for
QEH (1844–7).

At the top of Christmas Steps is the Chapel of the Three
Kings of Cologne, named after the statues of the Magi in
Cologne Cathedral. This (though restored with modern
statues) was the original chapel of Foster's almshouses
founded in 1504, but the almshouses themselves are a late-
Victorian rebuilding in a medieval French style. With their
patterned brickwork, wooden gallery and open spiral staircase, they are an attractive piece of work by the Bristol
architects Foster and Wood, who used a similar style for
Trinity Almshouses in Old Market Street. The firm contributed a good deal to the Victorian scene in Bristol, including
the Grammar School and, down by the Centre, the Colston
Hall (1873), in an impressive 'Byzantine' round-arch style.
The huge auditorium was burned out in 1898 and again in
1945, and although it has never recovered its first magnifi-
cence, it has benefited in acoustics and comfort from subsequent rebuildings and is today a first-class concert-hall,
acoustically excellent and seating over two thousand people. It
was acquired by the Corporation in 1920.

The Colston Hall was built on the site of the Great House,
which the merchant John Young erected in the place of the old
Carmelite monastery and in which he entertained Queen
Elizabeth in 1574. Further up on the hillside he built his Red
Lodge, which is in the Conservation Area and can be reached
by crossing the road from the top of Christmas Steps,
ascending another flight past the graceful curve of the old
horse-tram shed and turning left down Perry Road into Park
Row. The house is much altered externally, but inside are
some fine rooms with intricate plasterwork, carved chimney-
pieces, wooden panelling and Tudor furniture which can be
seen, free, on weekdays from 1 p.m. to 5 p.m. and are well
worth a visit.

Returning past the steps, we come to the foot of St Michael's
Hill, with a high pavement on one side and an attractive and
varied collection of early-eighteenth-century houses, many of
the older ones still with gables and timber frames. Several on
the west side have been renovated by the University. The first
buildings on the hill were Colston's almshouses, founded in
1691. Built round three sides of a courtyard, this low, two-

storey range, painted pink and white, and graced with clock and cupola, remains extremely attractive in spite of the flat-topped modern block which peers over it from behind. It was the first great gift of a man who, it has been calculated, gave some £100,000 in charities in his native city.

Edward Colston, whose fine tomb with a list of his beneficiaries is in All Saints', Corn Street, and whose statue stands in the Centre, was born in Bristol in 1636 and died in 1721. He lived most of his life and made most of his money in London, never held civic office in Bristol, although he was a freeman and Merchant Venturer, and after becoming MP for the city in 1710 appears never to have entered the place again alive. Yet so greatly was he esteemed that at his funeral in his native city thousands packed the streets, and the city bells tolled for sixteen hours. He had a strong interest in education of the High Anglican Tory variety and in 1710 established Colston's School in the Great House, which he had bought for the purpose. The trustees were the Merchant Venturers, who in 1891 were able to start a second school, for girls, in a new polychromatic building by Venn Gough in Cheltenham Road. In 1861 they moved the boys' school to its present site at Stapleton.

Near the top of St Michael's Hill the Hospital for Sick Children (1885) and the post-war Maternity Hospital are part of a complex of buildings which developed around the Bristol Royal Infirmary and now form the Bristol United Hospital Precinct whose large cylindrical chimney dominates the skyline. The Infirmary was started in 1737 and was one of the first hospitals for the poor outside London to be supported by voluntary contributions; Queen Victoria made it 'Royal'. It was rebuilt in 1786, with 'CHARITY UNIVERSAL' engraved over the porch, but the main development was the Edward VII Memorial Building of 1911, remarkably crisp and modern for its date. A recent, large, small-eyed extension has been made.

By the nineteenth century the need for a new hospital for the expanding city was evident, and in 1832 the BGH (Bristol General) was started in Guinea Street down by the New Cut. Whereas the Infirmary had the backing of the High Church Tories, the funding of the General represented the interests of the Whigs and Dissenters. It flourished and in 1852–7 was rebuilt to an ambitious design by William Bruce Gingell. The heavily rusticated ground floor with its round-headed openings is a reminder that Gingell's major additions to Victorian Bristol were factories, although probably his best-known work, in partnership with T. R. Lysaght, is the marvellously detailed bank (now Lloyd's) in Corn Street designed in the style of a Venetian *palazzo*. The BGH was important in relation to the development of a Medical School, which had been started in 1828 and was later to form a major element in Bristol University College. The College opened in a house, now demolished, in Park Row in 1876 with two professors and four lecturers. The first Principal was the eminent economist Alfred Marshall. In the 1880s the Medical School was given new Gothic buildings in red sandstone, designed by Charles Frederick Hansom, in University Road, and paid for largely by the generosity of local business concerns, particularly the chocolate-making Frys.

In 1908 came the event which was to lead to the present great University of some six thousand students. Plans had been discussed for turning the College into an independent university, but the £200,000 needed for the endowment could not be raised. And then, at the annual dinner of the University College Colston Society, Sir George Wills announced that his father, Henry Overton Wills, was offering a gift of £100,000 if a university were created by the amalgamation of the University College and the Merchant Venturers' Technical College.

The way open, a charter was obtained in 1909 and a new university was born, with most appropriately, H. O. Wills as its Chancellor. In 1912 his sons, Sir George Arthur Wills and Henry Herbert Wills, offered to finance new buildings as a memorial to their father. Gothic designs by George Oatley were approved, but work was interrupted by the war and not completed until 1925, when the new buildings were opened by King George V. Erected on the site of the Blind Asylum (1834–*c*1900), where Park Row and Park Street come together to form Queen's Road, the building is best known for its magnificent 215-foot-high tower with its deep-toned E flat bell, Great George, and its great hammer-beamed hall which was destroyed in the blitz and has been reconstructed in its old form, in accordance with the wishes of the then Chancellor,

Winston Churchill. Next door are two earlier buildings also of considerable worth, firstly another Wills gift, the Museum and Library (1904), in a Baroque style with high cool rooms, and next to that a splendid Venetian Art Gallery which Pevsner has called "the greatest compliment the West Country paid to John Ruskin". It was designed by John Foster and Archibald Porton and opened in 1871. War-time bombing caused it to lose some of its decoration and the whole of its interior, since adapted for use as a University canteen, but it is still an impressive building. The Museum was moved in with the Art Gallery and has not yet been given a new home. In spite of cramped conditions, standards of presentation are very high, and the museum is a valuable asset to the city and to education in the area.

Geographically and historically this is a nodal-point, for in every direction there is a slope and a different building-phase. Within a radius of a few hundred yards are Georgian squares, High Victorian neo-Gothic and neo-Classical terraces and villas, and post-war glass-and-concrete boxes. It is in one Conservation Area, Park Street and Brandon Hill, and on the edge of two others, St Michael's Hill, which has already been considered, and Clifton (with Hotwells). Brandon Hill has on one side, towards Park Street and Queen's Road, pleasant terraced streets, Georgian with some later insertions, the attractive Berkeley Square (begun in 1786) and the earlier elevated wide Berkeley Crescent in red brick. In Great George Street the 'Goergian House' built between 1789 and 1791 for the sugar-merchant John Pinney, was made into a museum in 1939 and is furnished as a Georgian home. It is open free on weekdays from 11 a.m. to 5 p.m. On the other side of the street is St George's Church of 1823. Surprisingly for a 'Commissioners'' church following the Act of 1818, it is in the Grecian mode, less surprising, however, when it is considered that it was designed by Sir Robert Smirke, architect of the British Museum.

Most of Brandon Hill, however, forms one of Bristol's invaluable open spaces. For centuries it was "a publick convenience to ye Cittie for ye use of drying Cloaths"; today it is a public park with trees and grass and shrubberies and seats, a children's playground, a ban on playing annoying football, and a prohibition on beating carpets between 6 a.m. and 9 p.m.

There are splendid views, principally over the dockland to Dundry Hill, but a wider panorama can be seen by paying 2p to pass through the turnstile and climb the 108 steps to the top of the Cabot Tower, one of the landmarks of Bristol. The foundation-stone of its pink sandstone tower in a fancy Gothic design by William Venn Gough was laid in 1897 to commemorate the four-hundredth anniversary of the discovery of Newfoundland by John Cabot, sailing from Bristol in the *Matthew*; which is why it has 'CCCC' on each face.

To the north-west can be seen the grey blanket which is Clifton and rising over it the soaring white top of Bristol's concrete cathedral church built to serve the Roman Catholic diocese of Clifton which was founded in 1851. Designed by the Percy Thomas Partnership team of Frederick Jennett, Ronald Weeks and Antoni Paremba, and built by John Laing Construction Ltd, this is the most striking modern building in Bristol. Whether considered beautiful or not—and people tend to hold very extreme views about this, it is undeniably impressive and is a brilliant answer to the problems of combining in one building the liturgical, business and social requirements of a great cathedral—just such problems as the medieval designers answered in the idiom and technology of their own age. Even the outside cladding of pink Aberdeen granite is functional in that it protects the polystyrene cocoon, itself a device for cutting down heat-losses. The lack of familiar decorative detail is something which many people find unpleasant, but the extraordinary quality of Henry Haig's coloured-glass windows in the Narthex (entrance hall) has been much admired. The cathedral was opened in 1973 and took over the functions of the old Pro-cathedral which stood on Honeypen Hill just north-west of Brandon Hill. The 'Pro' (that is, 'provisional') is a curious building, combining two designs, neither of which was completed. The extraordinary feature of giant uncapped columns along three sides under projecting eaves is left over from a massive Greek design by the Bath architect H. E. Goodridge in 1834, which proved too expensive to complete. Inside are the timber supports of the light roof which was added to make the building available for use in 1848, while at one end is a façade, side porch and single-storey room which are all that was built of Charles

Hanson's Romanesque design of 1876 for a complete re-modelling to include a tower and spire.

The Clifton townscape can happily accommodate these two strange buildings, for its own special and captivating quality comes from the complicated co-existence of a whole variety of intricate streetscapes and energetic designs. The street patterns are constantly providing surprises, whether they be little streets crammed with cafés, pubs and shops, terraces with first-floor canopied verandas in fancy ironwork, squares heavy with trees, or big villas—Palladian or Regency or Greek-revival or neo-Gothic or whatever. There are high pavements, some with railings and some without; there are steep streets and flat streets and straight streets and curved ones, and it is easy to come back, with surprise, to where you started from without having the least idea how you got there. There is Bath stone facing and rendering pretending to be Bath stone or else washed in off-white; there is a bit of brick and, principally in the late-Victorian villas to the north and east, a great deal of reddish sandstone. It has a nineteenth-century public school and a zoo and the longest crescent in England. It has Brunel's magical Suspension Bridge. More than anything it has homes—from the Lord Mayor's Mansion House to bed-sitters in basements.

It all started with a hot spring which bubbled up through the mud of the Avon floor and gained a reputation as early as the seventeenth century for curing all manner of ailments. The place was called, obviously, Hotwells, and in the eighteenth century it was much in vogue. The waters were bottled, to the advantage of the Bristol glass-industry, and many eminent people visited the place for the summer season, with the result that on the cramped site below the cliffs and climbing up the slope there were built the Georgian houses which survive in stone-faced Dowry Square (1725–50) and the red brick of Dowry Parade (1764), Albemarle Row (1763) and the charming Colonnade, a small, unfinished crescent of about 1786. It was in a house in Dowry Square that Dr Thomas Beddoes had his Pneumatic Institute and with his young assistant Humphrey Davy experimented with the 'laughing gas' (nitrous oxide) which sent Southey and Coleridge giggling into the night air.

Round the corner, as it were, a theatre was opened in 1729,

just out of reach of the Puritan power of the City. A tendency to riotous behaviour, particularly after a hatch had been cut through to the adjacent beer-shop, led to a serious fire in 1764. Meanwhile, liberalization of opinion in Bristol resulted in the building of a fine new theatre in the City, which opened in King Street in 1766. It received its Royal Patent from George III in 1778.

By the end of the eighteenth century the spa was no longer an attraction, for fashions were changing, the site was difficult to develop and, perhaps most important, it had been found impossible to stop the Avon mud from polluting the spring. And, as if all that were not bad enough, the place was getting a reputation for death. Meanwhile, building was spreading upwards to the plateau, as Bristolians learned to appreciate its healthy air and fine views. First came large houses, such as Clifton Hill (1746–50) and Goldney (1720 but much altered later), and then the first crescents and terraces, such as Windsor Terrace which was started in 1790 and ends in a great cliff of masonry, an extraordinary sight from the Avon valley below. As in Bath, which influenced, but not too strongly, its style and sent it much of its stone, this was speculative building which almost came to a stop with the financial troubles of the French and American wars, so that many of the schemes were not completed until the 1820s. Recovery was then rapid, and building continued apace until by 1841 Clifton had a population of fourteen thousand and in 1835, following the Municipal Reform Act, was brought within the boundaries of Bristol.

Most of the area belonged to the Merchant Venturers, and they took a keen interest in the environmental quality of the development, quite often refusing permission for buildings or uses which they felt would spoil the area. As early as 1813, for example, they would not allow Lady Miller to add a room to her house in Prince's Buildings as they considered it would be "a serious Evil to other houses by obstructing their view down the river".

The decay of opulent Victorian Clifton came with the advent of motor transport and the disappearance of cheap domestic labour, and by the 1920s comments were being passed on the shabbiness of buildings, while many of the big old houses were being split up into flats (a process which has accelerated since the Second World War), and there was a certain air of melancholy about the older terraces. Since the 1960s a pride has come back into the place and a quickening life. Developers have been resisted, and in 1972 Clifton was designated a Conservation Area with the general aim of furthering "the preservation and enhancement of [its] character and appearance".

What Clifton cannot do is expand, for on its northern edge lie the Downs. For centuries these had been an open, uncultivated space, and when Clifton building began to nibble at their edges, the Corporation grew alarmed and in 1861 acquired them for the citizens. Durham Down was bought from the Lords of the Manor of Henbury for £15,000, and the Merchant Venturers agreed "without any consideration to keep Clifton Down open and unenclosed as a place of public resort for the citizens and inhabitants of Bristol". It was an imaginative gesture which has benefited generations of Bristolians as they have strolled, courted, ridden, played football, gone to the Flower Show or the Circus, heckled the orators at Bristol's own Speakers' Corner or strolled across to the Sea Walls built by John Wallis in 1746 to stop people falling into the Gorge. And they can visit the Zoo, which was founded in 1836, fell on bad times, picked up again in the 1930s and now has an international reputation. It has very fine gardens and a remarkable collection of animals, but if you want to see Alfred, the famous gorilla, you have to go to the Museum.

The Downs make an enclave in the west side of Clifton, and here is an Iron Age Camp and an old windmill turned observatory with a *camera obscura*, and the Suspension Bridge. In 1753 a Bristol wine-merchant, William Vick, left £1,100 to the Society of Merchant Venturers to be invested until such time as a sufficient sum accumulated to pay for a bridge over the Avon at Clifton. Nearly eighty years later it was decided that the scheme could go ahead, and advertisements went out for a design competition which attracted the attention of a twenty-four-year-old half-French engineer, Isambard Kingdom Brunel. He sent in four designs which, with all the other entries, were rejected by the judge, the aged Thomas Telford. The Committee then commissioned Telford to produce a design himself, but his proposal, with enormous towers rising from the floor of the gorge, was so embarrassingly impossible that the competition was re-opened, and this time Brunel won. "I have to say," he wrote, "that of all the wonderful feats I have performed since I have been in this part of the world [Bristol] I think yesterday I performed the most wonderful. I produced unanimity amongst fifteen men who were all quarrelling about the most ticklish subject—taste." Unfortunately the following year saw the Bristol Riots, and work on the bridge did not start for some time. In 1840 the money ran out, the chains were sold, and for years the towers stood desolate on the heights above the Avon.

By that time Brunel was engaged in even greater matters arising from his contacts with Bristol, all, as he wrote, "resulting from the Clifton Bridge". First he was employed to improve the dock-gates and devise a system for scouring out the mud, which he designed with his usual ingenuity. This brought him to the notice of a group of local businessmen who were promoting a railway-line from Bristol to London. In March 1833, at the age of thirty, Brunel, who had no previous experience of railways, was appointed engineer to the GWR and ordered to complete his preliminary survey by May. Working up to twenty hours a day and travelling in the coach he had designed for himself, his famous 'Flying Hearse', whose accoutrements included a case of fifty cigars, he completed his task so well that in November the final plans were ready, and in March 1834 a Bill was before Parliament. It was rejected by the Lords, but in the following year a new version was successful, due largely to the expert advocacy of Brunel himself. "What a fight we have had," he wrote in his journal, "and how near defeat—and what a ruinous defeat it would have been."

By May 1840 the whole stupendous work had been completed, except for the section from Chippenham to Bath which involved cutting the Box Tunnel, nearly two miles long, longer than any previously attempted and in the opinion of many competent engineers an impossibility. It took 2½ years to complete and cost the lives of a hundred of the four thousand workmen employed, but in June 1841 it was finished and the line open the whole way from the great station which Brunel had built in the fields of Temple Meads. This is the Tudor-style 'Engineer's Castellated' Bath stone building on Victoria Street. Passengers passed through the booking-hall and then climbed steps up to where the platforms and railway were supported on arches 15 feet above ground-level and sheltered by a great shed with a magnificent 'hammerbeam' roof supported on iron 'Tudor' pillars. Brunel's station is now used as a car-park. The present station, with its bold Gothic clock-tower, was built in the 1870s, and on the right-hand side and lower down is a turreted mock-Jacobean block built as offices for the Bristol and Exeter Railway Company. The B & E got its Act in 1836 and by 1844 had reached Exeter, but, although a separate company, its engineer was Brunel, and initially the GWR worked the line. After a brief period of independence the B & E amalgamated with the GWR in 1876. Both lines were on Brunel's broad gauge of seven foot, whereas the rest of the country was being covered with Stephenson's 4 foot 8½ inches which he had adopted from the northern coal-tramways. In 'the Battle of the Gauges' the GWR lost and in the 1890s had to convert.

Meanwhile a scheme, half-jokingly suggested by Brunel, to extend the GWR to New York had been taken up seriously, and the Great Western Steamship Company was formed, for which Brunel designed a huge paddle-steamer, the *Great Western*, which was built in Bristol, fitted out in London and in 1838 made her maiden voyage in a famous race with the *Sirius*, under steam for Liverpool owners. Starting three days later than her rival, she docked in New York on the afternoon of *Sirius*'s arrival in the morning. The previous year the big Royal Western Hotel with its Ionic colonnade had been designed by Richard Shackleton Pope to accommodate passengers transferring from ship to rail. Unfortunately Bristol docks and the approach up the Avon were not suited to large ships, and moreover Bristol dock charges were much higher than those at Liverpool, with the result that the *Great Western* subsequently operated from the rival port. 'The Royal Western', having lost its chief reason for existence, subsequently became the Hydro Hotel, with Turkish Baths, and, renamed Brunel House, is now an office-block and much decayed.

The Great Western Steamship Company had planned to build two more ships like the *Great Western*, but this was dull stuff for a man of Brunel's eager spirit, and he persuaded them to invest in a ship such as there had never been before, a ship so large and so original that no one could be found to build it, and the Company had to excavate its own dock and arrange for the construction by the Bristol ship-builder William Patterson, under the direction of Thomas Guppy, an engineer and a Director of the GWR, Christopher Claxton, an ex-Naval officer, and Brunel.

Brunel's first design was for a paddle-steamer, but his attention was caught by the visit to Bristol of the *Archimedes*, which had a new type of screw-propulsion, and after carrying out tests he changed his mind, designed the first large propeller, six-bladed and 15½ feet in diameter, and adapted engines patented by his father Sir Marc Brunel, to drive it. Apart from the fact that, with a length of 322 feet, his ship was much bigger than any previously built and that it was made of iron, it was full of innovations, such as watertight bulkheads, a balanced rudder, hinged masts and a remote-indicating electric log. The great ship took four years to build, during which time its name was changed from *Mammoth* to *Great Britain*, and on 19th July 1843 Prince Albert came down on Brunel's railway, had lunch at Brunel's station and went to the docks to be present, along with thousands of Bristolians and their umbrellas, for it was a showery day, to see the launching of Brunel's ship. The *Great Britain* was then moved across to the present Gas Works Wharf to have her engines fitted and a year later into the river ready to leave the Floating Harbour— when she found she could not get out. Even after the top of the lock had been widened, she nearly stuck fast, but with the help of a high tide and a steam-tug the *Great Britain* steam-ship was on her way to astonish the world—"your magnificent ship", said Queen Victoria—and to bring financial ruin to the Great Western Steamship Company.

On 19th July 1970, on the anniversary of her launch, the *Great Britain*, with the Duke of Edinburgh aboard, eased into the Bristol dock where she had been made. Just as there had been many doubts as to whether it was possible or even necessary to build her, so there was a good deal of opposition and, worse, indifference to the project to bring her home from the Falkland Islands, where in 1937 she had been made Crown Wreck by being deliberately sunk in the shallow water of Sparrow Cove. And just as before, it was the vision, energy and efficiency of a few men which carried the work through to a triumphant conclusion. Outstanding among them were

Richard Goold-Adams who, as Chairman, organized the whole project, Ewan Corlett who made the first proposals and as a naval architect acted as technical adviser to the project, and Jack Hayward, a property millionaire, who promised to 'see the ship home' and gave £150,000 to make it possible. The vital question of finance was handled by the Honorary Treasurer, Eric Custance, and the highly responsible job of representing the Project in the Falklands was undertaken by Lord Strathcona. The actual raising of the ship and her towing to Britain on an underwater pontoon was done by the Anglo–German consortium of Risdon Beazley Ulrich Harms Ltd, and valuable assistance was given by the Royal Navy and Marines. These names are worthy of record in any account of Bristol, for they are of men who gave to the city, as to the nation, a tangible record of one of the great achievements of the past. Bristol itself seemed far from whole-hearted about receiving back her ship, and there was a strong possibility that she would go to London, but today she seems to be settled, and restoration work is progressing well. The ship, with the dock, dockside museum, restaurant and souvenir-shop, is open daily from 10 a.m. to 6 p.m. (5 p.m. in the winter). The 1976 Project Brief, for the City Docks Local Plan, includes the short statement that consideration should be given to "the continuing improvement of the SS *Great Britain* and the vessel's setting".

Brunel died in 1859, his end hastened by the worry and effort of building and launching the even bigger *Great Eastern*, and it was largely as a memorial to the great man that funds were raised and work restarted on his Suspension Bridge. Simpler in decoration than originally intended (the sphinxes, for example, were left off the tops of the 'Egyptian' towers), and using chains from Brunel's Hungerford Bridge demolished in 1861 to make way for Charing Cross railway bridge, it was finally opened in 1861, having cost £100,000. Since then its history has been undramatic except when people have flown aeroplanes beneath it or flung themselves from it. Extraordinarily, three people have been known to have fallen the 245 feet to the river and been saved by their long skirts, which acted as parachutes. Two were children flung over by a demented father, and the other was Sarah Ann Henley who jumped in 1885, after a tiff with her boy-friend, and lived to be eighty-five.

The bridge was, in fact, never a major transport link and was used mainly by local suburban traffic. More important was the route along the east side of Clifton which crossed the Downs and continued through Westbury-on-Trym towards Aust Ferry. The approach from the city was over St Michael's Hill to join what is now Whiteladies Road at the White Lady turnpike-house. Disadvantages in this route and the desire to open up new areas to building led to a move in the eighteenth century to construct a new link along the lines of the present Park Street and Queen's Road and to widen and improve Whiteladies Road itself, but progress was slow, and it was nearly a hundred years before there was a complete new, broad thoroughfare from the Centre to the Downs.

First to come was Park Street, named after Bullock's Park through which it ran. It was started in 1761, and although it took a long time to complete and has many Victorian intrusions and post-war reconstructions, it is still mainly late-Georgian with a pleasing simplicity of style in its stone-faced façade. At first mainly residential (although one of the first leases went to Hannah More's sisters for their school), it was rapidly invaded by commerce and is today mainly a street of shops and small restaurants, striving to maintain business against the disadvantages of steep slope and dense traffic, and the competition from booming Broadmead.

In 1845 the City's Improvement Commissioners obtained sanction for a number of important street-works, including an improved road from the top of Park Street which would carry traffic on to Whiteladies Road and then curve away at the junction to make a new and better approach to Clifton. Work started ten years later and produced Queen's Road with which the widened Whiteladies Road generated a long ribbon of late-Victorian building on an impressive scale, with important shopping developments at each end. The most spectacular building, however, the Victoria Rooms, in a Greek Revival style with a huge portico, pre-dates the improvements. Designed by George Dyer for the Tory gentlemen of Clifton, it was erected in 1840–42 on an open site near the gates of Tyndall's Park which swept up to the beautiful Georgian house which Thomas Tyndall built in 1761 on the site of the old Royal Fort. Thomas was the grandson of Onesiphorus Tyndall, a Gloucestershire farmer's son who sought, and found, his fortune in the city, and it must surely have been a source of satisfaction to him to set up in the style of a country gentleman. Yet in 1791 he sold his property for building development, which proved to be bad business, for the property boom was rapidly followed, as we have seen, by a slump, and the enterprise went bankrupt. Tyndall foreclosed on the mortgage and got his premises back in 1798. On his death the property went to auction and was bought by his son, and in 1799 the grounds were again laid out as 'Gentleman's Garden', so that it was not until later in the nineteenth century that streets and buildings came, the area being developed with large villas instead of the imitation Bath of crescents, squares and circles which had been originally planned.

The bridge that carried the bottom of Park Street over to College Green was not made until 1871. It still exists, but a similar one for Deanery Road on the south side of the Green has been filled in. The Green itself lies like an old-fashioned kite, with the Council House lining the curved end and traffic grinding along the sides to meet in frustration at the point where a stone Queen Victoria stands in impotent majesty like an ineffective traffic-warden. The red-brick Council House is in typical inter-war 'GPO Georgian', for it was started in 1938 although not completed until 1956 and is pleasant enough if not particularly distinguished or much in harmony with its surroundings. The worst feature is the cramped little shrine-like arch in the middle with its stone statue of a knock-kneed Tudor sea-captain with a dolphin up his leg, and the best, although some Bristolians did not think so at the time, the two 12-foot gilt unicorns standing against the sky. The Green itself has been lowered, and its trees and the Victorian copy of the High Cross have been removed, so that today it offers no privacy, interest or shade. The idea was to make it a kind of green forecourt to the Council House but, as its name suggests, it really belongs to the Cathedral which stands helplessly on the side, cut off by the stream of traffic. If, however, the proposed road-diversion through dockland takes place, the old unity might be re-established.

The Cathedral was originally the church of the little Augustinian abbey founded in 1140 by the Bristol merchant Robert Fitzharding who fourteen years later was granted the lands which made him Lord of Berkeley. It was built in his manor of Billeswick which lay west of the city and included the low-lying area by the Frome and Avon which became known as St Augustine's Marsh, or Canon's Marsh, the monks being popularly known as Black Canons. After the Dissolution the abbey church became the cathedral of the newly-created diocese of Bristol which had the geographical peculiarity of being mostly in Dorset. In 1836 the see was merged with Gloucester and was not re-established until 1897. Some Norman work from the early church still survives, principally in the superb Chapter House and the arches of the nearby Gatehouse, but the remarkable building east of the nave is mainly of the thirteenth and fourteenth centuries. The Norman nave was not rebuilt and rapidly became so ruinous that it was walled off from the choir and transepts, giving rise to the taunt during the merging of the see with Gloucester of "Half a church, half a bishop". Victorian civic pride would have none of this: funds were raised, the eminent architect George Edmund Street was commissioned, and work was begun in 1868, the west front towers being completed in 1888, seven years after Street had died and without the steeples he had proposed. It was altogether a highly successful enterprise.

Almost next to the cathedral is the Library of 1906, designed by Charles Holden, who is best known for his London tube-stations. With its oriel windows and vertical lines, it makes a companionable neighbour, in spite of the rather Art Nouveau feeling. The post-war extension is perhaps less happy if rather more functionally appropriate. The library, which is now run by Avon County, has, as might be expected, a notable quantity of material on Bristol which supplements the archives in the Council House. It also has in the Bristol Room a beautiful Grinling Gibbons overmantel from the Old Library in King Street.

On the opposite side of the Green was the Hospital of St Mark founded in 1220 by Maurice de Gaunt and Robert de Gournay, two grandsons of Fitzharding. It was bought by the Corporation at the Dissolution, and in 1721 the church, after being used by French Huguenot refugees, became their official place of worship and is usually called 'the Lord Mayor's Chapel'. The pretty little red tower is of 1487. It is interesting, if architecturally confusing church with much Victorian re-modelling and lots of monuments.

Down from College Green the road, considerably widened in and since the eighteenth century, leads to the Centre, which has gradually covered more and more of the River Frome. In about 1239 this was the scene of a quite remarkable piece of medieval engineering, by which the Frome, which had previously turned eastward and meandered uselessly through the marshes to Bristol Bridge, was diverted into an artificial channel straight to the Avon through land acquired from the Abbey. The result was to give Bristol merchants a new and better anchorage than their old one on the right bank of the Avon, and an advantage over the men of Redcliffe who had enjoyed a better position on the opposite bank. Indeed, Redcliffe, which with the adjacent Temple Fee was in Berkeley land, was at least as large and prosperous as Bristol and saw no need to help its rival. It took a royal command from Henry III to persuade its people to assist in the work and pay their share of the huge cost of £5,000. At the same time their ties with Bristol were strengthened by a reconstruction which transformed Bristol Bridge from a simple wooden affair to a four-arched stone structure carrying a double row of four- and five-storeyed timbered houses and a chapel to the Virgin Mary. It lasted until the reconstruction of 1768. To expose the river-bed for foundations, the Avon was diverted temporarily along a ditch cut along the foot of Redcliffe Hill from Temple Meads to Redcliffe Back, a route followed by the present Temple and Redcliffe Ways, and along this line a new town wall was built. At the same time Bristol made an outer wall across the marsh from the Avon to the new Frome.

It was along the line of this wall that a new thoroughfare, later known as King Street, was constructed in 1663. There was already a fourteenth-century chapel and seamen's almshouse at the western end, and this, which had been taken over by the Merchant Venturers, was enlarged in 1669–9 on land given by Edward Colston. It incorporated the Merchants' Hall which was rebuilt in 1788 and bombed so badly in 1940 that all that remains is part of the almshouses, prettily pink around an open courtyard. At the other end of the street St Nicholas's Almshouses, two-storeyed with gables, built in 1652 and recently restored, stand almost opposite the finest remaining half-timbered building in a city where this was once the characteristic style. Erected in 1669 as a row of houses, part of it became the Llandoger Tavern, now called 'The Llandoger Trow' and one of the chain of Berni Inns originated by two Italian brothers who started as restaurateurs in Bristol before the war. A trow is a flat-bottomed Welsh sailing-barge, and the waterfront round the corner from the end of King Street is the Welsh Back, worth visiting for its views along the river and for the fantastic polychromatic bastard-Byzantine warehouse built as a granary in 1869 to designs by Pontin and Gough.

There are more over-sailing, half-timbered ranges in King Street, but they are rather dingy, and the most striking buildings date from the eighteenth century, notably the former Public Library of 1739–40 and the big Coopers' Hall designed by William Halfpenny and erected in 1744, replacing four houses which were given to the Coopers' Company by the Corporation in exchange for their old Hall in Corn Street which was pulled down to enlarge the passageway by the Corn Exchange. The Company, like others in Bristol, was, however, nearing the end of its prosperity, and in 1785 they sold their new building. It has recently been adapted as a foyer and extension to its neighbour, the Theatre Royal.

The foundation-stone of this beautiful little Georgian theatre was laid in December 1764; the opening was on 30th May 1776, and in the following year it received its Royal Patent. At the end of the nineteenth century the theatre fell upon difficult times, but in 1942 it was bought for the City and leased to the CEMA (Council for the Encouragement of Music and the Arts, now the Arts Council). In 1946 the Old Vic was persuaded to start a daughter-company, the Bristol Old Vic, which rapidly earned a high reputation. In spite of this, the company had great financial difficulties and was disbanded in 1949. It was only because of a remarkable surge of national support that it was rescued from oblivion and re-launched on a course which has led to expansion and international acclaim.

Beyond King Street the marsh, which was used for sheep-grazing, began to develop as a favourite pleasure-ground for the citizens. A bowling-green was laid out; there was a bull-ring and a bear-pit and tree-lined walks and a pair of stocks for disturbers of the peace, and it was all quite pleasant but not particularly profitable to the Corporation. By the end of the seventeenth century it was ripe for development, and in 1670 the Corporation had the ground surveyed for building, plots to be let for three lives and houses to be made of brick. In 1702 Queen Anne visited the city, and in her honour the square "now building in the Marsh" was named Queen Square. The first house had been completed in 1701 for the Reverend John Reade, vicar of St Nicholas's, and another early one (demolished in 1889 to make way for the over-decorated design by William Venn Gough for the Port of Bristol Authority) was put up by Captain Woodes Rogers, best known as the man who rescued Alexander Selkirk, the original Robinson Crusoe. In 1711 Alderman Shuter built a house which in 1781 became the Mansion House, destroyed in the Riots of 1831, and although people were at first slow to take leases, the large and handsome square was completed by the end of the century. No. 37 had the distinction of being the first American Consulate in Europe in 1792, although Bristol does not have one today. Lined with impressive plane-trees and depressing parking-meters, Queen Square survived riots and fire, only to be torn asunder by pre-war planning which put a major road across one diagonal almost under the hoofs of Rysbrach's equestrian statue of William III which was put up in 1732–6 as a centrepiece to the green, much to the annoyance of local Jacobites who naturally looked on 'Dutch Billy' as a usurper.

Parallel to the west side of the square is Prince Street, named after Queen Anne's husband, Prince George of Denmark, and now full of decaying Georgian houses. It also has a post-war motel and a rather splendid old tea-warehouse of huge proportions, designed for J. & R. Bush in the early part of the nineteenth century and happily converted in 1975 for use as offices and the Arnolfini arts complex and restaurant.

Although the Avon anchorages were consequently used by coastal traders rather than by ocean-going ships, the flat land south of the river in Redcliff and Temple continued to develop industrially with a particular emphasis on weaving, soap-boiling and glass-making, with brewing along the river-bank. The tall chimneys which once lined the river like the masts of a great fleet have mostly disappeared, and the great cone-shaped furnaces of the glasshouses are now represented by a single base used to house the Kiln Restaurant of the post-war Dragonara

Hotel, but the area still retains a vigorous industrial life, and there has been considerable rebuilding, particularly in Temple.

Travel through this crowded area from Bristol Bridge became increasingly difficult, and in about 1865 a broad new highway, Victoria Street, was opened up as far as Temple Meads railway station where the route continued to the Bath Road. Originally lined with impressive, if gloomy, commercial buildings, it has not been noticeably improved by piecemeal post-war reconstruction. Incongruous but attractive, still stands the gabled Shakespeare Inn, first licensed in 1636 but much altered inside. Behind it the fifteenth-century tower of the Temple Church of the Holy Cross leans drunkenly beside the fine eighteenth-century Classical west doorway and in front of the church's gutted shell, on whose floor is marked the oval plan of the original church of the Knights Templar. The tower began to lean during its construction but was so well underpinned by the medieval builders that it has remained stable ever since, although there is a story that it narrowly escaped being blown up by the Army who thought that it was the bombing which had thrown it out of true.

West of Victoria Street and stretching to the big, abandoned, 'This Building is Dangerous' warehouses of Redcliffe Back, lie a jumble of mainly commercial and industrial buildings of no distinction or interest except for St Thomas's with its Perpendicular tower and Classical (1792) body, a nearby gabled range of about 1456 and the dominating shape of the fifteen-storey Robinson block, built in 1964 and voted by one engineering magazine as the third ugliest building in the country. Compared with others which have been put up since, it displays a remarkable elegance with its white pebbled surface, rows of arched windows and good proportions. Further south is a small building of some significance in the history of Bristol, the house built in 1749 by Giles Malpas "of St Thomas's Parish, Gent" as a dwelling for the master of the parish school. It was there in 1752 that Thomas Chatterton was born. The Classical façade of the school has been re-erected in front of the birthplace and looks blankly across the uncaring traffic of Redcliffe Way to the great church which inspired the boy to his Gothic forgeries and which remembers him in a simple oval plaque inscribed "Thomas Chatterton— of this parish—1752–1770—Poet".

Chatterton's importance to the development of the Romantic Movement seems now considerably less than many of his contemporaries thought, and he would probably have received much less attention if, at the age of eighteen, he had not Romantically killed himself with arsenic in a London garret. To Wordsworth he was the "Marvellous boy, the sleepless soul who perished in his pride", and even Dr Johnson gave grudging admiration: "It is wonderful," he said, "that the whelp has written such things."

The "things" were mainly a set of poems dealing with events in the history of Bristol, and particularly St Mary Redcliffe, which Chatterton wrote in 'medieval' language on parchment from the church's muniments room and passed off successfully as original discoveries. They have been responsible for a good deal of myth about the history of Bristol and in particular of the importance of William Canynge the Younger in the building of St Mary's, but even more damaging to Bristol's image was the invective which Chatterton directed against a Bristol society which was so easily deceived and yet so unwilling to be enthusiastic about the poetry he acknowledged as his own. To this day there lingers, perhaps unfairly, a feeling that Bristolians are more concerned with commerce than culture and will put economics before aesthetics any day of the week.

It has been argued that St Mary's itself is marked more by ostentation than by beauty (even today the interior dazzles with gilt and paint) and that there is something which smacks of over-much secular pride in a parish which erected what is virtually a small cathedral. This is a superficial judgement and ignores the frequency with which great shrewdness in business has been allied to genuine piety and the extent to which merchants and manufacturers have paid out of their own pockets for the better welfare of their fellow man or the greater glory of God—or both, as did Roger de Berkeley in 1190 when he gave the church a water-supply, and Lord Dulverton, of the Wills family, when he paid £8,500 in 1930 for the exterior restoration. Roger's effigy in the north transept shows him as a knight in chain mail with his feet resting pigeon-toed on a plump dog, and an even better exemplar of Mammon turned to the service of God is found in the two effigies of William Canynge in the opposite transept. The earlier is on the opulent tomb of his smiling wife and shows him in merchant's dress; in the other he is robed as Dean of the College of Westbury-on-Trym. The face with its big nose and chin is the same in both but looks more ascetic in the alabaster of the second version. He was one of the foremost Bristol merchants of his time, five times Mayor and twice Member of Parliament, but after the death of his wife he "was made preest and sange his first masse at our Lady of Redcliffe the yere following", an event which is commemorated every Whitsun when the church is strewn with rushes and a sermon is preached before the Lord Mayor.

Of the other monuments of historical interest may be mentioned the floor-slab to Admiral Sir William Penn (1670), father of the founder of Pennsylvania, and his armour hung on the tower wall, two fourteenth-century brasses from Temple Church, one of which is a palimpsest with a priest on one side and a woman on the other, and a brass to John Brook (1522) and his wife Joanna, whose father was Richard Ameryke (or ap Meryke) from whom Bristol derives its claim to have named America. He was Sheriff and Customs Officer at the time of Cabot's voyage in 1497 and responsible for paying the explorer, "him who found the new isle" (Newfoundland), the King's pension of £20 a year. It seems as likely a claim as that for the Italian map-maker Amerigo Vespucci.

Architecturally the church is notable, particularly in its splendid lierne vaulting, long row of flying buttresses, spire soaring to nearly 300 feet and fantastically carved doorway to the hexagonal north porch. The church's position in an industrial area, however, caused severe deterioration of the limestone fabric, and a great restoration was carried out by the specially formed Canynge Society between 1846 and 1877. This included repairs to the north porch carving and the replacement in 1872 of the top part of the spire which had been carried away by a great storm of 1446. Yet another restoration took place between 1927 and 1933, and further work was done after the war, including the removal of the Victorian reredos which had replaced a huge canvas triptych by Hogarth against the Lady Chapel, which had been blocked off when it was turned into a 'Grammar and Writing School' from 1766 to 1854. The Hogarth canvas is now in the excellent museum created near Bristol Bridge out of the bombed shell of St Nicholas's.

Clifton. At bottom right is Berkeley Square, bottom centre is Brandon Hill with the Cabot Tower. Roughly top left is the Roman Catholic Cathedral, above that Clifton College, and beyond lie the Downs.

The Cabot Tower, Bristol, built in 1898 to celebrate the fourth centenary of Cabot's voyage from Bristol and discovery of Newfoundland.

The Hatchet Inn (seventeenth-century), viewed between the Georgian buildings of Unity and Orchard Streets.

St Mary Redcliffe, Bristol. On the skyline left is the Cabot Tower and below it to its left the centre tower of the Cathedral. The chimney on the skyline right serves a hospital complex.

Bristol University (with tower) and Bristol Grammar School (top of picture). Left of the University Tower is the Museum and Art Gallery.

(*Overleaf*) Bristol from the air. See key on pp.212-13.

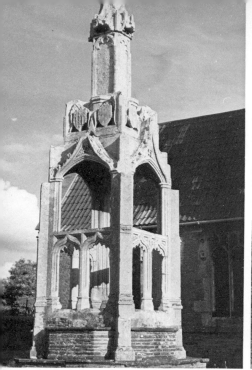

A churchyard cross (c1390) at Iron Acton.

The tower of Banwell church, 101 feet high. The niches contain figures of the Annunciation, and there is a lily in a vase carved on the window between.

Remains of the chapter house and refectory (right) of the Carthusian monastery at Hinton Charterhouse.

Chew Lake and Denny Island. The Mendip Hills form the skyline.

Burrington, Burrington Combe and Mendip top. The Twin Brooks
which come into the gorge are flowing over Old Red Sandstone.

Behind the churchyard with its embedded bit of tram-line
which was flung over the houses by the bombing on Good
Friday 1941, stretches the low sandstone plateau on whose
slopes the church was built and whose cave-ridden red rocks
can be seen down by the roundabout in the little garden made
out of the 1665 Quaker burial-ground which was given to the
city in 1950. Although much developed with new buildings
since the war, there is still a good deal of old Redcliffe to be
seen, including the splendidly re-furbished Georgian houses in
Redcliffe Parade and a small range of 1718 with Dutch gable
and carved figures over every window. A feature which was
destroyed to make way for the large but not unpleasing office
block of Phoenix House was the battlemented Shot Tower
which William Watts added to his house for the process he
patented in 1782 of dropping molten lead through a perforated
zinc tray to fall into a vat of water in the basement. Its
replacement down by the floating harbour was built in 1968.
Looking rather like a concrete barrel on a stalk, it won a Civic
Trust Award.

Over the hill the land slopes down to the muddy, canal-like
New Cut, which was made in 1804–9 to carry the tidal waters
of the Avon when the river was locked off to make the floating
harbour in a belated and not very successful effort to revive the
fortunes of the port. Here on the hillside and climbing on to
the plateau top is Bristol's first and most aesthetically successful large-scale high-rise housing development. Designed by
the City Architect, J. Nelson Meredith, and begun in 1953, it
still retains a bright, crisp appearance enhanced by the
maturing trees and well-established lawns. Incorporating a
mixture of low- and high-rise, a pub, a Methodist church,
shops and a secondary school, it achieves a high density
without being oppressive. Reactions to the high-level life are,
of course, varied but seem in general more favourable than
those frequently produced by tower-blocks.

South of the New Cut the land rises again in Bedminster
(Beda's church), which was not absorbed into Bristol until
1835. It was then little more than a village, and the present
dense pattern of terraced housing, shops and factories is
largely a late-Victorian creation whose growth was considerably accelerated after 1886 when the Wills tobacco firm moved
into the area. The factories moved out in 1976 to the W. D. and

H. O. Wills Estate at Bishopsworth, its brown box-like warehouses, factories and offices set in carefully landscaped surrounds. At its western end Bedminster merges into Ashton Gate, where Bristol City have their football-ground and where factories have spread along the low ground by Ashton Brook.

Eastward the Victorian streets continue steeply into Totterdown. The name conjures up struggling pedestrians, but it originally meant 'Lookout Hill' and its summit gives a view of the broad sweep of Bristol's eastern quadrant where close-packed residential streets and industrial buildings rapidly covered the fields in Victorian times, from the low, marshy region behind Temple Meads and along the Feeder Canal, up to Barton Hill, Easton, Eastville and St George's, on to the Frome valley with St Paul's and Baptist Mills (originally Bagpath, from the owner's name) and up again to Ashley Down, where the Gloucestershire cricket-ground sits next-door to Brunel Technical College housed in the gaunt, impressive buildings of the one-time Müller Orphanages.

The Reverend George Müller, born in Prussia in 1805, was not only one of Bristol's great philanthropists but unique in that he had no wealth of his own to bestow. He never asked people for money but, in his deep faith, depended on the power of prayer—and his prayers were answered. The orphanages cost £75,000 to build, and during his life, which ended in 1898, over a million pounds in voluntary contributions passed through his hands. From 1836 to 1955, when the orphans were rehoused elsewhere, over 3 million pounds were contributed, without solicitation, for maintaining the 17,317 children admitted to the homes. The road named in his honour was built between the wars as part of a City scheme to reduce unemployment.

The sturdy Victorian streets of the eastern quarter with their little gardens and bay windows and bits of stone carving, with corner shops and ornate pubs, big Board Schools and Nonconformist chapels, have meant home to thousands of Bristolians, and today the increasing spread of bright new paintwork and careful repairs shows a strong revival of local pride. Too frequently such regions have suffered from official neglect and planning contempt, but it seems that a new spirit is growing which respects the small-scale intricate relationships of community areas, and it may well be that there will be a halt to the Grand Planners who work on a God's-eye scale, the Great Pavers who cover the world in concrete, and the Insatiable Wreckers for whom 'old' means 'useless' and change must be complete and instantaneous, which it never is in practice so that unhappy stretches of wasteland are left to deteriorate for many years. Some pieces are of course irretrievable, because neglect has bitten too deep or because the buildings were rotten at the start or because they no longer can serve a useful function, but already there are small-scale replacements which fit comfortably into the older scene, adding new variety and pointing the way to a more humane treatment of the inner urban environment.

Beyond these areas, often without a break, lie the urbanized villages of outer Bristol where the ancient centre was expanded in late-Victorian times in brick and Pennant with high Victorian villas and terraces and smaller streets, with municipal parks and swimming-baths and libraries and schools, and, in the posher areas, trees in the streets. To this were added in the inter-war years the tidy lines of bay-windowed semis and red-brick shopping parades and uniform acres of Council housing contrasting with the Japanese cherries and laburnums of leafy 'Who's for tennis?' Betjeman-country suburbia. And since then have come the new shopping precincts, flat-faced housing, both low and high, municipal and private, the new schools, usually low and spreading in glass and white paint and dark brick and signposts because even the children do not know where everything is, and all the standard architectural clichés which belong to everywhere and nowhere.

In fact there is a great deal of distinctive individual character to be found in these urbanized villages, and the brief attention we can give them here cannot do them justice—they deserve a book to themselves, best compiled from original studies by folk who know them intimately. To generalize is to falsify, but, acknowledging that there must be considerable reservations, it can be said that there are basically three types. First are the villages of the old coalfield, often with old industries and ancient histories—Kingswood, for instance, which is not administratively in Bristol, and Fishponds, Stapleton and Hanham. Then to the south are the mainly post-war acres of housing, neat but too often characterless, at Bishopsworth, Withywood, Hartcliffe, Hengrove, the new Brislington and Whitchurch, none however without some point of interest. And thirdly, separated visually from Bristol by the ridge which runs from the Downs to Filton lie the suburban villages of the Trym valley and the King's Weston ridge which expanded between the wars on garden-suburb lines with a bias towards higher-priced commuter housing, although there were some important Council building as, for instance, at Sea Mills, a trend which has increased since the war. The tendency for these suburbs to coalesce into one large sea of housing has been held partly in check by the broken nature of the relief, but it is strong, has already triumphed on the eastern end with Southmead, Henleaze, and Horfield and arguably should be resisted. The designation of parts of Henbury, Shirehampton and Westbury-on-Trym as Conservation Areas holds out some hope that their individuality will be preserved.

Three features are of particular interest in the northern area—King's Weston House, Blaise Castle Estate and Westbury College. King's Weston House was designed by Vanbrugh and built between about 1710 and 1725. A rather plain building, its most remarkable feature is the combination of six chimney-stacks into an arched arcade, a feature visible from the M5. The house, after years of neglect, became a police college in 1970. Westbury College is another matter. Originally founded as a small monastery in about 962 by Oswald, Bishop of Worcester, it soon lost its importance as one of the pioneers of Benedictine revival in Britain and did not recover its significance until the end of the thirteenth century, when Godfrey Giffard, another Bishop of Worcester, elevated it into a Cathedral Chapter. Substantial growth did not however take place until the fifteenth century when John Carpenter, styling himself Bishop of Worcester and Westbury, undertook a rebuilding of the College for which Canynge provided a good deal of the money and, as his memorial in St Mary Redcliffe states, gave employment "by space of 8 years, 800 handy craftsmen, besides Carpenters and Masons every day 100 men". With the Dissolution in 1544, the buildings passed into the hands of Sir Ralph Sadleir and in 1643 were used by Prince Rupert as his headquarters during the Royalist attack on Bristol. When this succeeded, he had the

College fired to prevent its use in any Parliamentarian counter-attack. A more recent fire affected a good deal of what was left or rebuilt. In 1974 the remains of the buildings—a big gate-house and a couple of cylindrical angle-towers—were incor-porated into a pleasant design for old people's flats. The site has been since 1907 vested in the National Trust.

Blaise Castle, a Gothic folly of 1766, was incorporated in the landscaping by Humphrey Repton of the mansion designed by William Paty for the Quaker banker John Scandrett Harford and completed in 1798. To the house Harford later added a picture-room by Cockerell and an orangery and thatched dairy by John Nash, who was also engaged to design a collec-tion of cottages for retired workers from the estate. Called 'Blaise Hamlet', this is now the property of the National Trust and is a delightful essay in the Picturesque, with strange chimneys, oddly shaped thatched roofs and a little green. The estate was bought in 1926 by the Corporation, who turned the house into a Folk Museum in 1949. Entry is free; there is a car park; and the open grassy places and steep walks through the woods, together with the attractions of the castle, museum and lately installed Stratford Mill, make it a favourite place for family outings. Here too may be seen the great rock known as 'Goram's Chair', a reminder of one of those attractive pre-scientific explanations of natural features. Goram, the story goes, was a lazy giant who refused to help his brother Vincent in the job of cutting Avon Gorge but later, spurred to emulation by his brother's success, decided to dig one for the Trym, starting with a huge rock chair for his extensive rest-periods. Too indolent to get his own pick-axe, he shared his brother's, and they used to toss it to each other over the three-mile gap after giving a warning shout. One day Vincent gave his shout and threw his pick and killed Goram, who was asleep in his Chair. This so upset Vincent that he finished both gorges in double-quick time and went on to fabricate the stone circles at Stanton Drew and Stonehenge and the Giant's Causeway in Ireland. At least the story does not invoke visitors from Outer Space.

Beyond the northern ridge the land drops sharply to the lowlands of Severnside which belong physically to the coastal region but warrant consideration because economically and administratively they are part of the Bristol District and there is a continuous built-up area from Shirehampton to Avonmouth.

The docks at Avonmouth belong to the latest chapters of a history of the city and goes back at least to the Irish slave-trade in Saxon times. The Irish connection continued to be of importance, mainly for imports of fish, hides, timber, corn and linen and exports of salt, iron and woollen cloth. In the twelfth century came the beginning of a flourishing trade with Gascony, particularly in the export of cloth and the import of wine, and by a natural extension connections began to develop with the Iberian peninsula, particularly Castile and Portugal.

It was therefore the trade with the Biscay region and Ireland, with the addition in the early fifteenth century of Icelandic fishing, that formed the basis for the port's prosperity, and this was so greatly to its advantage when trade with north-west Europe became restricted that by 1500 Bristol was unquestionably the second port of Britain after London. It had also started its connection with North America: in 1480 there had been a Bristol attempt to find the 'island of Brazil', and it is possibly Bristol's interest in westward exploration that attracted the Genoese John Cabot to the city. With a patent from Henry VII and some financial backing from Bristolians, he set sail in the *Matthew* in 1497, with his three sons, Sebastian, Lewis and Sanctus, and a crew of eighteen, and discovered something—whether Newfoundland or part of the mainland is not certain. The results of a second voyage with three or four ships in 1498 are even more vague, and his subsequent history is unknown. Sebastian made a further voyage in 1509 to find a North-West Passage and may have penetrated the Hudson Straits before he turned back. This was an attempt which was to be taken up again in 1629 by a Bristol lawyer, Captain Thomas James, who took his ship into Hudson Bay, sank her in shallow water to prevent her being crushed by ice, wintered on the mainland, raised her in the spring and brought her home. The amazing feat is commemorated in the naming of James Bay, but the later exploitation of the discovery was to be the work of the London-based Hudson Bay Company. James wrote a book about the voyage, and it is not unlikely that it was this which inspired the 'ice imagery' in Coleridge's 'Ancient Mariner'.

These Atlantic ventures had a very minor effect on Bristol's commerce, apart from being a useful addition to the fish trade, but they did lead to some involvement with the colonization of America, a cause which was argued energetically by Richard Hakluyt who, from the time he became a canon of Bristol in 1582, was frequently in the city. It seems likely that his influence with the Merchant Venturers, who had received their charter in 1552, led to the voyage in 1603 of the Bristol seaman Captain Martin Pring, whose tomb, adorned with mermaids, can be seen in St Stephen's Church. Pring landed in northern Virginia, the present New England, and was able to stay there long enough to plant corn and to report favourably on his return. The first real Bristol attempt at colonization was in Newfoundland in 1610, but it was not a success. A second colony at Bristol Hope on land bought from the first was only a little more successful and eventually failed. Bristol never, in fact, established a permanent colony, but there were two Bristolians among the Pilgrim Fathers, and in the 1630s and 1640s many Bristolians took up land-grants in New England. Much of the promotion of these enterprises was financed by Sir Ferdinando Gorges of Wraxall, and in 1635 he was appointed Governor of New England but did not take up the appointment. Even more significant was the capture of Jamaica by the Bristolian Admiral Penn and the foundation of Pennsylvania by his Quaker son.

Bristol's American connections and her geographical position made her a major port for emigration, both free and forced, and some ten thousand emigrants passed through between 1654 and 1685—some of them as a result of the intense persecution of Dissenters in the Restoration period, many more by the actions of the city magistrates, who found it much more profitable to transport convicted criminals than to hang them. "Sir! Mr Mayor! You, I mean you, Kidnapper!" shouted Judge Jeffreys, come to Bristol to try rebels, "and that old Justice on the Bench, an old knave; he goes to the tavern, and for a pint of sack he will bind people servants to the Indies. A kidnapping knave! I will have his ears before I go forth to the town."

Meanwhile imports of tobacco and sugar were increasing, and to this was added in the later part of the century a lucrative slave-trade, illegal at first as a monopoly had been granted to the Royal African Company of which few Bristolians were members—Colston was an exception, but then he was operating from London. Later in the eighteenth century the trade was thrown open and Bristol's prosperity increased into what has been called her Golden Age of trade. Commerce with France, Portugal and Spain was still important, as was direct trading with the West Indies and America, where the colonies not only supplied sugar, rum, molasses, tobacco and fish but were large markets for manufactured goods. An important Baltic trade, particularly in timber, was developed. Indeed, the strength of direct trade, coupled with the very great importance of coastal shipping, was such that the rapid decline of Bristol's slave-trade after the 1760s, at a time when it was on the increase in Liverpool, had little effect on the city's prosperity, and its final abolition by law in 1808 was of no significance to the city.

With raw materials coming in at the front door and coal at the back, the eighteenth century was a time of flourishing industry in Bristol with brass- and iron-founding, soap-making, sugar-refining, leather-working, glass-making, wine-bottling, brewing, porcelain-making and shipbuilding. It was at that time that two of the best-known names in Bristol industry first appeared—Fry and Wills, both from Wiltshire families. In 1765 Joseph Fry, a Quaker apothecary with many business interests, bought Walter Churchman's patent for a chocolate-making machine and started the business which in 1777 moved to the newly-built Union Street. It was then a small business but expanded rapidly in the nineteenth century and in 1901 was accommodated in a large new red-brick factory in the Pithay. Designed by Sir George Oatley, its crisp lines and unadorned surfaces made it a remarkably modern building, all the more so as it came from an architect who was a master of the Gothic. The building is now demolished, Fry's having concentrated on the factory which they built in the 1920s on a green-field site by the Avon which they christened Somerdale. Today Fry's is part of the Cadbury–Schweppes combine.

The connection between the Wills family and the tobacco-business began in 1786, when Henry Overton Wills joined the firm of Samuel Watkins at 73 Castle Street. As with Fry's, the business migrated, first in 1789 to Redcliffe Street, then in 1886 to Bedminster, more recently, in 1977, to the southern suburbs at Hartcliffe.

Although Bristol's growth in industry and population in the nineteenth century was considerable, it was outpaced by the booming towns of the Midlands and the North. In particular it rapidly lost trade to Liverpool, a town with a better natural harbour, a more industrial hinterland and a greater freedom from ancient restrictions. It became vital to the economic health of Bristol to improve her docks.

William Champion, who had built a new dock at Hotwells in 1768, proposed a scheme for a floating harbour, but nothing happened until 1801 when a London engineer, William Jessop, was consulted and his plans adopted. The original intention had been that it should be a public venture, but in the event a private Dock Company was formed whose directors consisted of the Mayor and eight members of the Corporation, the Master and eight members of the Society of Merchant Venturers and nine members elected by the major shareholders. Work began in 1804 and was completed in 1809 at a cost of nearly twice the original estimate. A great loop of the Avon was locked off, by-passed by the New Cut and topped-up by the Feeder Canal which allowed barge-traffic to pass upstream to the navigable stretch of the Avon to Bath and so to the Kennet and Avon Canal which was opened in 1810.

Unfortunately, harbour-dues were made very high in an endeavour to recoup the cost of construction, and trade suffered. There were Town Dues, Mayor's Dues, Water Bailiff's Fees and Quay Warden's Fees, there were dues for Wharfage and Towage, and Carriage, and Cranage, and there were dues on ships and foreign goods, and tolls to be paid for use of the Feeder Canal. Often a ship had to pay twice as much as at Liverpool or London, and Bristol manufacturers would in some cases find it cheaper not to use their own port. There was therefore considerable criticism of the Company, and in 1848 it was taken over by the Corporation, who, by reducing the charges and carrying out a programme of improvements, succeeded in promoting a considerable revival in trade. It was however becoming increasingly clear, although not to everyone concerned, that the journey up the twisting tidal river was making access impossible for modern ships and that, in spite of talk of 'dockization' of the whole stretch, the future lay at the river mouth.

Private enterprise took the lead, and in 1877 the first Avonmouth dock was opened. Two years later a rival one, which had twice collapsed, was opened at Portishead, and in 1884 the Corporation, alarmed at the competition with the City docks, bought out both companies. Avonmouth continued to develop, the Royal Edward Dock being opened in 1908 and more than doubled in size by the opening of the Western Arm (Oil Basin) in 1921 and the Eastern Arm extension in 1928. Other developments include a 30,000-ton granary in 1966, a £2½ million Shell and BP re-development in 1972, and a £1 million Paktank liquid-storage installation in 1973.

In 1958 the Port Authority was already interested in development to the south of the Avon and started to acquire land—they eventually held some 2,000 acres. A scheme for a £27 million dock at Portbury was proposed in 1964 but rejected by the Government two years later. A smaller scheme was then proposed and rejected, but finally approval was obtained in 1970 for a West Dock and this was officially opened by the Queen as the 'Royal Portbury Dock' in August 1977. Trapezoidal in shape, it opens through the biggest dock-gates in Britain to an entrance-channel in King Road, where in the past vessels used to lie while waiting for the rising tide which would allow them to reach the City docks.

The development of the West Dock almost immediately sparked off controversy when Bristolians found their interests and sympathies once again at odds with Government opposing. The Japanese car-firm of Toyota wanted to use the dock as their major import-point, but the Government maintained that the final processes of preparing the cars at the port before they left for market constituted manufacture and that the installations therefore required an Industrial Development Certificate. This they would not grant, preferring that Toyota should go to Liverpool. The firm rejected the alternative, and Bristol, in a time of increasing unemployment maintained that it was being robbed of jobs, but Toyota did not come.

Apart from the power-station, opened in 1929, there has not been a great deal of industrial development in the Portishead area, although one firm does have the distinction of making most of Britain's horseshoes. Avonmouth, however, and the rather dismal flatlands of Severnside, is dominated by giant works and warehouses. Trade is mainly in imports, particularly bulk-cargoes of cereals, animal feeding-stuffs, wood and wood pulp, chemicals and fertilizers, petroleum products and tea, coffee and cocoa, and dominating the dockside are the bulky towers of the grain-silos and mills, including the largest animal-food compounding-mill in the world. Imported ores feed the smeltery of Rio Tinto Zinc which produces zinc and sulphuric acid and which worries local inhabitants about possible pollution hazards. The firm started as National Smelting during World War I, expanded to become Imperial Smelting and has since been taken over by RTZ. It has developed the Severnside Trading Estate on its own land, but further north the larger Chittening Estate belongs to the Port of Bristol Authority. Much of it is used for warehousing, but there is some manufacturing, including the making of carbon black by Sevalco (Philblack) Ltd. Rather more visually exciting is the ICI works with its assembly of geometric shapes like some child giant's construction-toy and its tall chimney with a long plume of orange smoke floating like a banner across the sky.

Growth potential in the Portishead and Avonmouth area has been increased by the construction of the M5 and M6, the north-south link being completed, after considerable delay, by the opening in 1974 of the great hump of the M5 bridge over the Avon, and it is with some justification that Bristol calls itself 'the Motorway Port'.

With all this river-mouth development, the death of the old City docks was inevitable, although like most things connected with the history of the port their final demise was the occasion of intense controversy, and it was not until 1971 that the necessary Act was passed and Casson, Conder and Partners were briefed to prepare proposals for the development of the site. Their Study was published the following year and approved in principle by the City Council, but with changes in local government and in planning law it became necessary to produce a District Plan. The brief for this, produced in 1976, makes admiring noises about the Casson offering but suggests that circumstances had changed so quickly that "some of the proposals must be recognized as impracticable". In particular it was considered that the balance must be shifted from office provision towards residence.

The aesthetic potential of this area is so tremendous that it is frightening to think what could be lost by insensitive redevelopment but exhilarating to contemplate the wonderful opportunity that Bristol has to create a new inner-urban townscape of world importance, the latest and most beautiful of its urban villages.

X

THE SOUTHERN HEARTLAND

This long rectangle, stretching some 20 miles from the moors to the trenched Limpley Stoke valley and filling the eight or nine miles from the Mendips to the lower Avon, is full of variety and surprise. Here, in contrast to the north, the streams flow east and west, corrugating the country and making switchbacks of the southbound roads which give glimpses of green fields and hedgerow timber, abandoned railways and canals, old coal-tips and a lakeland of man-made reservoirs. Abercrombie, in his *Plan for Bristol*, called it "Remarkable Country", and there is indeed much to be seen and appreciated. Mostly it is region of grey villages and good farmland, but there is sufficient distinction between east and west to justify a major sub-division roughly (very roughly) along the line of the A38.

What mainly distinguishes the west is the presence of the two mini-Mendips where the carboniferous limestone humps up through younger rocks. The most northerly is the Failand ridge, a well-wooded, pleasant area running from near Clevedon to the Avon Gorge and since the opening of the Clifton Suspension Bridge in 1864 increasingly favoured for expensive housing, well-illustrated in the two villages of Leigh Woods and Abbots Leigh. A 'leigh' was an open space in woodland, and the abbot was from St Augustine's, Bristol—his fishpond may still be seen in the village.

The village of Leigh Woods is a collection of large houses ranging from Victorian Gothic and Italianate through inter-war Various to rather dull post-war brick blocks of luxury flats. The setting is delightful. The red sandstone church of 1893 in rather uninspired Early English is relieved by a pretty wood-shingled tower and bell-turret. Off North Road are the University Botanic Gardens, open in the afternoons, and the nearby woods are National Trust property managed by the Nature Conservancy as the Avon Gorge National Nature

Reserve. They afford pleasant walks and are remarkably uncrowded considering their nearness to Bristol.

Abbots Leigh to the west is a linear village of biggish but unobtrusive houses in a pleasant rural setting. Here is another red sandstone church, Perpendicular but mainly rebuilt in 1847. Up on the main road and about a mile towards Bristol is a rather splendid Greek Revival gateway with giant Ionic columns, built as an entrance to Leigh Court, a Georgian mansion which is now a hospital. The previous Court became famous when in 1651 the Norton family gave shelter to the fugitive future Charles II, and in the village church this is commemorated on a Norton monument. Today the gate leads to Stoke Leigh Woods which belong to the Forestry Commission and are laid out in walks, with two small car-parks and pamphlet-guides on sale. The young, thin, tall deciduous trees give shade and a greenish light. A small look-out gives views over the Avon.

At the foot of the southern slopes of the ridge is a line of villages, the chief being Long Ashton and Wraxall. The former is now fortunately by-passed by the A38 and is a mixture of mainly eighteenth-century and Victorian buildings with newer houses behind. The fine early-Perpendicular church of All Saints' carried the arms of the de Lyon family on the tower, and inside are the tombs of Sir Richard Choke, Lord Chief Justice of England, who bought Ashton Court in 1454, and of the Smyth family, who held it from 1545 until it was bought by Bristol Corporation, who opened it in 1962 as a public park. In the porch are the tombs of the parents of Robert Southey, the poet. One of the best features of the church is a fine medieval rood-screen stretching across the full width. In the village a pretty row of almshouses, founded by Lady Smyth in 1902, bear the Smyth arms, and at the west of the village, in Wildcountry Lane, is the University of Bristol Horticultural Research Station which grew out of the National Fruit and Cider Institute.

Ashton Court, with its 300-foot-long front, has been restored and has a fascinating mixture of styles, half nineteenth-century Gothic and the rest partly fifteenth-century with Elizabethan additions, partly seventeenth-century Classical (the south-west wing, attributed frequently but without evidence to Inigo Jones). The Park, landscaped and treed by Repton, contains 840 acres, and deer have been re-introduced. There are several imposing nineteenth-century gatehouses.

Some of the buildings in Wraxall are along the main road, but the heart of the old village is round the church, which is finely set in a forest of stone and marble tombs and has a tall tower with vigorously sprouting pinnacles. In the churchyard is a small 'Gothic' school and by the gate a schoolhouse, both given by Richard Vaughan in 1823. The school was to be 'for ever' but was later superseded by a new one on the main road. Wraxall Court, nearby, is hidden by trees, but further along the road to Nailsea there is a view of the yellow medieval tower of Birdcombe Court. The astonishing Victorian Gothic of Tyntesfield (1862–4) is unfortunately hidden from view, and all approaches are private.

To the south of the ridge is a lowland with a narrow waist below Ashton Hill. The eastern part, Ashton Vale, is drained to the Avon by the Ashton Brook and followed by the A370; the western broadens rapidly into the flat clay lands of the coastal plain, intersected by rhines which feed into the Land Yeo and the Kenn, and from out of the moors there rises up to about 30 metres a patch of land from older times. This is Nailsea, 'Naegl's Island', where Pennant sandstone overlies the seams of coal which from 1768 to 1873 provided fuel for the making of Nailsea glass. The main product was green bottle-glass, and the better-known coloured fantasies of walking-sticks and other objects were 'friggers' made by workmen and apprentices to 'frig' away their spare time. There are fine examples in the collection at Clevedon Court as well as the remarkable work of the 'Potter Baron' Sir Edmund Elton (1846–1920).

The village of Nailsea has been swollen by post-war building and forms part of Bristol commuter-land. It has two centres, one on the south-west round the old church, the other to the north-east with a church of 1843. The old church, Holy Trinity, restored in 1861, is long and low, with a tall tower, while the new Christchurch has lancet windows and a bell-cote; behind it lies the shopping precinct of 1974 which clipped off the top of the small village green. The precinct is standard 1970s stuff in pale brick but is relieved by trees, flowers and coloured benches. It contains a library with hanging chains which are intended to carry rain from the roof but have an unfortunate habit of spattering passers-by, and for a time there was a rusty collection of boxes for a fountain which was so disliked that in 1977 it was spent to Spain. Another unusual feature, sited in the car-park, is a geodetic structure intended as an Exhibition Hall but at the time of writing occupied by a charity shop. Over the road sits a spreading modern school in light brick and white paint, and keeping an eye on everything is a dark brown police station with a pleasant grove of trees at its side and a telecommunications mast on its roof. All this is embedded in an anonymous matrix of housing estates.

North-west of Nailsea are Tickenham Court and church, both the subject of an interesting book, *The Story of a Manor*, by Denys Forest. The church, unusually dedicated to St Quiricus and St Julietta, child and mother reputed to have been martyred at Tarsus by the Diocletian persecution of AD 304, has a Norman chancel and nave. The Court, a private residence, has a hall of about 1400 and a solar of about 1500.

The carboniferous limestone reappears in a broad plateau which stretches southward from Lulsgate, with Bristol Airport, to Broadfield Down and whose western edge is steep, heavily wooded and deeply trenched by narrow valleys which include the beauty-spots of Brockley and Goblin Combes, similar in form though not in scale to Mendip's Burrington Combe. At its foot it is fringed with a narrow shelf of dolomitic conglomerate which gives a firm foothold above the moors to the A370 and a succession of villages from Flax Bourton to Congresbury.

The village of Flax Bourton ('the settlement by the hill where flax is grown') is on a loop north of the A370. Its church has a Norman doorway and chancel arch and a vigorous Norman carving of St Michael and the Dragon above the doorway. In Post Office Lane is a group of modern (1972) houses unlike anything else in Avon and remarkable, whatever you make of them. A mile to the east, Farleigh Hospital is the old Union Workhouse of 1837–8 in a Classical style.

The original centre of Backwell is also away from the main road, in this case up the hill where there is a Victorian school with modern additions and a pleasant group formed by Court Farm, a rather splendid stone barn and the church whose tower has curiously clumsy decoration. In the porch is a figure of St Andrew and the child, in touching memory of a ten-year-old boy who in 1956 fell from his bicycle on his way from choir-practice and died. Further south along the main road are Brockley, a scattered little village, and Cleeve, whose neo-Norman roadside church of 1840 by Manners, of Bath, has a certain stark attractiveness. Modern Cleeve is further south along the A370, and at this point a minor road which leads eastward to Wrington takes off and shortly passes a chapel and a disused quarry where there is parking. From there Plunder Street leads past the school to a broad path through Goblin Combe, a heavily wooded dry valley almost two miles long, with glimpses of bare limestone cliffs on either side.

The southernmost village, Congresbury (and so pronounced in spite of some attempts to make it 'Coomsbury'), grew up at a crossing-point of yet another Yeo (the Celtic name means 'forked stream') where it leaves the Vale of Wrington in its course westwards over the moors, and it was reached by small sea-going ships as late as 1900; the 1840 tithe-map shows a wharf behind the Ship and Castle Inn. Tradition attributes the founding of the village to St Congar, one of those remarkable Celtic holy men who specialized, with the help of miracles, in inhabiting unsuitable places. One version is that he fled from his father, the King of Cornwall (or, alternatively, Constantinople), arrived at the spot and was persuaded by a dream of a wild boar resting in rushes to set up house there, building himself a chapel of wattle, toughening himself up with a strict routine of small meals, cold baths and hair shirts, and in his spare time draining the marshes. One day he stuck his staff in the ground, where it took root, and today the ancient yew in the churchyard is known as 'St Congar's Walking Stick'. With the growth of the saint's fame, a settlement of 'Cungisberia' grew up, and the Saxon king of Somerset, Ine, granted land for a stone monastery of which, incidentally, no trace has been found. Subsequently, it is said, Congar founded another monastery in Wales, went to Jerusalem, died there and was brought back to Congresbury to be buried. There are suspicious parallels with the story of the Holy Thorn and St David's wattle church at Glastonbury, but that is not sufficient reason to discard completely the idea that Congresbury had some connection with a Celtic holy man.

Certainly the Celts were in the vicinity at the appropriate time, for a mile to the north of this water-place, which suffered severely in the floods of 1968, there is an isolated hill surmounted by an Iron Age fort, one of the many Cadbury camps in the West, which has revealed evidence of immediate post-Roman occupation.

As the village grew up at a river-crossing, the church, school, vicarage, market cross, inn and older houses are grouped near the bridge. Housing has spread along the B3133, and there is a fair amount of quite pleasant post-war development. Broad Street, behind the cross (actually a ball) is a quiet backwater with shops and a bank, and behind that is the large church with its narrow steeple, fine wagon-roof and pleasing wooden screen. The present main entrance to the church is through the north door, but it is worth going into the south porch to see the elaborate inner doorway with its ogee arch. Next to the church on its north-east side is the vicarage, which is partly a plain rectangular Regency building and partly, beyond, a house built about 1470 by the executors of Bishop Bekyngton of Wells. It has a fine two-storeyed gabled porch.

Out on the moor, where St Congar's work was completed under a Drainage Act of 1826, lay Congresbury Station on the Cheddar Valley line opened from Yatton to Cheddar in 1869 and continued in the following year to Wells. Once important for the carriage of Mendip stone, lowland milk and the seasonal traffic of Cheddar strawberries and Sidcot School scholars, it lost its battle with the roads and is now derelict. Another casualty of the transport war was the line from Congresbury to Blagdon, which opened in 1901 following a Light Railway Order of 1898. Intended for commuter and agricultural traffic which did not sufficiently materialize, it was never very profitable except for a short early period when it carried building-materials to build the dam on the Yeo which created Blagdon Lake. Beside that dam the Bristol Waterworks Company built two big red-brick halls in 1905 to house beam-engine pumps. They stopped work in 1955, but the two in the south wing have been restored and may be seen by prior application to the pumping-station, and the visit can include a sight of the trout-hatcheries from which the lake is stocked.

Along the northern side of the richly pastured Vale of

Wrington continues the limestone edge and its conglomerate girdle, again carrying roads and villages—big Wrington, little Redhill and tiny Barley Wood with the house, much altered, in which Hannah More lived after her move from nearby Cowslip Green. That remarkable lady, whose birthplace can be seen in Bristol behind the park in Fishponds, lived from 1745 to 1833 and had a varied and energetic career as blue-stocking, playwright, social reformer, educationalist, pamphleteer and founder of schools and women's clubs in the Mendip parishes. With her four sisters she is buried in Wrington churchyard, and there also, in the church, is a bust of the great seventeenth-century philosopher John Locke (1632–1704) whose birthplace in the village is marked by a plaque. On behalf of the Royal Society Locke once tried to take a barometer down one of the Mendip lead-mines to see what happened to air-pressure below ground, but the miners were highly suspicious of his instrument and refused to let him go down. Wrington, with its appropriately named Broad Street, has quite a small-town air about it, with some nice eighteenth-century houses and a church with an impressive 113-foot tower, built when the manor belonged to Glaston-bury Abbey. It is said that Barry used its proportions in his design of the Victory Tower on the Houses of Parliament; he certainly knew the church, for he designed its reredos in 1836.

Through Redhill, which probably takes its name from the rich colour of the conglomerate soil, the A38, the old Bristol–Exeter road, climbs northward onto the plateau and after a few miles runs beside Bristol Airport, successor to the earlier one opened in 1930 at Whitchurch (ST 4861) which has since been developed for housing and industry although still retaining a good deal of open space with playing-fields and a large Sports Centre which utilizes an old hangar. The Lulsgate field was developed during the war by the Air Ministry but then became derelict and was bought in 1955 by Bristol Corporation who spent £55,000 on it and opened it for com-mercial operation in 1957. There has recently been a good deal of controversy over the future of the airport and it has been argued, and recently supported by the Government, that regionally the main development should be at Cardiff Airport (Rhoose) which has become more accessible with the opening of the Severn Bridge. Proposals in 1979–80 to expand Lulsgate have been strongly supported by business interests who point to the rapid growth in passenger and freight traffic at the airport but opposed by other groups on environmental, social, and financial grounds—costs have been estimated at £5 million and £12 million according to which side is speaking. One particular problem is that extension to the runway would take it over the A38 which would have either to be diverted or taken through a tunnel.

Past the aerodrome the road swoops down into Lulsgate Bottom where it has junctions with roads going westward to Brockley Combe and eastward past a big quarry, a common and a church, to the Chew Valley, and it then climbs over the next ridge to the valley of Collier's Brook and the big Barrow Gurney reservoirs. There a stream valley gives a route westward through the linear village of Barrow Gurney to an interchange with the A370 near the entrance to Barrow Court, once the site of a nunnery and now a fine Jacobean mansion with delightful formal gardens of the nineteenth century. After the war Barrow Court was taken over as an outpost of the Diocesan Teacher Training College of St Matthias at Fishponds, Bristol, which in 1975, with Redland College, became part of Bristol Polytechnic; the future of Barrow Court is at the time of writing uncertain.

Of its history as a nunnery we have some information from the records of fourteenth-century bishops of Bath and Wells, for they found the nuns something of a problem. In June 1315, for example, Bishop Drokensford wrote to the Prioress warning her that she was in danger of excommunication if she did not give up her worldly ways and pay more attention to her duties. Apparently her nuns were going out in ordinary dress, often without leave, and were breaking the rule of silence. Some, too, were sleeping elsewhere than in the dormitory. His letter does not seem to have had much effect, for in the following month he appointed a male administrator, William of Sutton, to try to bring some order into the house.

The next year the Bishop managed to get rid of the worldly Prioress but then made the mistake of appointing an even more secularly-minded lady. Possibly he had no option, for the new appointment, the noble Joan de Gurney, was a relative of the patron of the establishment. In fact her appointment was illegal, as she had not taken her final vows, and that had hastily to be remedied. She was either uncaring or incompetent and in any case given to 'wandering', so in desperation the Bishop ordered the rectors of Chew and Harptree to take a hand. They proved no match for the Prioress, and the Bishop was forced to take the brave step of ordering her dismissal, at which she solved his problem by resigning. Unfortunately things had got so out of hand that the new Prioress was openly disobeyed, and so another letter went out from the Bishop ordering the nuns to behave. They seem to have paid little attention to orders from a mere man, even if he was a bishop, and it must have been with some relief that in 1327 Drokensford handed the problem over to his successor, who promptly appointed yet another prioress.

Things seem to have settled down after that, although some of the nuns still had their little peculiarities. For example, in 1398 the Pope himself was enquiring about Isabella Plyns and Joan Bazen who, complaining about the food, had taken themselves off to another house at Llandaff but were demanding to return to their old quarters—presumably the food at Llandaff was even worse. Again, in 1410, Bishop Bubwith had to deal with yet another prioress who, having retired, had assumed that she was absolved from being a nun at all. No more, however, is heard until 1536 when the house was dissolved, the property being assessed at £29 6s 8½d.

Returning from cloister to countryside, we find to the east of the Barrow reservoirs one of the most noticeable features of the western section, the long line of Dundry Hill, capped with the inferior oolite which provided the fine creamy stone for St Augustine's Abbey, now Bristol Cathedral, and St Mary Redcliffe, and for the splendid pinnacled tower of Dundry church erected by the Merchant Venturers of Bristol in 1484, some say as a beacon for sailors, although it is not easily visible from the channel. Like many hilltop holy places, the church is dedicated to St Michael, the captain of the heavenly host, for in ancient times it was believed that the hills were hollow and their tops in constant danger, especially on Midsummer's Eve, of being breached by the forces of malignant faery who dwelt within. At the far end of the ridge more secular warriors constructed the Iron Age fort of Maes Knoll. 'Maes' could be a corruption of 'Maeres', 'a boundary' (as we have seen, for example, in Marshfield), for here is the western edge of

Wansdyke, a linear bank and ditch which stretches to Bathampton Down and was a frontier line either between the Celts and the invading Saxons or between two Saxon factions.

East and south of Dundry lies a complicated country with a thick scatter of small settlements linked by a maze of minor roads and largely ignored by the major routes. Their lay-out is determined largely by three east-flowing streams, the Chew, the Cam Brook and the Wellow Brook, and the settlements are sited either in the valleys or on the plateaux between.

The Chew (whose curious name is probably connected with chickens or small fowl, although some like to derive it from Tiw, the war god) rises in the Mendips and starts by flowing north until at Chew Magna it turns abruptly eastward, passing through Pensford and Compton Dando before turning once again to the north and joining the Avon at Keynsham. At Chew Magna it is joined by a stream from the west which continues the valley line followed by the B3130 and contains the village of Winford, which was once important for its ochre-works, now closed, and its livestock market which has been moved to a more convenient site by the road to the east of the village and whose old site has been developed for housing.

Chew Stoke is just to the west of the dam which in 1956 created the Chew Valley Lake, which not only caters for the growing water-demands of Bristol but also provides a leisure amenity for fishermen, sailors, bird-watchers and picnickers, and for a few days provided holiday accommodation for a pelican which had managed to escape wing-clipping time at Bristol Zoo and doubtless thought he had flown to a pelican Heaven. The main road through the village reveals little, and to appreciate this pleasant place you need to walk round the back road to the street with its little bridge and pond, and Church Lane where the rectory is an extraordinary Victorian re-modelling of a sixteenth-century house. The church is in red sandstone, Perpendicular, with a striking spirelet to one corner of its tower, a porch with quatrefoil pierced parapet, and much Victorian work inside, including swarms of angels in the arcade. In the eighteenth century the village was famous for the work of the Bilbie family, bell-founders, who had a justified if sometimes immodest pride in their work. Bryan Little, in his *Portrait of Somerset*, quotes an example from a bell at Milborne Port, cast in 1736:

Come Here Friend Knight and Cockey too
Such Work as This You Cannot Do.

Chew Magna to the north was described by Leland,
antiquary to Henry VIII, as a "praty cloathing toun", but its
industrial days are long past, and its large Georgian houses
were built mainly for business and professional people from
Bristol—there is recorded on a gravestone an early commuter
who in 1814 was shot dead at Dundry by a highwayman.
Although still mainly a commuter village, it has retained a
good deal of character. The main street, with one pavement
raised, is pleasant, with buildings in red sandstone or colour-
wash and one or two large Georgian houses, but the most
interesting part is in a loop round the back of the church,
taking in Harford Square and Silver Street, although it is not
helped by a rather dull-looking church hall of 1923. The
churchyard is large and quiet, with an old preaching-cross,
and the church is mainly fifteenth-century with a large, rather
plain, tower. On the south wall, over a window, are the
initials of Thomas Bekyngton, the great building bishop of
Bath and Wells (1443–56), and inside are a number of interesting tombs which include a wooden effigy of knight in
fourteenth-century armour, cross-legged in a most uncomfortable position and labelled quite falsely 'Sir John de
Hauteville'. The origin and date of the figure are unknown,
but it was put there by a nineteenth-century rector of Weston-
in-Gordano who claimed descent from the Hautevilles, who
in the thirteenth century were Lords of the Manor of nearby
Norton Malreward. One of them, Sir John, was renowned for
his great strength, and legend has it not only that Maes Knoll
was formed by scrapings from his spade but that the big stone
near Stanton Drew was flung there by him, a distance of about
a mile; it is called 'Hauteville's Quoit'. By the entrance to the
churchyard is the restored and adapted church hall of about
1510 with a fine ogee gable over the entrance and the arms of
the St Loe family. Inside is an impressive timber roof. The
fifteenth-century Tun Bridge crosses the Chew on the road to
the south, and nearby is the water-wheel of the old Chew Mill.

'Stanton' in Stanton Drew is "the place of the stones", and
'Drew' comes from the family who held the manor in the
thirteenth century. Neither the name nor the stones has any-

thing to do with Druids, and the pub name, 'The Druids' Arms' is pure fancy. There are three circles of stones, a Cove (beside the pub), an Avenue down to the Chew and Hauteville's Quoit. The Great and North-eastern Circles and their Avenue share a field with cows and are under the care of the Department of the Environment (pay at the farmhouse). They are not very impressive, and little is known about them, but they are probably Neolithic and erected some time between 2000 and 1400 BC. More attractive are the legends: the Cove and Circles are, they say, a wedding-party petrified as a punishment for dancing on Sunday; the Cove is the parson, bride and bridegroom, the large circle the dancers, and the small circle the musicians. Hauteville's Quoit we already know about— there is no suggestion that he was throwing at the musicians.

The village is pleasant, with some good eighteenth-century houses, including the Court, beyond which a fifteenth-century two-arched bridge leads towards the thatched hexagonal turnpike-house. Church Farm shows traces of its medieval origin, but the church itself was extensively re-modelled in 1889. Upper Stanton Drew is not remarkable; Stanton Wick has a well-known pub-restaurant, and half a mile to the west of it is the tip from the Bromley Colliery which operated from 1860 to 1957.

A more impressive pit can be seen from the A37 south of Pensford where the first pit was sunk in 1909 and work continued until 1958, and although many of the mine buildings have been removed or put to other use, a certain amount remains to be seen. This and the other relics of the Somerset Coalfield are carefully recorded in *The History of the Somerset Coalfield* by Down and Warrington. Pensford is a rather confusing village as it is split by the New Road (present A37), a creation of the Bristol Turnpike Trust, and by the division of the Chew into a number of mill-channels, so that there are several little bridges, and the church, Victorian except for its tower and now abandoned, is almost islanded. The old bridge is mainly medieval with two pointed and one round arch and stood firm in 1968 when the floods washed away the nineteenth-century turnpike bridge, which was then replaced by another of severe and unattractive practicality. The flood-level, some seven feet above the street, is marked in two places.

East of the A37 the old road forms the High Street, which has some interesting houses and includes the eighteenth-century 'George and Dragon' with a coach-entrance. Nearby is the old village lock-up, its hemispherical roof surmounted by a stone ball. Most buildings are in Pennant, with a certain amount of lias and red sandstone, and there is not a great deal of modern development. The most outstanding feature of the village is the splendid railway-viaduct, now unused, which was built in 1873 to carry the line from Bristol to Radstock.

Eastward from Pensford the Chew valley, with increasing woodland, carries on past Publow with its fine Perpendicular church to Compton Dando, where the church has datestones of 1753, 1793 and 1905 but is mostly Victorian. It has, how-ever, one remarkable feature: built into the north-east buttress of the chancel is a block of stone with a figure carved on each of two sides—it matches two other stones found under Bath which were the corner-blocks of the Roman altar of Sul-Minerva and was probably carted as building-material to Compton, which belonged to Bath Priory. Moreover, 'Dando' is a corruption of 'd'Alno', and in 1261 the Prior of Bath was one Walter de Anno. The figures are much weathered, but the draped one, seated with lyre, is probably Apollo, and the nude man with a club could possibly be Hercules.

The Chew valley forms the bottom of one of the east-west corrugations, and the next south is the Cam valley with a string of villages from Hinton Blewett, with its pleasant triangular green called Forby and a fifteenth-century church with a striking lead roof, to Midford, where the castle is a piece of late-eighteenth-century Gothicry best seen from Midford Hill. Small and three-storeyed, its trefoil plan is said to commemorate, as an ace of clubs, its owner's gambling successes.

The A37 crossed the stream at Temple Cloud which derives its name from 'clud', a hill, and the fact that it once belonged to the Order of Knights Templar. This small place has a massive and fanciful police station and courthouse of 1857 next to a church, started in 1924, with an open bell-tower and narrow round-headed windows. Temple Cloud grew at the expense of Cameley to the west, which once had coal- and iron-mines, a brickworks and quarries, but when they closed in the nineteenth century, it became depopulated, and probably because of its relative isolation it lost out to Temple Cloud and nearby Clutton, another village with a 'clud' element in its name. Clutton also had the advantage of a railway, and the central feature of the village is not the church, which is peripheral, but the Railway Hotel, part eighteenth-century and part Victorian, with a fine Puffing Billy sign. The village became the centre of the Clutton Poor Law District, and the big workhouse, Cranbrook House, is about a mile away. This has retained its severe Classical façade but has been completely rebuilt behind to form a row of modern houses—an interesting and successful design.

The railway crossed the river at Hallatrow ('holy tree') where it was later joined by a line built along the course of the old Coal Canal, and although both lines are now dead, the Railway Hotel still lives. Of the other Cam crossing-places the most notable are Camerton and Combe Hay. Camerton is situated above the valley, which contains the remains of the canal and railway and the partly wooded tip of the colliery which operated until 1950. From 1800 to 1839 the rector of Camerton was the unhappy John Skinner, a difficult and conscientious man who had a terrible time with his children, his parishioners, the Lady of the Manor, the Noncomformists, the Catholics, the farmers, the miners and the mine-owners; in anguish he wrote that he would bear testimony that Camerton folk were as bad as the inhabitants of Sodom and Gomorrah. In the end he could bear it no longer, and in the wood by his house he took his own life. The ninety-eight volumes of his Journal he left to the British Museum but insisted that nothing should be extracted for fifty years in case anyone should be offended by what he had written. It is difficult not to believe that something went terribly wrong with a man who was basically good and considerate. He was also an ardent archaeologist, from whom no mound was safe, and although he left a lot of useful information, he also destroyed much evidence and propounded some theories which were without foundation.

At the bottom of Skinner's Hill, belatedly commemorating the parson, a signpost points down a lane to the church, which is mainly dull Perpendicular with a chancel and south aisle of 1891 and the pleasant Carew Chapel of 1640. The Court, visible from the field behind the church, was built in 1835 in a

Classical style. To the south-west of the village, around ST689564, on the Fosse Way, an important Romano–British site has been excavated, although there is nothing to see there now. (W. J. Wedlake published a very full report in 1958). It was Skinner who first investigated and wrote about the Roman site, but he unfortunately fixed on the idea that this, not Colchester, was Camulodunum. The history of the site, which was occupied for over four hundred years, is compli-cated, but certainly here by the great Roman highway were streets and houses, iron-working and pewter-making. Before this were Bronze Age burial-mounds and Iron Age huts, and after, a short distance away, a Saxon cemetery of the sixth and seventh centuries.

Combe Hay is tiny but has a splendid setting with woods on the north-facing valley side. The little church stands next to the Manor, a beautiful eighteenth–century house, part 1730 Palladian, part 1770 Adamesque. On the north side of the road 'The Wheatsheaf' is well-known for good pub-food, and nearby, north of the railway cutting, a very minor road takes you past the remains of the Somerset Coal Canal and a flight of locks in Bull Nose Valley.

The Surveyor to the Coal Canal was William Smith (1769–1839), widely and variously known as 'Fossil Smith', 'Strata Smith' and 'Father of English Geology', for he was the first to work out the sequence of geological strata by the identification of particular groups of fossils, a break-through in geological thinking which required both a deep knowledge of the subject and an original and powerful imagination. He lived for a time at Tucking Mill, near Monkton Combe, but later moved to Pulteney Street in Bath, and it was there, at the house of a friend, that he wrote down his table of strata. His original manuscript concludes with the words "This table of strata, dictated by myself, is in the hand-writing of the Rev. Benjamin Richardson at the house of Rev. Joseph Townsend, Pulteney Street, Bath, 1799."

The Coal Canal, built under an Act of 1794, entered the Kennet and Avon Canal near the Dundas Aqueduct, where the small basin can still be seen although the entrance-lock is hidden in an adjacent private garden. From there it ran back along the north side of the Midford Brook and the Cam to serve the collieries around Timsbury, Paulton and High

Littleton. This involved a drop of 130 feet, and it was decided to deal with it in a single descent at Combe Hay. The first attempt was to build a caisson-lock of which plans are given in Billingsley's contemporary *Agriculture of Somerset*. In this ingenious device of Robert Weldon's, the barge was floated into a large box which was then lowered down a water-filled masonry shaft. It worked for a short time and was then abandoned, as it could not be kept watertight. Next an inclined plane was tried, but that too was unsatisfactory, and the final solution was to make a flight of twenty-two locks, slow but reliable, round the little valley called 'The Bull's Nose'. This lies behind the old railway arch at ST 745604, and the remains of the narrow locks can still be seen. The scar left by the caisson is much more difficult to identify but is possibly in Engine Wood (ST 74605).

The Coal Canal was for a long time a financial success, but by the end of the nineteenth century it had outlived its usefulness. It was closed and much of its course incorporated in the GWR branch-line from Limpley Stoke to Hallatrow which opened in 1910. And now, like the Cheddar Valley, the Bristol–Radstock, the Wrington Vale, the Yatton–Clevedon, the Weston–Portishead Light, the much-mourned old Somerset and Dorset (the old Slow and Dirty) and all those rural railways which in the nineteenth century puffed into the lives of country folk, widening their horizons and galvanizing their economy, the line is dead, dead, dead, under a living shroud of brambles and young trees and wild flowers.

The Somerset and Dorset line used the next valley, the Wellow Brook. It was born of a canal venture from Glastonbury to Highbridge which sold out to the Bristol and Exeter and in 1854 became the Somerset Central. The company then pushed eastwards and met the Dorset Central with which it amalgamated in 1862 to form the S & D. Twelve years later the S & D had climbed over Mendip to Radstock, followed the Mellow valley to Midford, tunnelled under Combe Down and arrived at Queen Square Station, later named Green Park and now disgracefully decaying, which had been built by the Midland in 1869. The Midland then bought the S & D, and soon trains were running from Birmingham to Bournemouth and continued until closure in 1966.

The S & D from Radstock to Midford followed the towing-path of a branch of the Coal Canal, which never operated, although a tunnel, which still exists, was dug for it under the village of Wellow. At the Bath road entrance to Radstock, long bedevilled by a double level-crossing, one for the GWR and the other for the S & D, the line of the old tramway remains as a footpath crossing the pedestrian subway.

It is in the region of Norton–Radstock (a name dreamed up when Midsomer Norton and Radstock were combined in one District Council) that the mining past is most clearly evident, for it was the latest to develop, the first pit at Radstock being sunk in 1763, the deepest worked and the last to close— Camerton was in operation until the 1950s, and the last pit to close in Somerset was at Kilmersdon in 1974. Elsewhere the remains are scanty, hard to find, swallowed up by the trees and hedges and pastures and cornland of a rural landscape. Near Pensford the tip is just another hill; at Twerton another has been made into a playing-field. Opposite the Globe Inn at Newton St Loe the fields by the railway still turn black at the autumn ploughing, but of the eighteenth-century coal-works, which the Bath architect John Wood said would have been an object of admiration if they had been in Greece, nothing remains. Farrington Gurney has its 'Miners' Arms', Pensford its Miners' Institute', there are Coalpit Lanes and Engine Woods, and Colliers Fields and Paths, and many a small relic known only to the older villagers, but it is now difficult to realize that at the beginning of this century the coalfield was producing over a million tons a year and employing over six thousand people.

The rapid demise of the industry was not anticipated. One report at the beginning of this century forecast a life of 2,858 years, and in spite of drastic decline after the First World War, encouraging forecasts were again being made after the Second when a programme of modernization was introduced. Indeed, the Coal Board went so far as to encourage northern miners to settle in the Radstock area, where one can still be surprised by a Durham accent. It is, however, remarkable that it survived so long, for the seams are thin, tilted and made discontinuous by faulting. The coal itself is not of the highest quality and was generally used for household purposes, although in the nineteenth century a good deal was used for firing steam-engines and some was made into coke for the malting industry. In the last stages practically the whole of its output was crushed and fed as fuel to the Portishead power-stations.

Industry, never strongly developed on the coalfield, is now mainly concentrated in the Norton–Radstock–Paulton area, where products include flexible packaging, shoes, stationery, prefabricated buildings, animal-feed, metal products and books and colour-printing. Here and there in the region the traveller may be surprised by some small works tucked away in a valley, but in general post-war industrial development has not proceeded at the same pace as in the north-east Bristol fringes, nor have the villages, although predominantly occupied by commuters, been swamped by a flood of new housing.

At the northern entry to Radstock two large pubs, 'The Waldegrave Arms' and 'The Bell' (1880) stand guard over the now defunct level-crossings, and beside The 'The Bell' is a pleasant market building with a pretty clock-tower. Beyond is a small modern shopping centre, and up the hill an Italianate range put up for the Co-op in 1868. Little terraces in a rather staring white lias line the road towards Writhlington, and most of the modern development is along the Frome road. Writhlington itself is on the plateau top but also has a steep descent to the Wellow Brook and the coal-tips. Near the bottom the church (1874) is hemmed by trees and is now closed, as is the colliery whose buildings stand sadly derelict with every window smashed. At Clandown, which is vir-tually an extension of Radstock, there is an interesting bipartate lay-out. On the plateau-top, by the common, are a few rows of nineteenth-century houses, a church of 1840 with tower and bellcote, and the remains of colliery with large tree-clad tips; mining stopped in 1929, and the site is now occupied by a firm making concrete blocks for which all the materials have to be brought long distances by lorry. The head and middle of the valley are occupied by new housing, and in the lower part are more nineteenth-century terraces, such as Old Pit Terrace, a chapel and small industries, including aluminium- and zinc-works on the site of Middle Pit (c1800–1933), where there are several colliery remains, including a tall brick chimney of 1905. The metal-works also occupy the Old Gas Works which were by Middle Pit.

Just west of Radstock the Wellow Brook is joined by the little Somer and here is Midsomer Norton, although it seems that it takes its name neither from the stream nor, as Wesley suggested, because the roads were so bad that it could be reached only in midsummer, but because its church is dedicated to St John the Baptist, whose festival is on Midsummer Day. The Somer flows down one side of the main street and tends to cause flooding. It is neatly canalized, but too many people seem to regard it as a waste-paper basket. The church tower was rebuilt in the time of Charles II and carries his statue in a niche, but the rest is Victorian except for the later chancel (1924) and Lady Chapel (1936). On the western edge of the churchyard a gravestone records the death of twelve miners killed at Wellsway Coal Works in 1839; it was renewed in 1965 by 'the Somerset Miners'. The miners had fallen to their deaths as they were being lowered down the shaft. "The rope," says the inscription, "was generally supposed to have been maliciously cut."

Opposite the church the red sandstone tithe barn has been converted into a Roman Catholic church, which has a delightful interior but is rather spoiled outside by the metal boxes and tubes of the heating-system. In the main street is a big Gothic-type Methodist church of 1859. The old Town Hall is a large Italianate Victorian building with a balcony overlooking a tiny square called 'the Island'. It was built as a Market Hall and was bought by the Midsomer Norton Sanitary Board in 1873, who then found to their consternation that the Local Government Board in Whitehall had turned down their application for a loan of £1,250 for the purchase. They asked Whitehall if this refusal would absolve them from their contract to buy the place, but the Board refused to give an opinion, and they were in fact helped out by one of their own members, agreeing to repay him when funds were stronger. The Urban District Council which followed the Sanitary Board established itself in what are still District Offices in what is possibly the best building in the place, a plain early-eighteenth-century house which still proudly carries the old UDC title in wrought ironwork over the gateway. Along the ridge to the south of the heart of the town is a line of schools, Victorian building and factories, and all around are the remains of collieries and coal-tips, including the Old Mills

Colliery on the A362 which is now used for a large cash-and-carry store.

At the north-west tip of this southern industrial triangle lies Paulton, dominated by the large Purnell printing-works. Previously a mining town, it consists mainly of tidy Victorian terraces with a gloomy parish church of 1839 next door to a large one-time parochial school, unhappily decaying on a prime central site. As in all the mining areas, Nonconformity was strong, and there is a large and showy medieval-style Methodist church of 1894 next door to a Wesleyan school of 1843, now the public library, and further up the hill is a Baptist chapel of 1721 rebuilt in 1897 in an extraordinary mixture of Gothic and Classical styles.

Just as Paulton is situated on a watershed, or interfluve, between the Cam and Wellow brooks, so another village, Timsbury (the wooded or timber place), is on higher ground between the Cam and the shallower valley of the Newton Brook. The village has a skein of streets with no real focal-point. High Street, short and narrow, starts opposite the church, which is a rather dull Gothic effort of 1826–32 with fancier west end added in 1852 to designs by Sir George Gilbert Scott, the architect of the Albert Memorial. There are some Georgian houses, but most of the buildings are of the nineteenth century, and there is also a great deal of post-war all-sorts which infills and fringes the old mining and agricultural village. North of Timsbury the A39 crosses the brook at Farmborough where the stream flows down one side of the Street, and the houses are reached by little bridges. The Street contains the Manor House, dated 1667, with a big gabled porch, mullioned windows with dripstones, relieving arches in its lias walls. Once again there is much post-war housing.

North of Farmborough the main road leads to Marksbury, and from both villages minor roads connect eastwards to the brook at Priston Mill. Marksbury has a church by the main road which is noticeable mainly for its four pyramid pinnacles on the tower, each with a windvane, but the old part of the village is on a loop to the west and has a small green overlooked by a house dated 1668. Priston Mill has gained a reputation from the sale of stone-ground flour, and the working pitch-back wheel can be seen. Opening times are a bit complicated, but the mill and shop can usually be visited on weekdays from 2.15 to 5 p.m. Priston village itself is hidden in a tributary valley and has a church with a Norman nave (much restored) and a centre tower of 1751. Over the porch a sixteenth-century memorial starts with the exhortation "Priston repent . . .".

The small stream of the Newton Brook then wanders on to the outskirts of Bath where, set in a tributary valley, is Englishcombe with the scanty remains of the earthworks of a motte-and-bailey castle facing the parish church across a narrow valley. The church has interesting features, particularly the Norman blank arcading on the wall of the north aisle. In the field behind the church is a well-preserved section of the Wansdyke.

Englishcombe, like most of the villages of this southern quarter, or at least their older parts, is ignored by the main roads and sits in an older web of local communications which pre-dated the turnpiking of the through-ways in the eighteenth century which determined the main lines of the flow of motor-traffic of today. There were four Trusts involved—the Bristol (1727–1867), Bath (1707–1878), West Harptree (1793–1876) and Warminster and Frome (1752–1879), better known as 'the Black Dog' after the inn where its Trustees customarily met.

The Bristol Trust maintained the present main Bristol–Wells road, the A37, as far as Farrington Gurney, until 1778–9 when the Bath Trust took over the last section from White Cross (ST 632569) where the turnpike house still stands, although now a private house. Significant changes in line were made at Pensford, as we have seen. A second route managed by the Trust is now a minor road which runs over the top of Dundry down to the Chew Valley and through Chew Stoke on the West Harptree and the Mendips.

Bath Turnpike Trust was concerned with two major roads to the south, the present A39 through Marksbury to White Cross and the A367 to Radstock. The latter follows Fosse Way, but a number of deviations were made from the old Roman marching-line in order to ease the gradients for coaches. On either side of Dunkerton, for example, an easier route over the Cam valley leaves the Roman road as a track past Fosse Farm, and several changes were also made in the approach to Radstock. Although 'Radstock' means 'the place on the (Roman) road', the Fosse Way in keeping a straight line passed to the west of the settlement and in so doing had to traverse the very steep-sided valley of a tributary of the Wellow Brook, a valley into which is crammed the mainly nineteenth-century coal-mining village of Clandown. At first the new Bath road left the Fosse and followed an easier route directly south to Radstock, but it still had to rise over Round Hill before descending into the Wellow valley, and so the Trust altered the line to that of the present A367 by sweeping it round the western edge of the hill.

A further proposal for a major deviation from the Fosse which would have by-passed the present-day village of Peasedown St John was not carried out. If it had been, the village might never have existed, for in 1817 there were no houses there but only the Red Post Inn, which still stands today, an imposing building near a toll-house and one of the cast-iron parish-boundary-markers set up by the Trust. The toll-house was constructed, as was usual, to give views both up and down the road. The road made Peasedown, both in the nineteenth century and in its post-war expansion. 'Pease-down' was originally the name of a local field (where peas grew), and the 'St John' was tacked on after a separate parish was created in 1800.

The modern traveller does not perhaps sufficiently appreciate the debt he owes to the work of the nineteenth-century Trusts, and few motorists who drive along the A36 road to Warminster as it sweeps out of Bath along the side of the Avon valley realize that before this new line was engineered by the Black Dog Trust all traffic had to climb to Claverton Down up steep and winding Brassknocker Hill. Similarly, at the western exit from Bath, the broad Newbridge road was created by MacAdam for the Bath Trust in 1825.

Crowds of holidaymakers now follow the A368 to Weston-super-Mare, a road which was piked by the West Harptree Trust from Marksbury through Harptree and Burrington to join the Bristol Trust's road, the present A38, at what was then known as Fore Cross and now as Churchill Gate. The junction is now marked by traffic-lights, and the imposing old toll-house has been pulled down. Here the Bristol road did not originally take the present line past

Dolebury but detoured west to climb over the hill by Dinghurst Camp and descended the other side by what is now a track down to the Star Inn.

The Harptree Trust also operated a branch which, according to their return to the Clerk of the Peace in 1820, ran two miles from Stowey to Chew Magna. This fits a minor road from Sutton Farm (ST 597636) direct to Chew Magna, but later evidence indicates that they also operated the road along the Chew valley (B3130) and were responsible for the attractive and distinctive polygonal thatched toll-house at Stanton Drew. None of this Trust's activities seems, however, in spite of the coal-trade from the Bishop Sutton area, to have brought much wealth to the sixty trustees. The 1820 return gives an average annual income for the previous three years of only £401 8s 5d at a time when the Bristol Trust was making £21,766 and the Bath £11,870. Even the Black Dog, with a smaller mileage, was getting an average of over £3,000 a year.

The Trusts died a lingering death after the railways took away most of their income, and road maintenance reverted to the unwilling parishes, which in 1862 were grouped in Highway Districts, but these, through lack of funds, interest and expertise, were often inefficient, and at the end of the century their responsibilities were transferred to the newly-formed County and District Councils. It was not until 1936 that the Ministry of Transport, founded in 1919, became responsible for trunk-roads. It is these roads, however, which have saved the villages from depopulation by making them accessible by car from the major centres of employment—an interesting reversal of the condition in the eighteenth century when agriculturists were complaining that the new roads were making it too easy for people to go and live in the city. It remains to be seen what the effect of rising transport costs will be.

The activities within the southern heartland, both east and west, have, however, remained predominantly agricultural, depending on mixed farming with a strong emphasis on dairying. The balance between corn and animal husbandry has varied throughout history—sheep, for example, were more important until the advent of rapid rail-transport and an improved knowledge of bacteriology widened the market for milk—it was not for nothing that the GWR was nicknamed 'the Milky Way'. In recent years there has been something of a move towards beef-farming, and there has also been a considerable increase in poultry-keeping with the development of the battery hen. There has, however, been a considerable decline in the number of orchards as cider production moved from farm to factory, and there are now only a few places where locally produced 'scrumpy' can be had.

Generally speaking, the region was enclosed at an early date and is today a land of well-established hedges and trees, which still give a well-wooded look to the general view in spite of the recent ravages of Dutch elm disease—although it has been estimated that two thirds of the hedgerow timber is elm and ninety-five per cent of this is sick. On the whole, grain tends to be grown on the brown soils of the lias plateaux, and grass on the stickier red soils of the Keuper marl exposed in the valleys. With modern road transport, many of local markets have closed, and livestock marketing is now concentrated at the new Avon market outside Winsley. Important agricultural research establishments of Bristol University are for horticulture at Long Ashton and veterinary work at Lower Langford.

In accounts of the history of the nation, whether social or political, this quiet, moderately prosperous hill-and-valley country of the Southern Heartland is unlikely to get a mention. There is a Neolithic long barrow worth visiting at Stoney Littleton, and there are late Neolithic stone circles at Stanton Drew, which, however, lack the dramatic setting of Stonehenge and Avebury. There are Iron Age forts at Congresbury and Maes Knoll, the Roman Fosseway and traces of the Wansdyke, although it lacks the majesty of the Wiltshire counterpart making its way across the chalk hills. There are no great houses or castles or huge feats of modern engineering; it is not carved up by motorways or smothered in factories and supermarkets and tower blocks. It has no self-consciously pretty villages swamped by hordes of camera-clicking, ice-cream licking, car-parking tourists. It is a good place to live in.

It does have the modest remains of a priory, near Hinton Charterhouse by the A36, open from 2 p.m. to 6 p.m. on Wednesdays and Saturdays from April to October. It was the second Carthusian monastery to be established in England, the first being at Witham Friary in Somerset, and it was established in 1232 by Ela, Countess of Salisbury, widow of William Longespée (Longsword) on the same day as she founded a house of Austin nuns at Lacock in Wiltshire. There is a link with Thornbury in that a Hinton monk, Nicholas Hopkins, the 'devil monk' of Shakespeare's *Henry VIII*, was spiritual adviser to the Duke of Buckingham, so that when the Duke was arraigned for treason, Hopkins was imprisoned and the priory searched for correspondence. Buckingham was executed, and Hopkins died later, allegedly of a broken heart.

The priory just escaped the suppression of "lytell Abbeys and Pryoryes" in 1536 as its income was £48 over the £200 minimum, but its affairs were put into the hands of a lay steward, Sir Walter Hungerford. In January 1539 Commissioners Tregonwell and Petre arrived to accept surrender but found Prior Horde difficult to persuade, for he said that unless the King took his house "so it procedyd nott of his [the Prior's] voluntary surrender", he would not give it up. The Commissioners let him sleep on it, but in the morning they found him "of the same mind as of yesternyght or rather more Styff in the same". He continued to be Styff, and when his brother wrote to him from London urging him to give in, he replied tartly: "I marvelle gretly that ye thynk soo; but rather that ye wolde have thought us lyghte and hastye in gevyng upe that thynge which is not ours to give but dedicate to Allmyghte God for service to be done to hys honoure continuallye with other many good dedds of charyte which dayle be done in thys howse to our Christen neybors." In view of this, it would be interesting to know that persuasion caused the Prior and his sixteen monks to sign a deed of surrender in March. He got quite a large annuity of £44 a year and a cash gift of £11, while the monks were paid pensions of £6 13s 4d a year. Part of the buildings were sold to Sir Walter Hungerford, who complained that Sir Thomas Arundell, sent to survey the property, had "sold and carried away" quite a lot of the church and that the back door of the Prior's cell had been taken off and the documents of the house taken.

This is one local example of what, over the whole country, amounted to a massive nationalization and subsequent selling-off of monastic property, but there was another transference of land to the Crown in this region which had a different source and which explains why the Prince of Wales's feathers are emblazoned on cottages in Englishcombe and Farrington Gurney and why the iron gates at Newton Park bear the arms of Cornwall: the link is that the Prince of Wales is also Duke of Cornwall, and the story starts with the Gournay family whose lands included Midsomer Norton, Farrington Gurney, West Harptree and Englishcombe. During the reign of Henry III, Eva de Gournay, half-sister and heir to Maurice de Berkeley, also known as 'de Gaunt', married Thomas Fitz-John of East Harptree, who adopted the Gournay name. Their son Robert was co-founder in 1220 of Gaunt's Hospital in Bristol whose church is now the Lord Mayor's Chapel.

Robert's grandson, Sir Thomas de Gournay, had the bad judgement to side with Edward II's rebel wife, the handsome Isabella, 'she-wolf of France', and her lover Lord Mortimer, and was responsible for, or at least did not attempt to prevent, the murder of the King at Berkeley Castle. As a result, when Edward's son was old enough seize power, imprison Isabella and execute Mortimer, he also confiscated the Gournay lands. Sir Thomas, who had fled abroad, was recaptured but died on the way back to England, which was probably just as well for him. On the petition of Joan, his widow, the estates were restored and continued in the family until 1405, when Sir Matthew de Gournay, a famous fighter in the Hundred Years War, died at the great age of ninety-six and the lands were once again taken by the Crown and became part of the Duchy of Cornwall. When Newton Park, the property of Lord Temple, came on the market in 1940, it was bought by the Duchy, whose Englishcombe lands were on its border, and leased to Bath to be used as a teacher-training college—which explains why the College was opened by the Queen and its new Students' Union building by Prince Charles.

XI

THE MENDIP FRINGE AND WINSCOMBE VALE

For about a quarter of its length, between East Harptree and Sandford, the southern boundary of Avon follows the northern edge of Mendip and defines the edge of a ribbon region of limestone slope and conglomerate shelf similar to the one round Broadfield Down and with the same pattern of villages strung along a main road, in this case the A368. At Sandford, however, the boundary abandons the fringe and bends away to the southern Mendip edge, where it follows the hilltops as far as the Loxton gap. Here it picks up the River Axe and accompanies its windings to the sea by Brean Down.

The fringe region, abandoned by the boundary, continues westward and curls round the western edge of Mendip back along the south face as far as Loxton. Thus Western Mendip between the south and north fringes forms a separate sub-region centred on the valley of the Lox, or Winscombe Vale, and this will be considered separately towards the end of the chapter.

Central Mendip is an upfold or anticline of carboniferous limestone which has been eroded to form a plateau-top where in the highest part, Blackdown in Somerset, the underlying Old Red Sandstone has been exposed. The axis of the fold is roughly east-west, and the northern edge is therefore a steep slope formed by the downward-dipping limestone which disappears under the Wrington Vale and re-surfaces in Broadfield Down. Because of the slope there is little farming and a good deal of woodland, and access to the top is limited to a few minor roads. Where these minor roads join the main east-west route, villages have developed.

The most easterly of these is East Harptree, whose three parallel streets rise up the hill from the Jubilee Clock of 1897 ("Time Flies, Don't Delay") with the eastern one, Water Street, containing a small stream. In Church Lane the south-west corner of the village has a nice group of inn, farmhouse with a sundial ("*Sic Transit Gloria Mundi*") and church, whose porch contains a large monument of 1568 which portrays Sir John Newton and his twenty children. His wife Margaret is not shown—not, one hopes, and early example of male chauvinism. At the west end of the church are iron bars for the shutters which protected the windows when a ball-game similar to Fives was played against the tower. Inside is much Jacobean panelling and a display of part of the Harptree Hoard of Roman coins which were in a pewter pot dug up in 1887.

A track through the woods from the south-west corner of the village leads to the site of Richmont Castle, an adulterine (unlicensed) castle built by the de Gournays. It was captured by Stephen in the civil war of 1138–53 and was probably dismantled by order of Henry II, although at the time of Leland (*c*1540) part of the keep was still standing, and later in the sixteenth century a good deal of masonry was taken by Sir John Newton to build Eastwood House (ST 576553). Only a few fragments of a wall-base now remain, and the neighbouring aqueduct for the modern waterworks is more impressive. At the top of the hill is the solitary chimney of the lead-works which operated from 1867–76. The hill is Smitham Hill—'smitham' or 'smethum' was the name for small ore.

West Harptree, centred on the A368 which forms the broad main street, is built mainly of reddish dolomitic conglomerate, as are most of the villages of the Mendip fringe except where, more rarely, the grey carboniferous limestone is used. Most of the church is a rebuilding of 1865, but it has a Norman tower with a much later spire and memorial clock. Architecturally, the most notable features of the village are Tilley Manor and Gournay Court which face each other across the main road to the west of the church. The Manor is seventeenth-century with an eighteenth-century façade of almost Baroque fancy, while the Court retains its early-seventeenth-century front with gables and two-storeyed porch. To the north lies the Chew Valley Lake and under it the remains of a Romano–British settlement excavated in 1953; to the north-west, about a mile along the road to Chew Stoke, a track behind the Blue Bowl Inn marks the line of a Roman road which also disappears beneath the water.

The Roman road, which probably served the lead-mines at Charterhouse on Mendip top, comes down past Compton

Martin, named after its site, 'the place in the valley', and from the ownership of the manor in the time of Henry I by the family of Martin de Tours. The valley contains the headwaters of the Congresbury Yeo which feeds the village pond before entering Blagdon Lake. A major feature of the village is the church, which has an impressive interior with a good deal of Norman work, including a spirally fluted column and a clerestory which was preserved in the fifteenth-century Perpendicular rebuilding. The chancel is also Norman except for the east window, which was inserted in 1902, and the fifteenth-century attempt to remodel the entrance, which was abandoned as dangerous—the pillar on the south side leans outwards. There is a wall-tomb in the north aisle with a painted effigy of Thomas de Morton (c1290) whose hamlet of Horton was yet another sacrifice to the lake, and on the wall is a Russian ikon and a pleasant fourteenth-century Flemish carving of St Joseph taking the young Jesus for a walk. Outside, a door high up in the north wall of the chancel once led to a pigeon-loft.

Oddly-named Ubley was probably just 'Ubba's lea', or clearing, and its pleasant nucleus of red sandstone church and houses round a village across (re-erected in 1901), together with some new rather Mediterranean-looking housing, lies to the north of the main road, as do the two parallel valleys which make up much of bigger Blagdon, the village by the 'Bleak hill'. Blagdon church is worth mentioning, and if this section seems to be mainly a parade of churches, it is because firstly the buildings are of intrinsic interest and secondly they are usually the only ones available for public inspection.

Blagdon church has a very fine Perpendicular tower, 116 feet high, but most of the body was rebuilt in 1907–9 to designs by Sir Frank Wills, the architect member of the tobacco family. The interior is pleasant, which is more than 'The Churchgoer' could say in 1850 about the old one, which, he wrote, had "nothing whatever to boast of, being full of great pews which it required a person of considerable stature to peep over". He was already in a bad mood because he had been charged a Sunday double toll of 2d at the turnpike, in spite of being a parson; if he had been a local parishioner, he would have got through free. He noticed, however, that the view from the churchyard was "noble and extensive", which it still is, with the added bonus of a lake. Half a mile along the main road is Coombe Lodge, a large mock-Tudor building designed by Sir George Oakley in 1930–32 for the Wills family. It is now a Further Education Staff College.

The only major hillside valley in this area is Burrington Combe, a much-frequented beauty-spot with abandoned limestone-quarries where cars park and children climb in peril. It is followed by the B3134, which, near the foot, passes between the Rock of Ages, inspiration for the Reverend Toplady's hymn, and Aveline's Hole, once the home of Palaeolithic families. Less spectacular than Cheddar Gorge, but mercifully less commercialized, the steep-sided dry valley is well worth visiting and leads to interesting and exhausting walks on Mendip top. At the foot is the hamlet of Link (Old English 'hlinc', 'a hill') and a small Garden Centre. Slightly east of Link is the village of Burrington, named from the Iron Age fort, or burh, on the hill above. The village 'green' is all asphalt, and by it is the church with toothy monsters clasping the porch and a sundial which reminds us that "Life is but a Shadow". Inside, the elaborately carved bench-ends and screen are all modern, 1944, in memory of William Henry, Baron Winterstoke of Blagdon, the W. H. of W. H. & H. O. Wills. Also to be seen are the colours of the East Mendip Legion (motto "Who is Afraid"), raised in 1803 during the Napoleonic Wars.

One feature of the Combe is that the down-cutting of the valley has given access to caves in the limestone, notably Goatchurch Cavern, and Burrington is on the edge of an area famous for speleology. These caves were formed because the limestone has vertical fissures, or joints, down which slightly acidic surface-water travels, interacting with the limestone to form soluble calcium bicarbonate. In times of heavy rainfall the water-level in the caves rises at an alarming rate, and during the Ice Age water from melting snow rushed through the underground channels, filling them, buffeting the walls and roofs with the material it carried and greatly increasing the rate of erosion. Today, rainwater finds its way down a network of underground channels and emerges at the foot of the hill in 'risings' which are important as a source of water-supply. Such a rising may be seen by the bridge at Rickford, where it feeds a pond on the other side of the road, which was once used for the many paper-making enterprises along the

Mendip fringe. Another, for instance, was at Banwell, where the pond was later filled in to make a bowling-green. Blagdon and Chew Lakes are filled mainly by Mendip water, which, because of the limestone, is 'hard'.

Another limestone feature is the presence of veins of lead ore, which gave rise to a mining and smelting industry which lasted from prehistoric times to the seventeenth century, when drainage difficulties led to its abandonment. In the nineteenth century Cornish enterprise revived the industry, not by mining but by re-smelting the old slag. This ended in the twentieth century but has left many traces, mainly in the Somerset part of Mendip at Priddy and Charterhouse.

Another mineral of the hillside fringe which is no longer mined but was once of some local importance is ochre, a low-grade iron oxide used for making pigments, particularly the raddle, or ruddle, for marking sheep. It was while searching for ochre that some miners in the eighteenth century came upon a cavern or 'leer' at the western end of Banwell Hill (ST 3858) which was later 'lost' when the workings were abandoned and the shaft filled in. In 1824 a local farmer, William Beard, was inspired by his interest in archaeology and cave-discoveries which were being made elsewhere in Mendip to seek for the lost cavern. He found it and also and more significantly discovered a smaller cavern crammed with the bones of cold-climate fauna such as cave bear, wolf, Arctic fox, reindeer, bison and the huge wild ox, which apparently were washed into the hole. The house where Beard lived, on the right of the road from Banwell to Christon, is still called Bone Cottage, and a crude, grim-faced portrait bust of the farmer-archaeologist may be seen on his tomb near the porch of Banwell church.

The church itself has another of those fine Mendip towers, 101 feet high, although it does seem rather over-tall in proportion to the body. Its west face carries figures of the Annunciation and the east face a statue of the patron saint, St Andrew, although raising the nave roof has put him inside the church. Inside the large south porch, a piece of the old rood-loft was incorporated in a gallery in 1938, while in the church is a very elaborate screen of 1522, restored and resplendent in gilt and paint. The church interior is very fine and tall, with big clerestory windows and a wagon roof with angels. The upper part of the west gallery is Elizabethan.

The village has spread along the six roads which meet there, and the main street, suffering badly from traffic in summer, is the A371 to Weston-super-Mare. Horse-drawn traffic caused its own problems in the past, and Butstone House in the main street has a lump of rock in the pavement, a 'butstone' or 'glancestone', placed there to bounce wheels away before they hit the wall. One of the roads leads up over the hill to Winscombe, and at the top is the sprawling, castellated Banwell Castle, which is Victorian and bears the notice telling passers-by that the place is of no historical interest, reminding them that 'An Englishman's Castle is his Home'.

Before they were beheaded by the new county-boundary, all the fringing parishes included a substantial portion of Mendip top, which until the nineteenth century formed an important element in the village economy by providing common land for summer grazing. This open area was enclosed for corn during the Napoleonic Wars and a completely new landscape created of large rectangular stone-walled fields, straight roads and new farmhouses. For example the Blagdon Award of 1787 maps over a dozen new roads which can be traced to date even though some are no more than tracks.

For an Award the Commissioners had to find out who were the Commoners and what, expressed in 'stints', was each individual's right of common so that appropriate areas could be allocated. Rights of common on Mendip, as on the lowland moors, went with the occupation (not ownership) of ancient or 'Auster' tenements. An example comes from a late (1913) Award for Burrington Ham and Havyat and Langford Greens, where each Auster tenement, including the church and school, irrespective of its size or value, carried twenty-five stints. One stint gave the right to pasture a sheep (no rams); five were needed for a bullock or heifer (no bulls—obviously there was to be no sexual permissiveness) or one pony or donkey; a horse needed seven, and a pig (who must have a nose ring) two. One stint also equalled three geese or twenty fowls.

Provision was often made for a parish quarry or gravel-pit, and this was the case at Blagdon and also at Weston-super-Mare, where the quarry which scars the hillside provided much of the grey stone from which the town was built. Some land was usually allocated to provide an income for relief of the poor, and other parts were sold by the Commissioners to defray expenses. A grant of land on the old common carried a statutory obligation to enclose it with walls or hedges, and as this was an expensive business, the poor usually sold out to the wealthier landowners, and their small fields marked on the maps of the Award never materialized.

In effect, enclosure often meant that the poor were deprived of their one little piece of independence and cushion against unemployment. 'Improving' landlords, however, argued that this would make for a better-disciplined and harder-working labour-force. "In sauntering after his cattle he acquires the habit of indolence," wrote Billingsley, himself a Mendip farmer, "Day labour becomes disgusting: the aversion increases by indulgence, and at length sale of a half-fed calf, or hog, furnishes the means of adding intemperance to idleness." "All I know," said one labourer, "is that I had a goose and now I have no goose."

On Mendip top the new fields, planted year after year with grain and lacking the benefit of manure from stock, became exhausted, and much of the land reverted to poor pasture, while other parts were let out as potato-patches to the villagers. From this state the region has been restored by piped water-supply for cattle, motor-transport for milk, chemicals for restoring fertility, and Government grants to help with costs. At one time Mendip was a battleground of interests between royal foresters, miners and commoners; today the clash is between farmers, quarrymen, tourists and Water Authorities.

The fertile conglomerate shelf is now mainly grassland, and there is today no trace of the once important teasel crop specifically mentioned by Billingsley in 1795 as being "much cultivated" in the parishes of Blagdon, Ubley, Compton Martin, 'Harptry' and over the valley at Wrington. The seed was sown in April on old grass leys or wheat stubble, and the crop harvested the following year in July, when the heads were cut with a knife at fortnightly intervals, dried and made into packs—'kings' with nine thousand heads and 'middlings' with two thousand. Production was often on a share-cropping basis, the farmer providing the land and ploughing and the cropper the seed and labour; the market proceeds were shared equally. Teasels, used for raising the nap on cloth, were sold to the mills of Somerset and Wiltshire and sent as far afield as Yorkshire. Billingsley, as was to be expected from an 'improver' and leading light of the Bath and West Agricultural Society, recommended seed-selection. Equally predictably, his advice was not taken.

Today the A368, without a teasel in sight, continues westward to Churchill Gate. The village of Churchill is on a minor loop, and where this takes off is a pleasant clock-tower built to celebrate sixty years of Victoria's "benificent reign" (1897). It was provided by Sidney Hill, and a little further along, the graveyard of a Gothic Methodist chapel of 1871–81 contains an obelisk to his family. Sidney Hill also built Jubilee Almshouses at Langford. His home, Langford House, large and Italianate, built in 1850 with wings added in 1903, is now the Bristol University School of Veterinary Science.

In Churchill parish church is some armour of Sir John Churchill, Master of the Rolls in 1685, and a 1572 brass to Ralph Jennys and his wife. It is claimed, though not proven, that this Churchill was an ancestor of the Duke of Marl-borough and the Jennys of the Duke's wife, the redoubtable Sarah.

Passing through linear Sandford and Banwell, the main road crosses the M5 and heads out across the moor for Weston-super-Mare, passing the Air Force camp and by-passing Locking village, which is on the Old Banwell Road and has been considerably enlarged by pleasant modern housing. When Woodspring Priory was founded in 1230, Geoffrey Gilbwyne gave them "the manor of Lokyng and all belonging to it", and it is possible that the monks founded Locking church, although the nave and chancel were rebuilt in 1816 and 1833 respectively, and the north aisle, separated from the nave by two plain Tuscan pillars, was added in 1814, a date recorded on a large drainhead together with the names of the builders and plumber. There is a fine, gaily painted, fifteenth-century octagonal stone pulpit.

The fringe route continues as a minor road past the war-time ordnance factories which now house the Bristol Aerojet Rolls Royce Engine Division, picks up the A370 for a while and then branches off to Bleadon. The alternative routes from

Oldmixon or from Hutton go over the top of the hill and afford some splendid views southwards over the moors. Bleadon is perched on the side of a valley between Bleadon Hill and the small outcrop of South Hill with its old carboniferous limestone quarry. Most of the buildings are in limestone, but some, such as the post office, are in the red dolomitic conglomerate. The minor road continues along the foot of Bleadon Hill to Loxton, which is the last Avon village on the southern Mendip fringe and is sited beside a gap where the Lox Yeo breaks through the hills to join the Axe. It has fine views across the gap over the M5 to impressive Crook Peak and below it the gabled Webbington Country Club, built as a private house in 1907. The church, interesting but not exciting, is down a side road by a farm and is twice signposted in the village. It has a Norman doorway partly obscured by the tower arch and a much restored wooden screen with linen-fold panelling and Gothic tracery.

The road northward through the gap takes us to Christon, with its sturdy little Norman church, much restored in 1875. There is a splendid Norman south doorway and renovated Norman arches to the crossing, which has a very simple vault with the ribs resting on dragons. The nave and east windows are neo-Norman, but the side windows of the chancel are of about 1300. There are good views over the valley to the Loxton gap and Crook Peak, which may take its name from the British '*cruc*', a hill, or from its resemblance to the curve of a shepherd's crook.

The Winscombe Vale, spread out below Christon and ringed by hills, was formed when the over-arching limestone was so heavily eroded that the central plateau was reduced to a broad valley and the limestone left as a girdle of upland. At the western end of the Vale the M5 cuts its way through the northern limb of hill and goes out through the Loxton gap, but it uses the valley without serving it, and service is provided by the A38 which climbs in at the eastern edge under the Iron Age ramparts of Dolebury Camp, where legend says there should be treasure:

> If Dolebury digged were,
> Of gold would be the share,

and exits over the low col at Shute Shelf. This exit was also used by the Cheddar Valley Railway which went out through a tunnel, having come into the Vale through the broad Sandford gap to the north.

Fortunately neither the intrusion of the humming motorway nor the expansion of Winscombe by post-war housing has seriously disturbed the quiet charm of the valley with its broad hills, part-wooded, part-open, circling the good green pasture and hedged fields of the floor. The lower western end is filled with Keuper marls and a smear of alluvium; the higher eastern part is dolomitic conglomerate; and at the junction, on a large patch of Head down-sludged from the hills at the end of the Ice Age, sits Winscombe. This village was originally called Woodborough, and Winscombe, which has the fine parish church, was a separate settlement on the conglomerate shelf to the south. The name-change was caused by the railway. At first the station was called, quite properly, Woodborough, but this caused confusion, particularly with the mail, as there was a Woodborough Station in Wiltshire. So in 1869 the station and postal address were changed to Winscombe.

Mention of Winscombe church is unavoidable, for it has a magnificent position, visible from much of the valley, and one of those splendid towers, 100 feet high. Like Banwell's, the tower had images of the Annunciation, of which a lily in a pot remains, and a statue of the patron saint, in this case St Peter. The tower was probably built between 1380 and 1440, and six of the bells were cast in 1770 by the famous Bilbies of whom we have heard at Chew Stoke. There are interesting windows in the church, notably the 'golden window' of the Saint Peters (the Deacon, the Apostle and the Exorciser) given by Peter Carslegh, Vicar of Winscombe from 1532 to 1550, fifteenth-century windows in the south chapel, and a chancel east window attributed to William Morris and his firm. "It is," writes Pevsner, "one of the best examples of Morris glass in existence and quite unrecorded."

On the conglomerate, just off the A48, is the hamlet of Sidcot, and it was there at the beginning of the nineteenth century that the Society of Friends, commonly called Quakers, founded a boarding-school whose fine playing-fields lie over the main road by the Winscombe turning. At first there were separate boys' and girls' schools on the same campus, but soon the school became fully co-educational, as it is today. In its Quaker simplicity of building it avoided the neo-Gothic excesses of many of its contemporaries. The old school front, Italianate and painted white, is of the 1820s; the reddish dolomitic conglomerate building by the side road is an 1890 extension, and there is an amount of post-war building, including a footbridge over the main road. The Meeting House is mainly of 1817 with a front extension of 1926—the 1961 date on it refers mainly to the addition of an internal gallery.

It was a Sidcot schoolmaster, F. A. Knight, who at the end of the nineteenth century applied principles of local study in two books, *Heart of Mendip* and *Seaboard of Mendip*. It is an ex-Sidcot schoolmaster who has been pleased to extend those methods to making a portrait of a county Francis Knight never knew.

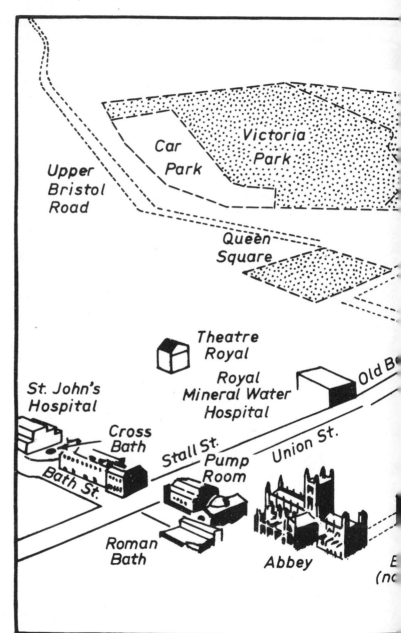

Upper Bristol Road

Car Park

Victoria Park

Queen Square

Theatre Royal

Royal Mineral Water Hospital

Old B

St. John's Hospital

Cross Bath

Stall St.

Pump Room

Union St.

Bath St.

Roman Bath

Abbey

E
(no

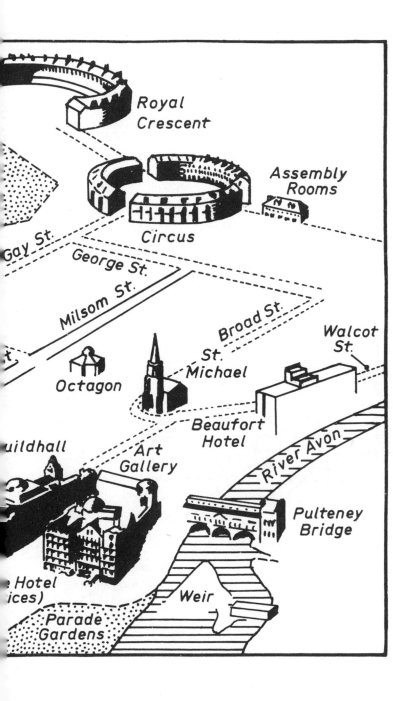

Royal Crescent

Assembly Rooms

Gay St.

Circus

George St.

Milsom St.

Broad St.

Walcot St.

St. Michael

Octagon

Beaufort Hotel

uildhall

Art Gallery

River Avon

Pulteney Bridge

e Hotel
ices)

Weir

Parade Gardens

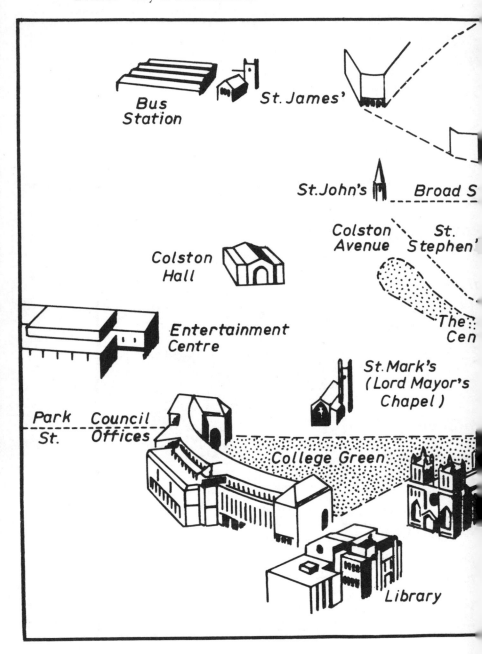

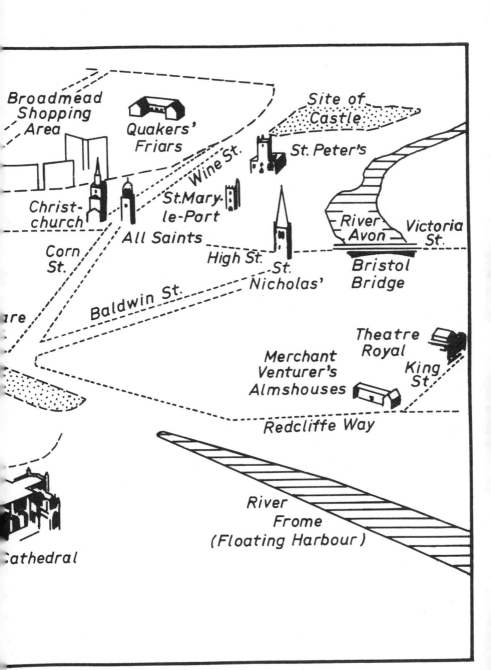

INDEX

215